EXCEL-BASED DECISIONS IN MANAGERIAL ACCOUNTING

WEDGEWOOD CANDLE COMPANY

TERESA STEPHENSON
AND JASON PORTER

Images used under license from Shutterstock.com.

ISBN 978-0-912503-49-3

Printed in the United States of America.

CONTENTS

CHAPTER 3 — Using Job-Order Costing

CHAPTER 4 — Using Process Costing

CHAPTER 6 — Joint and By-Products

CHAPTER 7 — Allocating Service Department Costs

SECTION 2 — Using Cost Information to Improve Business Decisions

CHAPTER 8 — Determining Transfer Pricing

CHAPTER 9 — Performing CVP Analysis

CHAPTER 10 — Performing Variance Analysis

CHAPTER 11 — Making Tactical Decisions

This page is
intentionally blank.

About the Authors

TERESA STEPHENSON, CMA, PH.D., is an Associate Professor of Accounting at the University of Wyoming. She joined the faculty at UW in 2005, less than a year before completing her doctorate at the University of Kentucky in 2006. Prior to her doctoral work she worked as an independent consultant for small business managers and owners. In 2000, she earned a Master of Professional Accountancy at Indiana University.

Teresa has taught management accounting and taxation at several schools including University of Wyoming, Indiana University, University of Kentucky, Sullivan University, and Ivy Tech. In 2010 she was the recipient of the "Top Prof" award given by the University of Wyoming Cap and Gown Chapter of the Mortar Board Society.

Teresa has published articles appearing in journals such as *Strategic Finance*, *The CPA Journal*, *Accounting Horizons*, *IMA Educational Case Journal*, *Midwestern Business and Economic Review*, *Practical Tax Strategies*, *Academy of Educational Leadership Journal*, and *Journal of Accounting Education*. She is also a co-author of the annual edition of the *Multistate Tax Guide to Pass-Through Entities* published by CCH. In 2011, she was awarded the University of Wyoming's College of Business Outstanding Junior Research Award.

JASON PORTER, PH.D., is an Associate Professor of Accounting at the University of Idaho. He joined the faculty at UI in 2006 after completing his doctorate at the University of Georgia. Prior to his doctoral work, Jason earned his Masters of Accountancy from Brigham Young University.

Jason has taught management and financial accounting at several schools including University of Idaho, University of Georgia, Brigham Young University, Salt Lake City Extension, Piedmont College, and Utah Valley Community College. In 2012 he was the recipient of the "Presidential Mid-Career Award" given by the University of Idaho. In 2010 he was awarded the College of Business and Economics "Teacher of the Year" award by the students of the college. He has also won the "Outstanding Accounting Faculty Award" multiple times.

About the Authors, *cont.*

Jason has published articles appearing in journals such as *Issues in Accounting Education*, *Global Perspectives in Accounting Education*, *Strategic Finance*, *IMA Educational Case Journal*, and *Journal of Global Business Issues*. He has served as a member of the Steering Committee for the Conference on Teaching and Learning in Accounting (CTLA) since 2010 and is an editorial review member for the *Journal of Accounting Education* as well as an ad hoc reviewer for other academic outlets.

Authors' Prior Collaboration

In addition to collaborating on this book, Teresa and Jason won the American Society of Business Publication Editors' (ASBPE) Northeast Regional Gold Award in 2011 for best feature series (in *Strategic Finance*); and in 2012 they won a Lybrand Certificate of Merit for another series of articles on variance analysis (again in *Strategic Finance*).

Acknowledgements

We greatly appreciate the help and support of Carol Borsum and Randal Elder, without whom this project would not have been possible. We are also grateful to Patricia Naretta for her careful editing of every aspect of the project and to Lynne Wood for her preparation of the manuscript. Finally, we appreciate the efforts of Jennifer Leverett for production coordination and Aaron Borsum for valuable comments and corrections throughout the process.

Finally, we appreciate the encouragement and support of Carrie Porter, Jeremy and Travis Huey, and other family, friends, colleagues, and students who have listened to and read through many different aspects of this project through the process.

Thank you all for helping us make this dream into a reality.

This page is intentionally blank.

CHAPTER 1

INTRODUCTION

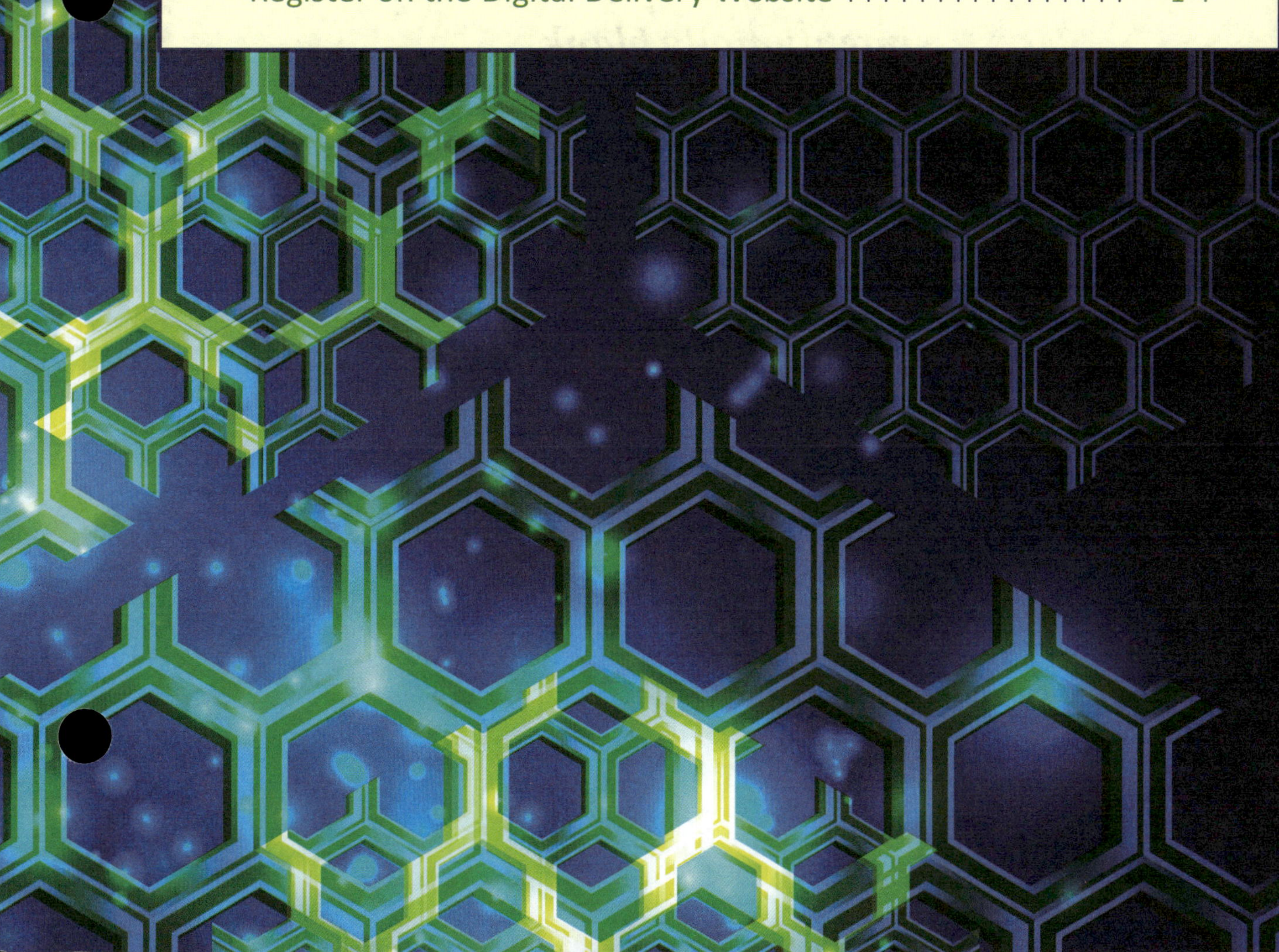

This page is intentionally blank.

CHAPTER 1

Introduction

What's in the Book?

Managerial accounting can be one of the most useful tools in business, but only if it is used correctly. A good managerial accountant or consultant, or any accountant that might be asked for advice on business matters, should have a thorough understanding not only of how to explain these important tools, but also how to use them. This book builds upon the accounting concepts you are learning by providing you with ten projects, each designed to help you use Excel to master a topic in cost or managerial accounting. In the process, you'll not only practice managerial accounting, but you'll also improve your Excel skills.

Each project introduces a challenge faced by Wedgewood Candle Company, a small company that makes specialty candles. The company, which has had a long and successful history, now finds itself struggling to compete against growing competition and rising costs. Your job, as a managerial accountant working for Wedgewood, is to use the skills you are learning in your managerial accounting class to help the company overcome its challenges. In a real company, you would have to tackle all of these projects at once, since they are typically interconnected. For this project, though, each problem will be largely independent of the others. Depending on what your instructor decides, you may cover all of the questions and problems or only do a few. Of course, you are welcome to do them even if they aren't required in class. After all, what better preparation can you have for the real world than dealing with a specific problem facing a company?

So, are you ready to use your managerial accounting tools to make some decisions? Good. Let's go!

Microsoft Excel®

One of the skills employers seek when they hire accountants at any level is good spreadsheet skills. Accountants use spreadsheets as decision aids and to document when and why they made a decision or implemented a strategy. Furthermore, good spreadsheets are easy for nonaccounting users to read and understand. Excellent spreadsheets allow nonaccountants to intuitively enter information and data from their own departments, saving accountants time and energy, not to mention reducing the number of explanations that need to be made. Since Microsoft Excel® is the most widely used spreadsheet program in the accounting profession, improving your Excel skills will greatly increase your value in the marketplace.

To help you gain these skills, you will use Excel to complete each of the projects in this workbook. In addition, if you aren't as savvy with Excel, we will provide detailed guidance for each of the methods used for Excel 2010. We will also mention any significant differences from the 2010 methods to those in Excel 2013. While we will discuss specific Excel skills in each chapter, the Index of Excel Functions and Commands located in the back of the book provides you with a quick reference to the Excel instructions for all eleven chapters. Because we may introduce an Excel concept in an earlier project, we suggest referring to the Index if you are unclear of how to proceed with your spreadsheet project. In addition, the Armond Dalton digital delivery website includes the data you will need for each project.

The sticker in the lower-left corner of the front cover of this book includes the one-time-use serial number you will need to access Armond Dalton data files online via a secure digital delivery website (www.armonddaltonsoftware.cdtdigital.com). The serial number is hidden by a silver scratch-off coating in the middle of the sticker. Information about how to use the serial number begins on page 1-4.

Organization

This book contains two sections. In the first section, Understanding and Allocating Costs, you will concentrate on cost behavior and assigning costs to different cost objects. First, you will learn how to separate costs into mixed and variable components and to create a total cost equation that you can use to predict future costs. Next, you will work on job-order costing, process costing, and activity-based costing. While each of these three projects stand alone, they all use the same basic data, allowing you to analyze the three different methods as part of a larger project for class or to simply gain a better understanding of how the three methods compare. Assigning costs to joint products and by-products comes next, followed by assigning service department costs to production departments. These are important topics that help complete your understanding of cost behaviors and assignment of costs, especially since many textbooks only briefly cover these subjects.

The second section, Using Cost Information to Improve Business Decisions, starts with transfer pricing and then moves on to discuss flexible budgeting, one of the most important tools in preparing for a new period. No managerial practice set would be complete without discussing cost-volume-profit (CVP) analysis; this chapter includes common metrics used in business decision making such as breakeven point, margin of safety, target profit, and even adds in tax effects for an advanced understanding of CVP principles. After that, you will use Excel to perform variance analysis, one of the best tools available for continuously improving business performance. The last two topics deal specifically with financial decision making, or how to use accounting information to improve decision making. First, you will make tactical decisions for short-term decisions such as make-or-buy, special orders, and keeping or dropping a product line. Second, you will develop a spreadsheet for use in making long-term capital budgeting decisions, including calculating a project's net present value, internal rate of return, and payback period. For more fun, we mix up these last decisions with non-uniform cash flows and tax effects, since that is how those decisions must be made in the real world.

We hope, whether you work through one project or all ten, that this book will improve your Excel skills and will also help solidify your understanding of managerial accounting and how important it is in the business world!

Wedgewood Candle Co. — The Sample Company

Wedgewood Candle Co. produces and markets scented candles for spas, boutiques, and specialty shops throughout the U.S. Because of their high quality, the candles traditionally sell for a significant premium over other brands of candles.

For the most part, the company produces different sizes of pillar candles. These candles have a standard diameter, but varying heights. Wedgewood's candles are all one and one-half inch in diameter. This non-standard size, coupled with a unique marbling effect in the candles' coloring, makes the candles easy to spot in stores and adds to their appeal.

Because of their niche market and focus on high quality, the company has stayed relatively small in the 75 years since it was originally founded. The owners, all members of the original (but growing) founding family, have been reluctant to allow the company to grow significantly, fearing that they would be unable to maintain sufficient control over expanded production. They have long felt that without their personal oversight, quality would diminish and so would their unique market position.

Recently, however, one of the Board members, George Wedgewood, has become convinced that growth in the family would either require the company to expand or to deny some members of the family a part of the business. No one was in favor of pushing family members out, especially since most of the new members were the fifth generation coming of age and interested in the family business. Based on George's recommendation and compelling evidence that their own incomes would soon decrease as ownership became spread among more family members, the Board voted to create a new department that would produce a line of specialty candles. The new department's management team has been encouraged to focus on maintaining the company's reputation for high quality as its primary goal. The Board believes that cost efficiencies can be achieved once the new line is established and the new managers sufficiently trained.

Traditionally, the company has focused on making candles, and their process has been carefully handed down from Candle Master to candlemaker and from candlemaker to apprentice since the firm was created. However, as more family members have decided to join the firm, Wedgewood's Board has found itself in need of specialized help that the family cannot always provide. For example, even though the Controller, Josey Wedgewood, is the great-granddaughter of the founder, she can no longer do all the accounting herself. Thus, the company has been forced to hire several new accountants to provide the information they need.

Using Your *One-Time-Use* Serial Number to Register on the Digital Delivery Website

> **Note:**
>
> For the entire project, the following symbol is used to indicate that you are to perform a step using your computer:
>
> Whenever you see this symbol in the left margin, you should complete the related step, which is shown in italics. You should not begin doing an activity with your computer until the symbol is shown.

As explained on page 1-2, the sticker in the lower-left corner of the front cover of this book hides a one-time-use serial number that you will need in order to register on the digital delivery website. The serial number will not be visible until you scratch off the silver coating in the middle of the sticker. **Note:** Simply use a coin and gently scratch off the silver coating to reveal the serial number; **DO NOT TRY TO REMOVE THE STICKER.**

Do not register on the digital delivery website until you are ready to download the data files. Registration is covered next.

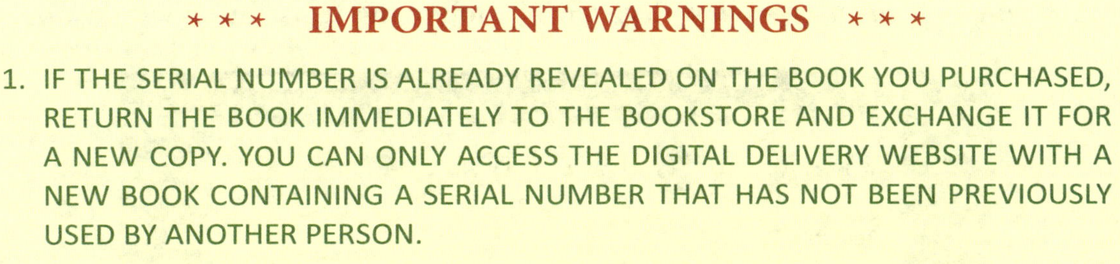

*** * * IMPORTANT WARNINGS * * ***

1. IF THE SERIAL NUMBER IS ALREADY REVEALED ON THE BOOK YOU PURCHASED, RETURN THE BOOK IMMEDIATELY TO THE BOOKSTORE AND EXCHANGE IT FOR A NEW COPY. YOU CAN ONLY ACCESS THE DIGITAL DELIVERY WEBSITE WITH A NEW BOOK CONTAINING A SERIAL NUMBER THAT HAS NOT BEEN PREVIOUSLY USED BY ANOTHER PERSON.
2. THE EXCEL FILES CAN ONLY BE LOADED ON ONE COMPUTER, SO BE CAREFUL TO CHOOSE THE COMPUTER THAT YOU WANT TO USE TO COMPLETE THE ENTIRE PROJECT.

After you reveal the serial number, go to the following website:

www.armonddaltonsoftware.cdtdigital.com

The main window opens as shown below.

If you have previously registered on the Armond Dalton digital delivery site for this book or any of our other books, you do not have to register again. Simply log in using your previously registered email address and password. This will take you to the Armond Dalton software window shown on the bottom of page 1-7.

If you are a new user who has never registered before on the Armond Dalton digital delivery site, click Register. The following registration window opens:

Type all information requested on the registration screen, including the email address and password that you want to use for signing into the digital delivery website. Be careful if you use Google Chrome Autofill settings because sometimes the Autofill feature is not accurate.

AFTER YOU DECIDE WHICH EMAIL ADDRESS AND PASSWORD TO USE, WRITE THEM DOWN IN THE SPACES PROVIDED BELOW. IF YOU FORGET THIS INFORMATION YOU WILL NOT BE ABLE TO DOWNLOAD THE PROJECT DATA FILES. THE SPACES BELOW PROVIDE A CONVENIENT PLACE FOR YOU TO RECORD THEM.

Email address used to register: ______________________________

Password used to register: ______________________________

Click the checkbox next to "I agree to the terms and conditions governing the use of this site" and then click the Register button, which opens the Terms of Use window.

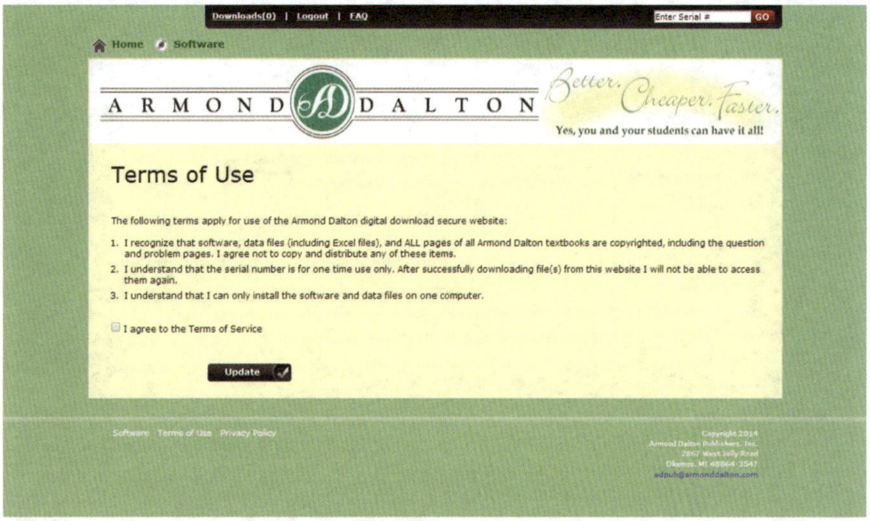

Read the terms of use carefully, especially the one about not copying ANY of the pages in this book. All of the Excel files and pages of this book are copyrighted material and cannot be copied without expressed written permission from Armond Dalton Publishers.

After reading the terms of use, insert a check mark next to "I agree to the Terms of Service" and then click the Update button. A welcome window opens.

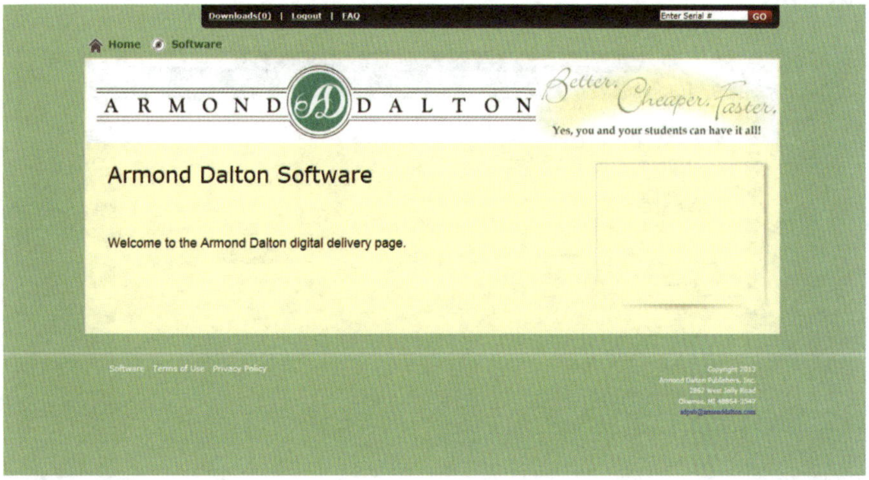

 *Click Software in the upper-left corner of the window (next to Home) to open the Software window shown below.*

The window shown above is used for all of Armond Dalton's books, so you can ignore the ACL 9 Software file listed, as well as all of the other books listed on the left side of the window. DO NOT CLICK ANYTHING UNTIL INSTRUCTED TO DO SO IN THE NEXT STEP.

 *Select the Managerial Excel option on the left side of the window.* When you do this, the window now shows Managerial Accounting in the middle of the window.

Click the View Now button to open the serial number window.

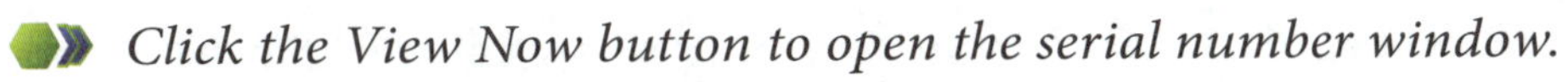

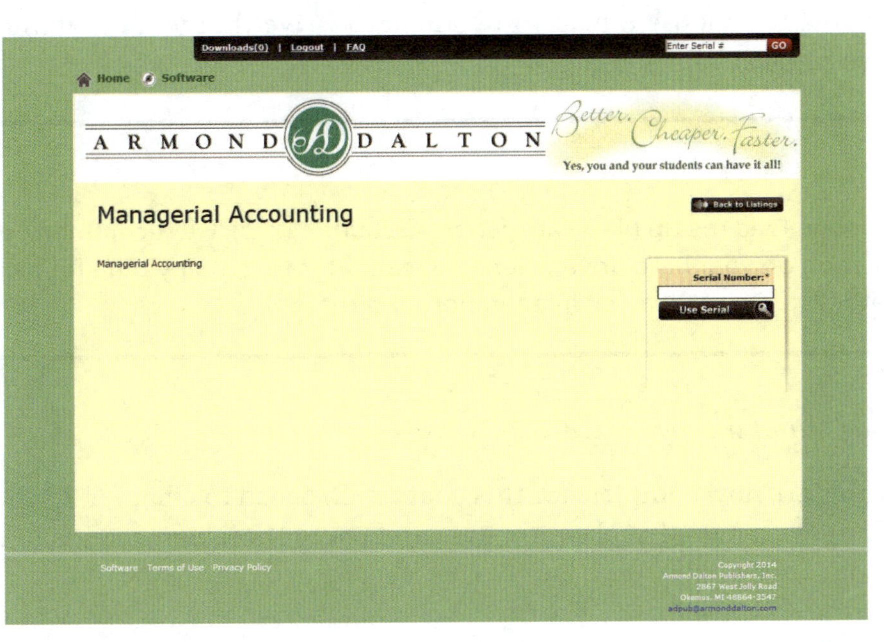

Type the serial number from the lower-left corner of your book in the Serial Number box. **Note:** The serial number is case sensitive.

Click the Use Serial button. The Data Files download window opens next.

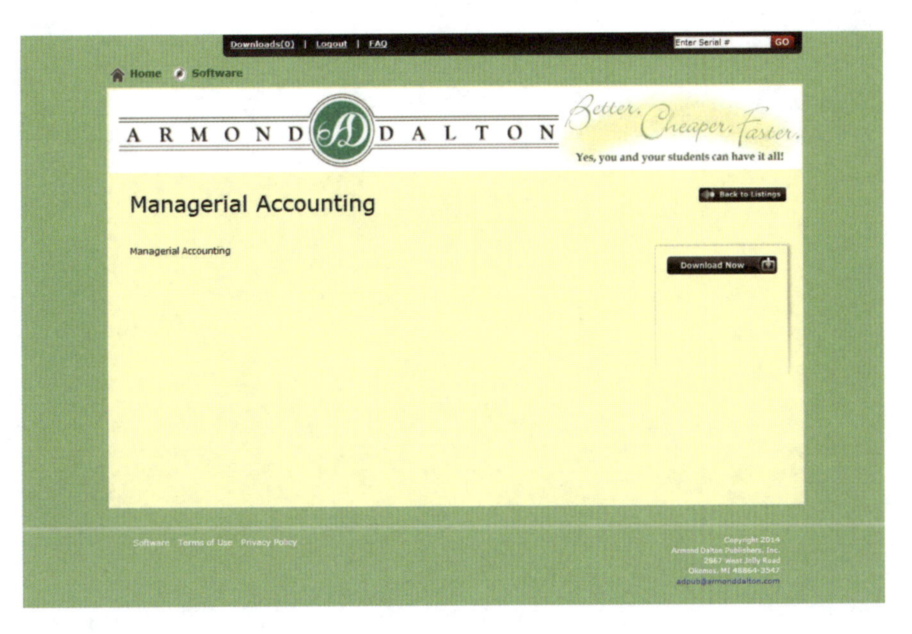

 *Click the Download Now button.* If you have a choice (if Save As option is available), choose a place on your hard drive that you can remember later. We suggest your Desktop.

Note:

After you download the zip file (Managerial_Accounting.zip), we recommend extracting it to a location on your hard drive where you can refer to it at any time for a clean copy of the data files. Do not leave it in a temporary directory.

Log out of the digital delivery website.

All procedures are now complete for this chapter. Proceed to Chapter 2, where you will begin working with basic Excel commands and using those commands to understand cost behavior.

UNDERSTANDING COST BEHAVIOR

This page is intentionally blank.

CHAPTER 2

Understanding Cost Behavior

Objectives

Excel Skills

- Perform basic formatting
- Insert columns in a spreadsheet
- Sort data for analysis
- Perform basic calculations
- Perform basic regression and statistical analysis

Accounting Skills

- Classify manufacturing costs as Direct Materials (DM), Direct Labor (DL), and Manufacturing Overhead (MOH)
- Classify MOH as variable, fixed, or mixed costs

Mastering Excel

Each of these chapters start with an Excel lesson that covers spreadsheet skills that will either be specifically required in that chapter's assignment or that will just be useful to you throughout your career in either accounting or business. Depending on your experience level with Excel, these skills may be a review that you can skim through quickly. For others, these Excel skills will be one of the most important benefits of completing these assignments. Either way, we hope you will soon come to enjoy playing around with Excel as much as we do. In this chapter, you will learn to use multiple spreadsheets in an Excel workbook, insert columns, name tabs, sort data, use various formats, and, finally, perform basic regression analysis. Let's get started!

Basic Formatting

The first step, of course, is to start Excel. When you open a file in Excel, it is called a *workbook*. So, go ahead and open this chapter's practice file or workbook. You'll find it in the downloaded files as **C2 Excel Practice Sets**. Each page in a workbook is called a *spreadsheet*. If you look in the bottom-left corner of the screen, you will see two tabs called "Basics" and "Regression." These are the two spreadsheets that make up this first Excel workbook. The third tab, the one on the far right, allows you to easily create new spreadsheets, which we will address later. For now, the Basics spreadsheet should be highlighted in white. This means that you are working on that spreadsheet. Now that we've covered a few basic Excel terms, let's get to work.

At the top of the Basics spreadsheet, you should see the beginning of a data table that looks like the one pictured here.

	A	B
1	General Le	Amount
2		
3		

The first two cells (A1 and B1) of this spreadsheet are the titles, or *headers*, of the first two columns of a table. Unfortunately, you can't really see the headers because of the current formatting. Let's take a second and fix that.

Excel starts out with a standard format. The column widths are all the same, the font is all the same, and numbers are all formatted the same way, etc. As you type, Excel allows your words and the numbers to run into the next cell, until you type over it. That's what has happened here. Let's try it, and we'll show you what we mean.

Note:

Any text that is to be typed using your computer keyboard or keypad is shown in THIS FONT. Whenever you see this blue font style, you should type the blue characters/letters using your keyboard or keypad.

Click in cell A2 and type I love accounting.

As you type, you should notice two things. First, the text is running from column A into column B. Second, all of the text appears in a text box at the top of the screen.

In cell B2, type Spreadsheets are fun.

Again, you should notice a few things. First, you can no longer see all of the text from cell A2. You probably only see "I love acc". Excel is showing you as much as it can with the current formatting. Go ahead and click in cell A2 again. Notice that in the textbox at the top of the screen you can still see everything in that box, even though you can't see it in the spreadsheet. That's one of the things that makes this general textbox so important—you can always see what you have typed into the box, regardless of the formatting below.

Now that we've covered the basic formatting provided by Excel, let's change the formatting to better suit our data.

- *Delete those phrases that we just typed into row 2 by clicking on cell A2 and pressing the [Delete] key, then repeating for cell B2.*
- *Click on cell A1.*

In the general textbox you can see that the full title is "General Ledger Number." There are two ways that we can fix the spreadsheet formatting to make the header visible. First, we can resize the column. Second, we can reformat cell A1. Because the general ledger numbers that we will type in later tend to be short, we don't really need a wide column. Keep in mind that when you start making columns wide, you can see less of your work on the screen (the columns to the right get pushed off the screen), so we typically try to avoid that first option when possible. Let's do the second option instead.

- *With your cursor still on cell A1, find the Wrap Text command ( ) in the middle of the ribbon (that's what Microsoft calls the menu bar at the top of the screen) and click it.*

The Wrap Text command should be located about the middle of the ribbon in the Alignment group. So, if you can't see it, make sure that you have the Home tab at the top selected. The Excel ribbon is broken down into general tabs, which appear at the top of the screen, and groups, which appear at the bottom of the ribbon. Excel normally has eight tabs: File, Home, Insert, Page Layout, Formulas, Data, Review, and View. Depending on what else is installed on your computer, you may see other add-ins, such as Acrobat or QuickBooks. Each tab is then broken down into several groups. On the Home tab, you should see groups for Clipboard, Font, Alignment, Number, Styles, Cells, and Editing. In the bottom-right of each group is a small box with a diagonal arrow. If you click on this box, you get more commands than appear on the ribbon.

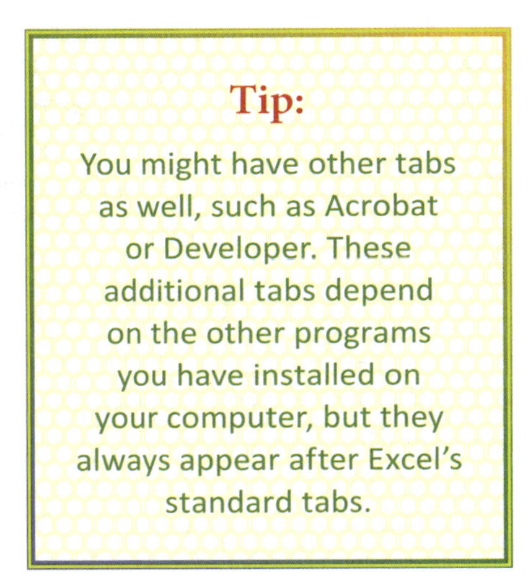

Tip:

You might have other tabs as well, such as Acrobat or Developer. These additional tabs depend on the other programs you have installed on your computer, but they always appear after Excel's standard tabs.

Let's go back to formatting our column header. After you wrap the text, the row height should automatically increase, and you can now see the whole header. You've just done your first formatting!

Entering Data

Now that we have legible headers in our table, we need to type some numbers into each of these columns. Let's start with the general ledger numbers.

- *Type in the following general ledger numbers, starting in cell A2 and pressing [Enter] after each number:* 5311, 5313, 5315, *and* 5317.

- *Type the following amounts in column B, starting in cell B2 and moving down:* 24000, 360000, 474000, *and* 12000.

As you typed, you probably noticed that some of those numbers were hard to read. Your readers will feel the same way when they look at your spreadsheet, so let's take a minute and format them so that they will be more legible. The general ledger numbers in column A are formatted just fine the way they are. They don't need dollar signs or commas because they are easy to read and aren't dollar amounts. However, when you use financial information in Excel it's nice to format the numbers so that a reader can easily see that they are in dollar amounts. Let's go ahead and format the dollar amounts in column B.

- *Click on cell B2, hold down the left mouse button, and drag your cursor down to cell B5.* You should now have all four cells *selected* or highlighted.
- *Right-click on one of the highlighted cells and two formatting menus will pop up. The first of these menus contains a set of quick format tools. The second, down below, is a more comprehensive list of formatting commands and options. You can see these two menus below.*

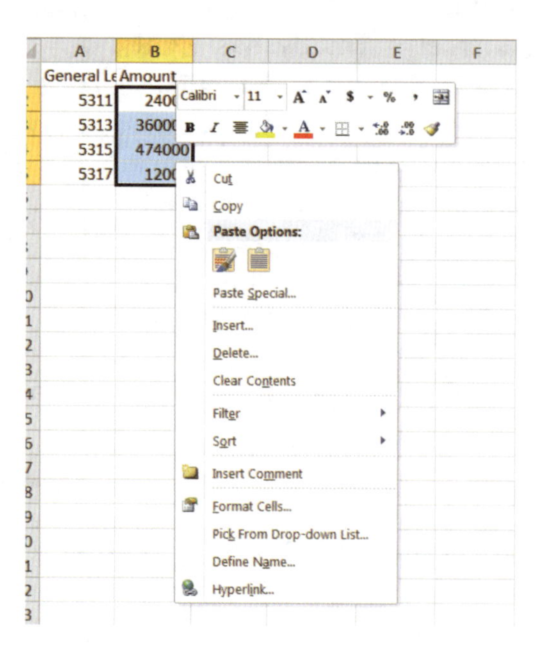

- *Click on the dollar command (**$**) in the middle of the top row of the first pop-up menu. When you did that, most of your numbers were probably replaced with ########.* This is Excel's way of telling you that you have numbers in a cell but that the formatting makes it impossible for Excel to display those numbers. When this happens, you need to resize the column. *(For Excel 2013, you need to choose the format from a drop-down menu instead of the quick link.)*
- *Place your cursor on the line between the column labels for columns B and C. Your cursor should change from a white plus (✚) to a black line with arrows pointing right and left (✥).*
- *Click on that black line and drag right or left to increase the size of our columns, or you can double-click and Excel will automatically make the column wide enough to show all of your numbers.*

Go ahead and play around with your column widths for a minute. We'll wait for you....

Now that you have increased the size of column B, you can see that all of our numbers now have a dollar sign, commas, and two decimal places, and they are much easier to read. You can leave your numbers just like this, but most Excel users prefer to eliminate decimal places when they are not actually being used (meaning we are working with whole numbers or can view the numbers rounded off to whole numbers), since it gives spreadsheets a cleaner look.

- *Right-click again on the four selected cells.*
- *Click twice on the Decrease Decimal command (←.0 .00), the second to last command on the second row of the top pop-up menu.* You can also find these types of formatting commands in the Excel ribbon under the Number group of the Home tab.

Inserting a Column

Often as we start entering data we realize that we missed something or have some other data that we need to put into a table. In this example, it would be helpful to include the account names instead of just the account numbers. We could, of course, put the account names at the end of the table, in column C, but that really wouldn't make much sense to a reader trying to match up titles and account numbers. So, instead, we'll insert a new column with the account names next to the general ledger numbers.

- *Place your cursor on the B at the top of the second column. Your cursor should change from the white plus to a black arrow pointing down (⬇).*

- *Right-click and choose Insert from the second or lower pop-up menu. A new column appears immediately before the Amount column. This is now column B, and the amounts are now in column C.*
- *Type the header* Account Name *into the new cell B1 and, if necessary, format the cell to wrap text to see the full header name.*

Now let's type the following account names into our table.

- *Input the following labels starting in cell B2 and working down (B3, B4, etc.):* Cleaning supplies, Depreciation, Indirect salaries, *and* Insurance.

Notice that the column is not wide enough to read the names of each of these accounts. Now we have a choice. We can use the Wrap Text command or we can resize the column. We have to decide, basically, if we want wider columns or thicker rows. What will be easier to read? Most accountants prefer thicker rows for headers and wider columns for data. Not only does this help set off the headers, but it also makes it easier to quickly skim through long lists of data without having to scroll though lots of blank space. While you are welcome to do whatever you prefer in your own work, for now let's use this opportunity to practice resizing columns again. Go ahead and make column B big enough to read the account names by either manually resizing the column or double-clicking the line between the column B and column C titles, as we described in the previous section.

Sorting Data

Right now our spreadsheet is sorted by account number, a pretty typical way for accountants to think about various accounts. However, most managers don't think about accounts that way. Instead, they tend to prefer to see the accounts in alphabetical order or sorted by size. For our example, let's sort the accounts so that the account with the highest dollar amount comes first.

- *Select all of the active cells.* An *active cell* is one that has something in it. *For our example, we want to click and drag from cell A1 to cell C5.*
- *Click on the Sort & Filter command (AZ) in the Editing group (usually the commands on the far right of the Home tab). The default for this command is to sort the first column from smallest to largest or in alphabetical order. In this case, though, we want to sort based on the third column, so we need to use the Custom Sort option.*
- *When the Sort pop-up window appears, make sure that the box at the top next to "My data has headers" is checked (because we want the headers row to stay where it is).*

- *In the Sort by drop-down box, choose Amount.*
- *The next drop-down box should have Values preselected; that's what you want, so leave it alone (or select Values, if it's not already chosen).*
- *In the third drop-down box, select Largest to Smallest.*
- *Click OK.*

Your data should now be sorted so that the account with the largest dollar amount (indirect salaries) appears first and the account with the smallest dollar amount (cleaning supplies) appears last. Here's what ours looks like.

	A	B	C
1	General Ledger Number	Account Name	Amount
2	5315	Indirect salaries	$ 474,000
3	5313	Depreciation	$ 360,000
4	5311	Cleaning supplies	$ 24,000
5	5317	Insurance	$ 12,000
6			

Performing Basic Calculations

The next Excel skill that we need to develop is using formulas. This is actually one of Excel's most powerful tools, but many people have a hard time trusting Excel to do calculations when they first start using it. They type numbers into Excel, and then use a calculator to do all of their calculations, then type the results into Excel as well. Not only is this a waste of time, but it actually keeps you from using the real power in Excel: automatic updates and flow of information. The sooner you get out of this beginner's habit, the more productive you will be with Excel. To practice, let's figure out the cost per hour for each of our expenses.

- *In column D, type the header* Direct Labor Hours *and then enter the following hours:* 6,500; 7,900; 9,800; *and* 12,000 *in each subsequent row of the that column. We have shown the commas here to make the numbers easier to read, but you don't need to type the commas when you input the numbers into Excel. Instead, use Excel's formatting commands to show symbols and punctuation, like dollar signs and commas.* You'll notice that Excel either didn't format your cells or it made them into dollar amounts.
- *Select the four amounts you just typed and right-click.*
- *In the box that appears, select Format Cells, then choose Number from the category box. Then, decide how you want the numbers to appear. Because*

these are labor hours, choose Number as the main format and use the options for 0 decimal places, the 1000 Separator, and put any negative numbers in parentheses and red font like this: (1,234).

 *Click OK, and your cells should be formatted in a way that makes them much easier to read.*

All right, now that we have our data, let's type a header into column E called Cost/Hour. Because we want to calculate the cost per hour, we are going to divide the total cost by the DL hours we just added.

- *Start with your cursor in cell E2 and then find the [+] key on your keypad. If you prefer, you can use the [=] sign to start an equation instead.*
- *Press [+] and then your left arrow (which we will show as [←] from now on) twice (to put a dashed box around the amount). Note that you can press [+] and then click on cell C2 to accomplish the same thing.*
- *Type [/] (forward slash, which is also on the keypad).*
- *Type [←] once to select the DL hours. Note that you can type [/] and then click on cell D2 to accomplish the same thing.*
- *Press [Enter]. Your new equation divides the amount in cell C2 by the amount in cell D2.*
- *Format that cell to appear as dollars and cents with two decimal places.*

At this point you have two options. You can work your way through the other three cells, typing in the equation each time, or you can use the power of Excel to really speed up the work. With just a few simple steps, you can copy the equation or formula so that Excel calculates all of the costs per hour automatically. There are at least three ways to do this. Why three? Probably because some users prefer to use a mouse, some prefer to use the keyboard, and some prefer to use the ribbon commands. Here's the first way:

- *Click on cell E2.* This highlights the cell with a black box.
- *Click on the top edge of the highlighted box and move the $72.92 to cell F2. Excel will update all of the equations automatically, so you can move things around in any way you wish to improve the formatting of your spreadsheet. Now, move the equation back to cell E2 so that we can finish practicing our copy commands.*
- *Select cell E2 and notice that the lower-right corner of the highlighted box has a separate black square.*
- *Click on that square and your cursor will change to a + sign.*

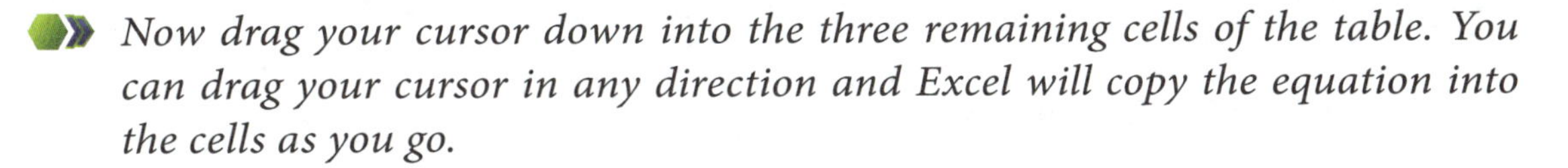

- *Now drag your cursor down into the three remaining cells of the table. You can drag your cursor in any direction and Excel will copy the equation into the cells as you go.*

When you copy a cell, instead of moving it, Excel automatically updates your equation so that it refers to new data. So, our first equation is C2/D2, the second equation (in cell E3) refers to C3/D3, the third (in cell E4) refers to C4/D4, and so on.

Here's the second way to copy your work:

- *Click on the cell you want to copy (E2) and use the keyboard command [Ctrl] [C] (hold down the [Ctrl] key while typing [C]).*
- *Select all four cells from E2 through E5 and use [Ctrl] [V] to paste the equation.*

Here's the third way:

- *Click on the cell you want to copy (E2), then click on the Copy command ( ) from the Excel ribbon (Home tab, Clipboard group).*
- *Select the cells to which you wish to copy the formula (cells E2 through E5, for our example).*
- *Click on the Paste command ( ) from the same area of the Excel ribbon.*

All three of these methods for copying accomplish the same thing. You'll probably quickly decide that one is your favorite, but you will want to learn more than one method because each method is more convenient in some circumstances. Your table should now look like the one pictured here.

	A	B	C	D	E
1	General Ledger Number	Account Name	Amount	Direct Labor Hours	Cost/Hour
2	5315	Indirect salaries	$ 474,000	6,500	$ 72.92
3	5313	Depreciation	$ 360,000	7,900	$ 45.57
4	5311	Cleaning supplies	$ 24,000	9,800	$ 2.45
5	5317	Insurance	$ 12,000	12,000	$ 1.00
6			$ 870,000		

You can do any arithmetic in Excel using this basic format. You can also use pre-specified equations, called *functions,* built into the program to help speed up the process. The most commonly used function is AutoSum. Let's say that we wanted to get the total cost from our table. There are many ways to do this as well.

Here's the first way:

- *Type* `=C2+C3+C4+C5` *into cell C6.*

Here's another way:

- *Type in cell C6* `=sum(C2:C5)`. In English, this means *sum all of the numbers in the cells from C2 through C5.* Note that even though you typed the command in lower case, Excel automatically changes all Excel commands to upper case.

Yet another way:

- *Type* `=sum(` *and then click and drag over the cells you want to add and press [Enter].*

Finally, our favorite shortcut:

- *Place your cursor in cell C6.*
- *Click on the AutoSum function (Σ) in the Editing group of the Home tab. Excel will make a guess at the cells you want it to sum. If you have selected the cell at the bottom of a column of numbers or at the right of a row of numbers, Excel will assume that you want to sum the column or row. When you try this, you'll notice that a box appears around the cells that Excel assumes you want to sum. You can use the squares in any of the four corners of this flashing box to adjust the cells that Excel will sum. After you have selected the cells you want summed, press [Enter].*

Whichever option you choose to use, you should end up with a total cost of $870,000. Play with the options. Give them all a try. We'll be right here waiting for you when you feel comfortable and are ready to move on.

Performing a Regression Analysis

Now that we have created a simple cost table, we have only one more Excel skill to learn in this chapter. In order to really understand cost behavior, we have to be able to create a cost equation or formula. A cost formula shows the fixed and variable components of the costs and allows managers to estimate total costs for budgeting and other planning purposes. When you have a mixed cost, the best way to create this formula is by performing a regression analysis, and the easiest way to do that is in Excel. As a quick refresher (just in case it's been a while since your last statistics course), regression analysis uses one set of data (called an *independent variable*) to predict another (called the *dependent variable*). When you run the regression, the equation breaks down the dependent variable or data into the fixed portion (called an *intercept*) and the variable portion (called a *beta*).

In managerial accounting, we use a cost driver as the independent variable to predict total costs. We've provided another set of data for you to use while practicing these steps. At the bottom of your Excel file, you'll see a set of arrows and several named spreadsheets. The default names are Sheet1, Sheet2, etc. However, naming them makes it easier to know where to look for information. For the first part of our practice, we have been in the Basics spreadsheet. Now, we want to switch to the Regression spreadsheet. To switch, just click on the tab you now want to work on. This Excel file, or *workbook*, only has two spreadsheets, but you can have hundreds (although we don't really recommend trying to keep track of that many).

- *Click on the Regression spreadsheet, and you should see a three-column table all set up and ready to go.*
- *Click on the Data tab at the top of the Excel ribbon.*

The group at the far right side of the ribbon should be the Analysis group. If the Analysis group doesn't show up, you can easily add it using the Excel Options menu. Here's how:

- *Click on the File tab, and then select Options.*
- *Click on Add-Ins (it's in the menu on the left of the command box that opened).*
- *Verify that the Manage drop-down box shows Excel Add-Ins.*
- *Click Go.*

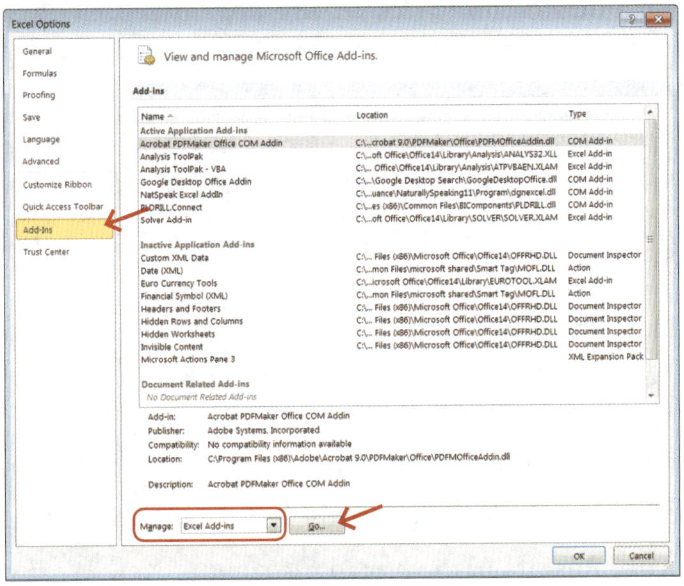

- *Check the boxes next to Analysis ToolPak and Analysis ToolPak–VBA on the final command box and then click OK.*

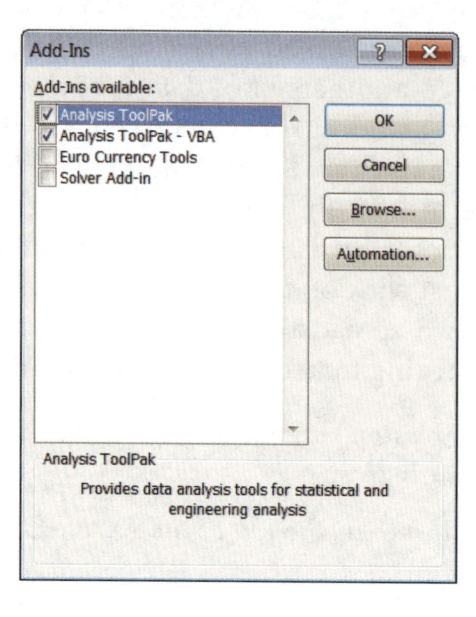

Now, when you select the Data tab, you should see the Analysis group on the far right. Let's go back to creating our regression.

- *Click on Data Analysis and examine the dialog box with all of the statistical analyses you can do in Excel.*
- *Scroll down and select the Regression tool.*
- *Click OK.*
- *Find Input Y Range and click in the box to the right with the red arrow in it. This is where we will put the dependent variable, which is the cost information.*
- *Highlight the cell containing the word Overhead and then drag the cursor down so that you have all the cells containing the dollar amounts highlighted.*
- *Click on the second box with the red arrow, right below the first box that you just used.*
- *Find Input X Range and input the independent variable the same way. This time, though, make sure you use the DL hours in cells C1 through C13, the header (DLH), and all 12 values.*
- *We included the headers in our data, so check the box marked Labels.*
- *Check the New Worksheet Ply option in the Output options section.*
- *Type the word* Results *in the box to the right of New Worksheet Ply.* You don't have to put anything here, but we decided to name ours just to make it easy to find.
- *Click OK.*

We now have a new spreadsheet containing our regression output, but the information here doesn't look very user-friendly. Let's do some formatting to make it easier to read.

- *Click on the Results spreadsheet tab, if it's not already open.*
- *Right-click on the triangle in the upper-left corner of the spreadsheet, above the number 1 row label and to the left of the letter A column label.* We've pointed out its location with an arrow in the illustration below.
- *Click on the comma icon (,) on the right side of the pop-up formatting menu.*
- *Highlight all of the active columns by clicking and dragging across column labels A through I.*
- *Double-click on a line between any two columns.*

Your regression output worksheet should now look like the spreadsheet pictured.

	A	B	C	D	E	F	G	H	I
1	SUMMARY OUTPUT								
2									
3	*Regression Statistics*								
4	Multiple R	0.80							
5	R Square	0.64							
6	Adjusted R Square	0.60							
7	Standard Error	1,448.96							
8	Observations	12.00							
9									
10	ANOVA								
11		*df*	*SS*	*MS*	*F*	*Significance F*			
12	Regression	1.00	37,037,744.61	37,037,744.61	17.64	0.00			
13	Residual	10.00	20,994,714.31	2,099,471.43					
14	Total	11.00	58,032,458.92						
15									
16		*Coefficients*	*Standard Error*	*t Stat*	*P-value*	*Lower 95%*	*Upper 95%*	*Lower 95.0%*	*Upper 95.0%*
17	Intercept	237.84	3,401.76	0.07	0.95	(7,341.77)	7,817.44	(7,341.77)	7,817.44
18	DLH	5.07	1.21	4.20	0.00	2.38	7.76	2.38	7.76

Your managerial accounting instructor or textbook will probably cover most of the features of the regression output shown here, so we are only going to discuss a few of the most commonly used items. First, the R-square value of 0.64 (found in cell B5 in our figure), means that 64% of the variation or change in overhead expense is explained or predicted by the change in DL hours each period. This is a reasonable value and tells us that we have probably selected an appropriate driver for predicting our future costs.

Second, the P-values shown in column E (rows 16 through 18 in our figure), tell us how likely it is that these results occurred strictly by chance. In this case, the chance that overhead costs aren't related to the change in DL hours is about 0%. Of course, there is slightly more than a zero percent chance. If you move your decimals out far enough (using the Increase Decimal command), you will see that there is a small value of about 0.0018, but that is small enough that we can call it zero. In other words, we are pretty confident that the change in DL hours each period is a good predictor of how overhead costs will change.

Third, the coefficients in column B (found in rows 16 through 18 in our figure) form the building blocks for a cost equation or formula. The coefficient to the right of the word Intercept is our estimate of the company's fixed costs. The easy interpretation of this value is that even if the company used ***no*** DL hours for the period, they would still pay $237.84 in monthly overhead costs. The coefficient to the right of "DLH" represents the company's variable costs. The easy interpretation of this value is that for each additional DL hour used during the period, the company's overhead costs will go up by $5.07. With this information, we can write the cost equation for the company: Total Overhead Cost=$237.84+($5.07×DL hours used).

Wrapping Up Our Excel Work

That's the end of our Excel lesson for this chapter. As you move into the Wedgewood case, use the questions asked as an opportunity to practice these Excel skills. Remember, the fundamental goal of managerial accounting is to provide information that decision makers can understand and use, so make sure that your spreadsheets look good!

Wedgewood Candle Co.

Determining DM, DL, and MOH

Josey sighed as she looked at the list of numbers in front of her. As the company controller, she had better things to do with her time than fight with these small details. While figuring out the cost breakdown was important to analysis and budgeting, it wasn't something that she should be wasting her time on. What she needed was an assistant.

There was a knock on her door, and Josey looked up to see Sam Rindlesbacher, the head of Human Resources and Josey's brother-in-law, standing there. "Sam, what are you doing here?" she asked.

"Bringing you a present, and from the look on your face, you look like you can use it," Sam walked into the office followed by a nervous looking young man. "This," Sam said gesturing behind him, "is Jordan Leavitt, and he's your new staff accountant."

"New staff accountant? I don't remember.... Oh wait," Josey smiled at the young man. "I do remember. We talked about it after the last executive meeting, right after we discussed the creation of the new division. I said I was super busy, and you said that we didn't have anyone in the family interested in accounting."

"Right," Sam agreed. "So, we decided to look outside the family to find you some help. I sent you several emails asking what you were looking for in an assistant, but you never answered." Josey grimaced. "I assumed that since you were too busy to even answer my emails, I'd better get right on it. Anyway, Jordan has just graduated with an undergraduate degree in accounting from the University of Wyoming. He doesn't have any experience yet, but he earned good grades and is excited to work in the same firm as several of his family members. His dad is a Candle Master, been with Wedgewood for over 20 years. Right, Jordan?"

The young man nodded. "Yes, sir," he said in a polite voice. "My family has worked for Wedgewood since it was founded. When I went into accounting, I didn't think I would be able to work here, so I was really excited when a position opened up."

"Well, that settles it," Sam said with a nod. "I'll be in touch to make sure things are going well. Enjoy!" And with that, Sam was gone.

Josey stared at her new assistant for a few moments. "Um," she finally said, "I really wasn't prepared for this. Since accounting never gets any new hires, I started filtering Sam's emails, so I had no idea that he was moving forward on finding me some help." Jordan looked a little crestfallen. "But, that's okay," Josey went on quickly. "I do have a project ready for you to get started on." Jordan immediately brightened up.

"We need to break down our corporate costs so that we can do some analysis and get ready for the next budget. Here's the data." She handed him a spreadsheet. (This workbook is in your downloaded files. Open the workbook called **C2 Cost Behavior** and make sure that you are on the Last year's data spreadsheet. The table pictured below shows what the spreadsheet should look like.)

	A	B	C	D	E	F	G
1	General Ledger Number	Last year's manufacturing expenses	Amount		Last year's miscellaneous information:		
2	5110	Wax	$ 3,000,000		DL Hours	36,250	
3	5120	Scent	$ 480,000		Batches	125,000	
4	5315	Indirect Salaries	$ 474,000		Candles	1,500,000	
5	5313	Depreciation	$ 360,000		Average Candle-inches	6,000,000	
6	5130	Wicks	$ 300,000				
7	5220	Candlemaker Labor	$ 183,750				
8	5323	Shipping Costs	$ 180,000				
9	5140	Coloring	$ 120,000				
10	5230	Candle Master Labor	$ 112,500				
11	5210	Apprentice Labor	$ 105,000				
12	5321	Rent on warehouse	$ 72,000				
13	5325	Utilities	$ 60,000				
14	5193	Information Stickers	$ 45,000				
15	5311	Cleaning supplies	$ 24,000				
16	5192	Packaging Boxes	$ 18,750				
17	5319	Parts and Repairs	$ 18,000				
18	5150	Clips	$ 15,000				
19	5191	Cellophane	$ 15,000				
20	5317	Insurance	$ 12,000				
21							

"I need you to classify the direct materials, direct labor, and overhead components. After we have that, then we'll move on to breaking down our overhead."

Stop here and answer questions 1 through 4 on assignment page 2-21 before continuing.

Rapid Review:

Direct materials, direct labor, and manufacturing overhead make up the three parts of production costs (or the costs to produce a product). ***Direct materials*** refer to the raw inputs bought from suppliers and used in production. ***Direct labor*** refers to the wages, overtime, and benefits paid to line workers that produce the products. ***Manufacturing overhead***, often referred to simply as ***overhead***, is everything else spent on production. These are the different costs of running a production plant, including the plant manager's salary, utilities, security, depreciation on machines, and many other costs. If it is spent on production, and it isn't direct materials or direct labor, then it is classified as overhead.

Classifying Fixed, Variable, and Mixed Costs

Later that afternoon, Jordan was back in Josey's office with his completed analysis. Josey looked over his classifications, and then leaned back in her chair. "Good work. I figured a straightforward assignment like this would be a good way to get you started. Now, though, I need to you to work on something a bit more challenging." Jordan nodded, eager to impress his new boss. "As you can see, manufacturing overhead is a significant portion of the expenses at Wedgewood, but up until now we have just applied it to production using candle inches. Since all of our candles are a standard width and the work is very standardized, height has been a reasonable measure for assigning most of our overhead costs to our candles."

"Like a cost driver?" Jordan asked. "We usually used direct labor hours in our managerial accounting classes."

Josey nodded. "It is a cost driver, but for us candle height has traditionally been a much better driver than direct labor hours. You see, a three-inch candle takes three times as much materials, labor, and other inputs as a one-inch candle does, and a six-inch candle takes twice as much as a three-inch candle. Since all candles are manufactured using the same basic processes, this has worked fairly well." She shook her head. "But, now we are developing a new specialty candle division, so candle height might not be the best driver for us anymore. A three-inch specialty candle will absorb more inputs and resources than a three-inch regular candle. Because of the change, we are going to have to start using direct labor hours as our driver, at least for now.

"Anyway, because of the change, all of my cost equations are now wrong, so I need you to classify these overhead costs as variable, fixed, and mixed and then calculate the cost equation for each one."

Jordan looked again at his spreadsheet. "Why do you need cost equations for each cost? In school we just did them for total overhead."

Josey smiled. "You know, that's a great way to estimate total costs for next year, but it doesn't work well for budgeting purposes." Seeing Jordan's confused look, she continued. "Assume that we pay a base fee for our phone service, plus $0.06 per minute. That's a mixed cost, since it has both fixed and variable components. So if I renegotiated our phone contracts, it could change both my fixed cost and my variable cost estimates. It's easy to incorporate those changes into the equation for the phone service cost, but it can get confusing to do it for a total equation, especially since some costs change every year while others stay constant. The changes can also start to offset each other."

Jordan nodded. "I get it," he said. "If you have it all broken down you can just change each component, then add them all up...."

"And you get the total fixed and variable estimates for the period." Josey finished.

"Okay. I'll get started on those classifications, but," Jordan paused, "I don't think that I have enough information here to do that. I mean, I know that DM and DL are variable by definition, but without being able to see how the overhead costs changed with production, I have no way of knowing if they are fixed, variable, or mixed."

Josey smiled. "Good catch. You do need more data, but I'm afraid I haven't gathered it all for you this time. You'll have to get what you need out of our general ledger, which will not only save me some time, but it will also give you a chance to get to know our books a little bit." She handed him the general ledger printout. (You have a copy of this document at the end of the chapter directly after the assignment pages. Find the report called **Wedgewood Candle Co. 2015: General Ledger Report – Quarterly Selected Accounts.**) "You'll have to type some of those numbers into Excel so that you can get the classifications. Also, remember that those costs that don't change based on production are fixed. Those are the easiest to find.

"Take the Cost Behavior spreadsheet that I gave you and add a column next to the amount. Classify each cost as Variable, Fixed, or Mixed. Even though direct labor and direct materials are always variable, make a note of that anyway in your new column. Then move on to the overhead items."

"How can I tell the difference between variable and mixed costs?" Jordan asked.

"Well, first you get the total direct labor hours per quarter from the Quarterly Labor Report, since that's our new cost driver. (You have a copy of this document at the end of the chapter directly after the assignment pages. Find the report called **Wedgewood Candle Co. 2015: Quarterly Labor Report**.) Then you divide the cost each quarter by the direct labor hours per quarter. Remember to use the total direct labor hours from all three levels of labor. If the quarterly cost per hour is constant, then it is a variable cost. If the cost per hour changes, then you have a mixed cost. With the mixed costs you run a regression analysis in Excel. The constant is the fixed portion and the coefficient is the variable portion.

"Once you have classified all of the costs, I need you to also create a cost equation for each one. Do you remember what a cost equation is?"

"Not really," Jordan confessed.

"Don't worry about it," Josey said. "We'll get you up to speed yet. A cost equation summarizes each cost so that you can predict future costs for budgeting or for calculating predetermined overhead rates. The basic setup looks like this." She wrote out the equation on a piece of paper:

$$\text{Total cost} = \text{fixed cost} + (\text{per-driver variable cost} \times \text{number of drivers})$$

"Oh," Jordan said. "I've seen that before. I assume you want me to make you one of those as well?"

"Not one, Jordan. Several. I want one for each overhead cost. I need to be able to predict each type of cost for my budgets individually. But don't worry. We can easily add up the results of each equation so that we get the total estimates for the period. Since the number of drivers will be the same for each cost, you will only need two new columns in your table: one for the fixed component and one for the variable component for each cost."

"And each equation will be different, right?" Jordan interrupted, "I mean, for the fixed costs the variable portion will be zero and for the variable costs the fixed portion will be zero."

"Right!" Josey continued. "When you are all done, add a row at the bottom called 'Total' and sum each of the two new columns. We can quickly use these figures to estimate any individual cost or total costs if we know how many direct labor hours we will have in a period. Actually… " she thought for a moment, "what we will need is a total for all costs, but a separate total for just the overhead costs as well. Think you can handle that?" She sketched out an idea of what she had in mind. (See top of the following page.)

	A	B	C	D	E	F
1	General Ledger Number	Last year's manufacturing expenses	Amount	Variable, Fixed or Mixed	Variable	Fixed
2	5110	Wax	$ 3,000,000	Variable	$ 82.76	$-

Jordan nodded. "I'll get right on it."

Stop here and answer questions 5 through 8 on assignment pages 2-23 through 2-27 before continuing.

Rapid Review:

All production costs can also be split up as fixed, variable, or mixed costs. A ***fixed cost*** is a cost that doesn't change with production, like a plant manager's salary. It doesn't matter if 1 unit or 10,000 units are produced; her salary isn't going to change. A ***variable cost*** is a cost that does change with production. For every one unit made, we will incur a specific amount of variable costs. Direct materials is a great example of variable costs, because for every unit produced, we will need the same number of inputs. For example, for every cheeseburger a fast-food restaurant makes, they need one bun, one burger, one slice of cheese, and one blob of ketchup. If you don't make the burger, you don't use the ingredients, so you don't incur the costs.

A ***mixed cost*** has both a fixed and variable component. Josey uses the example of the phone service. Wedgewood pays a base amount, say $300 per month, plus $0.06 per minute. That's a mixed cost, because there is a fixed amount ($300) plus a variable amount ($0.06 per minute). Another good example would be a delivery service that receives $5.00 per delivery plus $0.30 per ounce of weight.

Making Cost Predictions

Josey poked her head into Jordan's office a little while later. "How's it going?"

"Just fine. I think I'm just about done with the cost equations."

"Excellent! Then I just have one more job for you to do before calling it a day. I'm predicting that we will use 45,000 direct labor hours next year. Using your equations, estimate the total amount we will spend on manufacturing overhead and how much we will spend overall next year. After that's done, go ahead and call it a night and I'll see you tomorrow."

Stop here and answer questions 9 and 10 on assignment page 2-29.

Rapid Review:

A ***cost equation*** shows the fixed and variable cost portions of an expense. It is always set up in the format Josey showed to Jordan in the middle of page 2-18. For a fixed cost, the variable portion is $0.00, for a variable cost, the fixed portion is $0.00, and for a mixed cost you will have values for both fixed and variable costs. You can use a cost equation for each cost or for all of the costs combined (usually called a ***total cost equation***).

Cost equations have two purposes: to show the breakdown between fixed and variable costs and to estimate future costs. Once you have the variable cost per unit and total fixed cost portion of the total cost equation, you can input the number of drivers you think you will use in the upcoming period and solve for total cost. If you have chosen a good driver, then the result will give you a good estimate of the total costs that will be incurred in the upcoming period.

Name:

Questions

Note: *For questions and problems that require calculations, attach a copy of your spreadsheet to the related assignment page and hand it in to your instructor.*

Determining DM, DL, and MOH

Q-1. Using the information from Josey's spreadsheet, calculate Wedgewood's total direct material (DM) cost for last year.

____

Q-2. What was the company's total DL cost for last year?

____

Q-3. What was the company total MOH cost for last year?

____

Q-4. What do you notice about the relationship between account numbers and your classifications?

____

____

____

If required by your instructor, print out a copy of your spreadsheet before moving on to the next set of questions.

Name:

Classifying Fixed, Variable, and Mixed Costs

Q-5. Using the list of general ledger accounts and the DL report available in the documents at the end of the chapter, determine which of Wedgewood's MOH costs are:

a. Fixed

b. Variable

c. Mixed

Name:

Q-6. Create a cost equation for each of the expenses in Excel. To calculate the variable expenses, divide the quarterly costs by the quarterly total labor hours. Wax, for example, is as shown in the diagram here. Because the amount per hour is $82.76 for each quarter, this is a variable cost with the following cost equation: Total Wax Cost=$0+$82.76x. A fixed cost will be the same each quarter, and so, for instance, insurance will be $3,000 every quarter and the cost equation will be: Total Insurance Expense=$3,000+$0.00x.

Wax		Hours		
$	540,000.00	6,525.00	$	82.76
$	660,000.00	7,975.00	$	82.76
$	810,000.00	9,787.50	$	82.76
$	990,000.00	11,962.50	$	82.76

Complete the following table for a sample of the cost equations. Print out a copy of your full spreadsheet with all of your cost equations if required by your instructor.

Cost		Cost Equation
Example: Wax	=	*$0+$82.76x*
Cleaning supplies Expense	=	
Rent on warehouse	=	
Wicks	=	

Name:

Q-7. Based on the R-square values from your regression analysis, for which mixed costs is DL the best predictor?

For which is it the worst predictor?

Explain.

Q-8. Add up the fixed and variable components of your individual expense cost equations and create a total cost equation for:

a. MOH only

---

b. Total Production Costs

Name:

Making Point Predictions

Q-9. How much should Jordan estimate that Wedgewood will spend on MOH next year if they use 45,000 DL hours (round to the nearest dollar)?

Q-10. How much should Jordan estimate the company will spend on production next year using the 45,000 DL hour estimate (round to the nearest dollar)?

Name:

Problems

Critical Thinking Issues

In the case, Josey decided to switch from the company's traditional cost driver (candle inches produced) to a new cost driver (DL hours) because of the possibility that the new line will make candle inches a less effective driver.

The following table presents Wedgewood's total production costs, total candle inches produced, and total DL hours for the past five (5) years:

Year	Total Production Costs	Total Candle Inches Produced	Total DL Hours
2015	$5,595,000	5,300,000	36,250
2014	$5,200,000	4,700,000	35,360
2013	$4,750,000	4,000,000	27,075
2012	$4,000,000	3,500,000	28,000
2011	$3,275,000	2,800,000	19,650

Problem #1

Using this information, perform two regressions. Both will have production costs as the dependent (or Y) variable, but one will use candle inches and the other will use DLH as the independent (or X) variable. Then use this information, as well as the information from the case, to write a memo to Jeremiah Wedgewood, the current CFO of Wedgewood Candle Company, discussing which driver you suggest the company use. Remember that your memo is going to a senior member of the management team, so you will need to provide adequate support for your arguments, *and* provide a polished final product. You can use the space below to prepare an outline of your memo.

Name:

Ethical Issues

"Josey," Jordan asked with a puzzled look on his face. "I don't understand these regression results for our mixed costs."

"What seems to be the problem?" Josey asked, looking over his shoulder at his spreadsheets.

"Well, I used direct labor hours, like you said, and it seems to be a great driver for cleaning supplies and a pretty good driver for parts and repairs, but it isn't a good driver for our utilities bill."

"What's wrong with that?"

"Well, I would have expected our utility bill to be pretty constant. I mean, the lights are pretty much always on, the water usage is pretty constant, and none of our machines are that energy intensive. So, why is it jumping around so much?"

"Well," Josey said sitting down in a nearby chair. "The utility bill itself is pretty constant. But I use the utility expense account as kind of a 'miscellaneous expense.' Any time I have to buy miscellaneous items for the office, or when we have an office party for a holiday or celebration, I just debit utilities expense."

"Why?" Jordan asked, obviously confused.

"Well, for one thing it's easier. For another, no one really looks at utilities expense, so I don't have to spend a lot of time explaining those costs."

"Doesn't that mess up our numbers and our budgets?"

"Not materially. Because the cash flows are all accounted for and since everything balances, I just decided that it wasn't worth my time, not with everything else I have to do with only you to help me."

Problem #2

a. What concerns do you have about Josey's response to Jordan's questions?

____

____

____

____

____

Name:

b. What are the consequences of recording these expenses inappropriately? Do you really think it makes any difference to Wedgewood?

c. What consequences might Jordan face if he continues to argue with his new boss?

d. What options does Jordan have for resolving this issue? Which of your options do you think he will choose?

Wedgewood Candle Co. 2015

General Ledger Report - Quarterly Selected Accounts

General Ledger Number Account Description		Date	Reference	Description	Debit	Credit	Account Balance
	5100						
Wax		1/1/2015		Beginning Balance			0.00
		3/31/2015		Total Quarterly Activity	540,000.00		540000.00
		6/30/2015		Total Quarterly Activity	660,000.00		1200000.00
		9/30/2015		Total Quarterly Activity	810,000.00		2010000.00
		12/31/2015		Total Quarterly Activity	990,000.00		3000000.00
	5120						
Scent		1/1/2015		Beginning Balance			0.00
		3/31/2015		Total Quarterly Activity	86,400.00		86400.00
		6/30/2015		Total Quarterly Activity	105,600.00		192000.00
		9/30/2015		Total Quarterly Activity	129,600.00		321600.00
		12/31/2015		Total Quarterly Activity	158,400.00		480000.00
	5130						
Wicks		1/1/2015		Beginning Balance			0.00
		3/31/2015		Total Quarterly Activity	54,000.00		54000.00
		6/30/2015		Total Quarterly Activity	66,000.00		120000.00
		9/30/2015		Total Quarterly Activity	81,000.00		201000.00
		12/31/2015		Total Quarterly Activity	99,000.00		300000.00
	5140						
Coloring		1/1/2015		Beginning Balance			0.00
		3/31/2015		Total Quarterly Activity	21,600.00		21600.00
		6/30/2015		Total Quarterly Activity	26,400.00		48000.00
		9/30/2015		Total Quarterly Activity	32,400.00		80400.00
		12/31/2015		Total Quarterly Activity	39,600.00		120000.00
	5150						
Clips		1/1/2015		Beginning Balance			0.00
		3/31/2015		Total Quarterly Activity	2,700.00		2700.00
		6/30/2015		Total Quarterly Activity	3,300.00		6000.00
		9/30/2015		Total Quarterly Activity	4,050.00		10050.00
		12/31/2015		Total Quarterly Activity	4,950.00		15000.00
	5191						
Cellophane		1/1/2015		Beginning Balance			0.00
		3/31/2015		Total Quarterly Activity	2,700.00		2700.00
		6/30/2015		Total Quarterly Activity	3,300.00		6000.00
		9/30/2015		Total Quarterly Activity	4,050.00		10050.00
		12/31/2015		Total Quarterly Activity	4,950.00		15000.00

(continued on reverse)

General Ledger Number Account Description	Date	Reference	Description	Debit	Credit	Account Balance
5192						
Packaging Boxes	1/1/2015		Beginning Balance			0.00
	3/31/2015		Total Quarterly Activity	3,375.00		3375.00
	6/30/2015		Total Quarterly Activity	4,125.00		7500.00
	9/30/2015		Total Quarterly Activity	5,062.50		12562.50
	12/31/2015		Total Quarterly Activity	6,187.50		18750.00
5193						
Information Stickers	1/1/2015		Beginning Balance			0.00
	3/31/2015		Total Quarterly Activity	8,100.00		8100.00
	6/30/2015		Total Quarterly Activity	9,900.00		18000.00
	9/30/2015		Total Quarterly Activity	12,150.00		30150.00
	12/31/2015		Total Quarterly Activity	14,850.00		45000.00
5210						
Apprentice Labor	1/1/2015		Beginning Balance			0.00
	3/31/2015		Total Quarterly Activity	18,900.00		18900.00
	6/30/2015		Total Quarterly Activity	23,100.00		42000.00
	9/30/2015		Total Quarterly Activity	28,350.00		70350.00
	12/31/2015		Total Quarterly Activity	34,650.00		105000.00
5220						
Candlemaker Labor	1/1/2015		Beginning Balance			0.00
	3/31/2015		Total Quarterly Activity	33,075.00		33075.00
	6/30/2015		Total Quarterly Activity	40,425.00		73500.00
	9/30/2015		Total Quarterly Activity	49,612.50		123112.50
	12/31/2015		Total Quarterly Activity	60,637.50		183750.00
5230						
Candle Master Labor	1/1/2015		Beginning Balance			0.00
	3/31/2015		Total Quarterly Activity	20,250.00		20250.00
	6/30/2015		Total Quarterly Activity	24,750.00		45000.00
	9/30/2015		Total Quarterly Activity	30,375.00		75375.00
	12/31/2015		Total Quarterly Activity	37,125.00		112500.00
5311						
Cleaning Supplies	1/1/2015		Beginning Balance			0.00
	3/31/2015		Total Quarterly Activity	4,700.00		4700.00
	6/30/2015		Total Quarterly Activity	5,500.00		10200.00
	9/30/2015		Total Quarterly Activity	6,400.00		16600.00
	12/31/2015		Total Quarterly Activity	7,400.00		24000.00

(continued on the following page)

General Ledger Number Account Description	Date	Reference	Description	Debit	Credit	Account Balance
5313						
Depreciation	1/1/2015		Beginning Balance			0.00
	3/31/2015		Total Quarterly Activity	90,000.00		90000.00
	6/30/2015		Total Quarterly Activity	90,000.00		180000.00
	9/30/2015		Total Quarterly Activity	90,000.00		270000.00
	12/31/2015		Total Quarterly Activity	90,000.00		360000.00
5315						
Indirect Salaries	1/1/2015		Beginning Balance			0.00
	3/31/2015		Total Quarterly Activity	118,500.00		118500.00
	6/30/2015		Total Quarterly Activity	118,500.00		237000.00
	9/30/2015		Total Quarterly Activity	118,500.00		355500.00
	12/31/2015		Total Quarterly Activity	118,500.00		474000.00
5317						
Insurance	1/1/2015		Beginning Balance			0.00
	3/31/2015		Total Quarterly Activity	3,000.00		3000.00
	6/30/2015		Total Quarterly Activity	3,000.00		6000.00
	9/30/2015		Total Quarterly Activity	3,000.00		9000.00
	12/31/2015		Total Quarterly Activity	3,000.00		12000.00
5319						
arts and Repairs	1/1/2015		Beginning Balance			0.00
	3/31/2015		Total Quarterly Activity	3,850.00		3850.00
	6/30/2015		Total Quarterly Activity	4,456.00		8306.00
	9/30/2015		Total Quarterly Activity	4,722.00		13028.00
	12/31/2015		Total Quarterly Activity	4,972.00		18000.00
5321						
Rent on warehouse	1/1/2015		Beginning Balance			0.00
	3/31/2015		Total Quarterly Activity	18,000.00		18000.00
	6/30/2015		Total Quarterly Activity	18,000.00		36000.00
	9/30/2015		Total Quarterly Activity	18,000.00		54000.00
	12/31/2015		Total Quarterly Activity	18,000.00		72000.00
5323						
Shipping Costs	1/1/2015		Beginning Balance			0.00
	3/31/2015		Total Quarterly Activity	32,400.00		32400.00
	6/30/2015		Total Quarterly Activity	39,600.00		72000.00
	9/30/2015		Total Quarterly Activity	48,600.00		120600.00
	12/31/2015		Total Quarterly Activity	59,400.00		180000.00
5325						
Utilities	1/1/2015		Beginning Balance			0.00
	3/31/2015		Total Quarterly Activity	11,172.00		11172.00
	6/30/2015		Total Quarterly Activity	14,997.00		26169.00
	9/30/2015		Total Quarterly Activity	12,336.00		38505.00
	12/31/2015		Total Quarterly Activity	21,495.00		60000.00

Wedgewood Candle Co. 2015

Labor Report - Quarterly - By Type of Labor

Labor Type Rate		Quarter 1 Hours Payroll	Quarter 2 Hours Payroll	Quarter 3 Hours Payroll	Quarter 4 Hours Payroll	Year Total Hours Payroll
Apprentice		2,700.00	3,300.00	4,050.00	4,950.00	15,000.00
$	7.00	$ 18,900.00	$ 23,100.00	$ 28,350.00	$ 34,650.00	$ 105,000.00
Candlemaker		2,700.00	3,300.00	4,050.00	4,950.00	15,000.00
$	12.25	$ 33,075.00	$ 40,425.00	$ 49,612.50	$ 60,637.50	$ 183,750.00
Candle Master		1,125.00	1,375.00	1,687.50	2,062.50	6,250.00
$	18.00	$ 20,250.00	$ 24,750.00	$ 30,375.00	$ 37,125.00	$ 112,500.00
Total		6,525.00	7,975.00	9,787.50	11,962.50	36,250.00
		72,225.00	88,275.00	108,337.50	132,412.50	$ 401,250.00

CHAPTER 3

USING JOB-ORDER COSTING

This page is intentionally blank.

CHAPTER 3

Using Job-Order Costing

Objectives

Excel Skills

- Review basic Excel formulas
- Create a new spreadsheet
- Write formulas that pull information from other spreadsheets
- Format a worksheet so that it is easier to read
- Practice skills in formatting, use of lines and outlines, colors, and shading

Accounting Skills

- Identify and compute the value of direct materials (DM) and direct labor (DL) applied to a job
- Calculate the pre-determined overhead rate (POHR) and apply manufacturing overhead (MOH) to a job
- Determine the per-unit and overall cost of a job

Mastering Excel

In order to do job-order costing in Excel, we need to learn two important Excel techniques and practice several that we've already mentioned. Specifically, we will discuss linking information on multiple spreadsheets and creating user-friendly places to input data and turn that data into information. If you are familiar with these topics, then you can just skim over this section. However, if these are new skills for you, the best way to learn them, or review them, is to actually use them. Let's get started!

Reviewing Basic Formulas

Open the workbook called **C3 Excel Practice Sets** from your downloaded files. We're going to demonstrate how to create multi-spreadsheet formulas using a job-order costing example, and we'll also give you a quick refresher on job-order costing before you get started on the Wedgewood case.

Notice that there are three spreadsheet tabs at the bottom of the page: DM, DL, and MOH. Let's start on the DM spreadsheet. In this spreadsheet, we have provided you with some sample data. It's just like the materials we've discussed for Wedgewood, but they don't have nice names like "wax" and "wicks." Instead, we just use DM1, DM2, etc. Each material has a per-unit cost (if it is added to each product the company makes) or a per-batch cost (if it is only applied to a batch). For example, if we were to produce pens we would add plastic and ink to each pen, but normally we don't sell just one pen. Instead, we would sell them by the dozen in formed plastic boxes that allow customers to see what the pens look like. In this case, the box would only be added to each batch of a dozen pens.

There are also two departments in our example: Department A and Department B. In Department A, two of the DM costs are per unit and two are per batch. Notice that the batch size for our practice product is 100 units. In Department B we have two costs, one of which is per unit and one of which is per batch.

Now let's take a look at the DL spreadsheet to see the labor costs for our example company. Of course, we still have two departments that our products will need to pass through, and each department has two classifications of labor. In this example, workers complete multiple units each hour, which is typical for high-volume, low-margin items (like pens or candles). Large items (like computers or cars) work the other way: each employee puts in multiple hours for each unit.

Now let's look at the MOH spreadsheet. On this spreadsheet we can see the two key components of allocating MOH: the total estimated MOH cost that each department will spend during the upcoming year and the total estimated drivers that each department will use. In this case, the company uses the same driver for each department: direct labor hours (DLH). That's not always the case. Typically companies will find that different drivers are more appropriate for different departments or divisions. The method stays the same when a different driver is used for each department. You just have to add an additional line to your spreadsheet for each driver.

With this information we can calculate our POHR for the coming year, and that's going to be our first step in working with Excel. A POHR is used to allocate overhead costs to each department or each product throughout the year. The basic equation is estimated MOH cost ÷ estimated units of the cost driver. In this case, we will use estimated MOH ÷ estimated DLH. Throughout the year, every time a department uses one driver, the accounting department will allocate one POHR of MOH to that department. To calculate the POHRs:

- *Type the row header* POHR *in cell A4.*
- *In cell B4, divide $1,500,000 by 50,000. Don't do this with a calculator or in your head! Use the following equation in Excel:* =B2/B3. *(Remember to click on*

cells B2 and B3 when you come to them in the formula. That way, if the estimated overhead or estimated labor hours change, you can just update the data and it will automatically change the POHR without requiring you to make a manual adjustment.)

 *Copy your equation from cell B4 into cell C4.*

Now you have the two POHRs and we are ready to move on to multi-spreadsheet formulas.

Creating New Spreadsheet Tabs

For this example, let's assume that during the current week the company produced 4,000 units. Our goal as good managerial accountants is to compute a total cost of production and a per-unit cost for those products. There are two options to calculate these measures. Under the first option we would calculate the total DM costs on the DM spreadsheet, the total DL costs on the DL spreadsheet, the total MOH costs on the MOH spreadsheet, and then add them all up. However, that method is hard for others to follow, especially if they aren't familiar with Excel. A better option is to put all of those calculations on one separate spreadsheet. Not only does that make it easier for others to follow but it also allows us to keep all of our equations on one spreadsheet, making it easier for us to update and "tweak" our work when necessary. Because this second option is typically the most effective, let's create a new spreadsheet. Creating a new spreadsheet is easy.

- *Click on the very last spreadsheet tab at the bottom of your workbook. It appears immediately after the MOH spreadsheet tab and has a small box with a star in the upper-left corner. A new spreadsheet will be added to your workbook.* (In Excel 2013, this is a circle with a plus in it instead of a small box with a star.)
- *Double-click on the name of the new spreadsheet tab (Sheet1) and type in* Cost. *You now have a new spreadsheet ready to go!*

Using Multi-Spreadsheet Formulas

With all of the cost information typed into your first three spreadsheets and a new spreadsheet ready to go, you are ready to calculate the total production costs and per-unit costs for this example company. The first piece of information that we need is how many units were produced.

- *In cell A1, type the row header* Units Made.
- *In cell B1, type in* 4,000.

To make our spreadsheet easier to read, let's drop down a couple of rows to separate the raw data (units produced) from the calculations.

Tip:

If you include the comma when you type in a number, then Excel will automatically format your cell as a number rounded to the nearest whole unit. If you just type in "4000", then you will have to format the cell yourself. Both ways work; just remember that we are trying to make a spreadsheet that others can easily use, so we want to make sure that it is well formatted and easy to read. As part of making things easy to read, make sure that all of the columns are wide enough so that you can easily read all of the headings and numbers.

- *In the third row (cells A3 through D3), type in the following headers:* Cost, Per Unit, Per Batch, *and* Total.
- *Select all four cells, center them, and add a bottom border to set them off as column headings. To do this, use the Center command in the second row, left side of the Alignment group of the Home tab of the Excel ribbon at the top of your screen. The Borders command is in the Font group of the Home tab and looks like a table with a drop-down arrow to the right. Typically the Excel default is bottom border, but if you don't see a bottom border in the four squares of the command symbol, click on the drop-down arrow and choose the bottom border.* Your headers are now good to go.
- *In cell A4 type the row header* DM, *because that is the first of our production costs.*

Now, starting in cell B4, we are going to gather the information from the DM spreadsheet.

- *Press either the [+] key or the [=] key and then click on the DM spreadsheet tab.*
- *Click on cell B3, then press [+], then cell B4 (make sure you are still on the DM spreadsheet), then [+], then cell E3, and then finally press [Enter].*

When you press [Enter], Excel takes you back to the Cost spreadsheet. If you have summed up the value correctly, you should have $11.15 as the per-unit cost in cell B4.

- *If necessary, format cell B4 as currency so that those reading your work will know what they are looking at.*
- *Put an equation in column C that multiplies the amount in B4 by 100 to get the total cost per batch. (Remember, you can put in this formula by typing* =B4*100 *and then pressing [Enter].)*

The other two DM costs are batch costs instead of unit costs, as we discussed earlier. That means that we will need to divide those costs by 100 units (the standard batch size for this company) to get the per-unit costs. To do this, let's sum up the three batch costs, but this time we'll put it in column C, our Per Batch column.

- *In cell C5, type [=] then go to the DM spreadsheet and sum up the three batch costs just like we did with the per-unit costs.*
- *Press [Enter] to get back to the Cost spreadsheet.*
- *Type a formula in cell B5 that divides the amount in C5 by 100.*

Now we want to get the total costs for our DM. To do this, we simply multiply the per-unit costs by 4,000 for the total column. Make sure, though, that you link your total column equation to cell A2, which shows the 4,000 we typed in at the beginning of this section, instead of typing in the 4,000 manually (so this formula should be =B4*A2). You should end up with a total cost of $44,600 for the first DM row. Take a minute and complete the second DM row as well.

The nice thing about using formulas that pull data from other spreadsheets is that when you update the information on those other spreadsheets, Excel automatically updates the formula. Let's try it.

- *Go to the DM spreadsheet.*
- *Change the cost of DM6 to be $25 per batch.*

When you return to the cost spreadsheet, you'll see that the amounts in row 5 have been automatically updated. The per-unit cost is now $1.57, the per-batch cost is now $157, and the total costs is $6,280. After you have those numbers, go back and change the cost of DM6 back to $15 per unit. Now let's move on to our DL costs. Leave a blank row to make your work easier to read.

- *Type* DL *into cell A7.*

Just as we did with our batch DM costs, we have to adjust the data provided in the DL spreadsheet to give us what we need for our calculations. In this case, to get the per-unit labor costs for all four different types of labor, we're going to have to divide the hourly rate by the number of units completed per hour. Let's walk through the first one together.

- *In cell B7, press [+] or [=] and go to the DL spreadsheet.*
- *Click on the rate for the first labor type in Department A and divide by the number of units per hour.*
- *Press [Enter].*

You should be back on the Cost spreadsheet and you should see a cost per unit of $0.33 (after you format the cell, of course). With the DM costs we were able to combine all of the per-unit cost and the batch costs, but we can't do that this time. The DM costs were standardized for each unit or each batch. The DL costs are different because each employee completes a different amount of time on each unit. If we had multiple employees or employee classifications that spent the same amount of time on each unit, then we could combine those costs.

In the next three cells down (cells B8 through B10), calculate the cost per unit for the remaining three labor types. After you have that done, then you can multiply the per-unit DL costs by 100 to get the batch costs and by 4,000 to get the total costs.

Last but not least, we need to calculate the MOH costs.

- *Type the row header* MOH *into cell A12.*

As you probably remember, applied MOH is POHR multiplied by the actual driver units used. Stop for a moment, and see if you can figure out on scratch paper how much MOH would be applied to one unit of production in Department A. Did you get $2.20? If so, good job! If not, see the tip box on the following page. Now let's walk through the process in Excel.

First, we will start with the calculation for DL1. In cell B12, we need to calculate MOH per unit for the first driver, namely the DL1 hours used. To do this, we first need to calculate how many hours of this individual's time are spent on each unit. Because he works on 25 units each hour, he spends 1/25th of an hour on each unit. So, the first part of our equation is to take 1÷25, but in a way that links our information to the DL spreadsheet. Again, we link everything so that we can easily update our numbers. Next year, he might speed up and do 26 units in an hour, or we might have to hire someone new who can only work on 14 units each hour. Either way, we want the information to flow automatically into our calculations. After we have the numbers or hours, or fraction of hours in this case, we multiply that amount by the POHR for Department A. In Excel, we can do all of this with just one formula.

- *Click on cell B12 and, this time, type in* =1/ *but don't press [Enter] yet!*
- *Go to your DL spreadsheet and click on cell B3, but still don't press [Enter].*
- *Type [*] to multiply, but still don't press [Enter].*
- *Go to your MOH spreadsheet and click on cell B4 and, finally,*
- *NOW press [Enter].*

Your formula should look like the one pictured here.

12	MOH	=1/DL!B3*MOH!B4

Notice that when you use a number from a spreadsheet other than the one you are currently working on (the MOH spreadsheet in this example), the name of that spreadsheet appears as part of the formula. The formula pictured shows that we pulled one number from the DL spreadsheet and one from the MOH spreadsheet. For the most part, you can just let Excel worry about this; just be careful if you have to edit your equation.

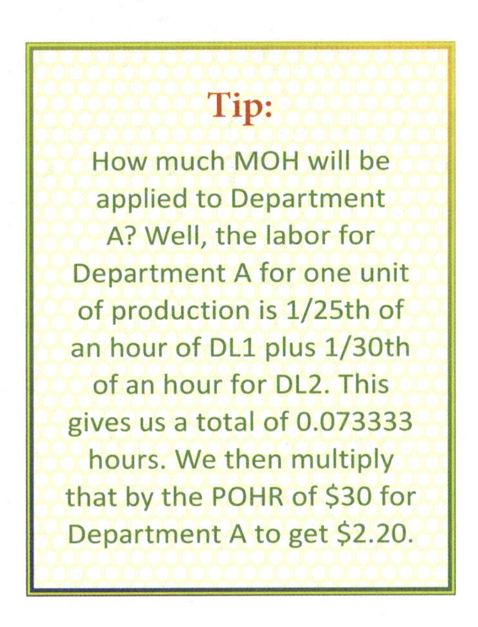

Tip:

How much MOH will be applied to Department A? Well, the labor for Department A for one unit of production is 1/25th of an hour of DL1 plus 1/30th of an hour for DL2. This gives us a total of 0.073333 hours. We then multiply that by the POHR of $30 for Department A to get $2.20.

Now that we have done the basics, go ahead and calculate the amount of MOH that will be applied based on the other three types of labor. Make sure that you switch to the Department B POHR when appropriate.

To finish off our MOH section, we need to multiply each of the per-unit costs by 100 to get the per-batch amount, and by 4,000 to get the total production amounts.

Our original assignment was to figure out the cost per unit and the total production costs. We are now ready to do that.

- *To start, type* Total *as the new row header in cell A17. Then, you can use the AutoSum command to calculate a total for each column (B, C, and D). As a refresher, click on cell B17, then click on the AutoSum command in the Editing group of the Home tab in the Excel ribbon. When you use the AutoSum feature, Excel always tries to guess which cells you want to sum, but it always stops when there's a blank space. Because you want to sum all of the numbers in rows 4 through 15, you'll have to select those cells yourself.* We now know that the per-unit cost is $16.51, the cost per batch is $1,651.43, and the total cost for production this week is $66,057.24.
- *For another check, change the number of units made to 5,000.* Did your total cost change to $82,571.55? Good!
- *You can undo that change by clicking the Undo button (↶) at the top-left of your screen. It looks like an arrow pointing left in the very top left corner of your screen. Alternatively, you can just press [Ctrl] [Z] to undo the last entry.*

Formatting an Excel Spreadsheet

What we've created is a solid set of numbers that we could provide to management, but take a look at your spreadsheet. If it is anything like ours, it isn't too pretty at this point. Part of working in Excel includes creating forms and tables that are easy to read and follow, and that's what's missing here. Our form is functional, but not easy to read. We need to spruce it up so that it looks good for management. Remember, the easier you make life for your manager, the quicker you'll get promoted!

Excel offers a multitude of options for formatting our work, and we aren't going to try to cover all of them here. Instead, we'll just cover a few that will allow us to make our work look great. Let's start out by typing in a title.

- *Right-click on row 1 header (the gray cell on the left of the screen that says 1).*
- *Choose the option to Insert and a new row will appear.*
- *Do this twice so that Units Made now appears in row 3.*
- *In the new cell A1, type in the following title:* Production Cost Information.

Now we have a title, but it still doesn't look very good. The first thing we need to do is to center it over the columns in our table.

- *Select cells A1 through D1, then click on the Merge & Center command in the Alignment group of your Excel ribbon.*

Now your title looks a little better, but it still needs to be set off a little bit so that it doesn't just look like normal text. You can do this in many ways, but let's use Excel's standard formatting options.

- *With the cells still selected, click on the Cell Styles command in the Styles group.*

You should see a number of different format options. These are pre-formatted cell styles that you can use to automatically format your cells. They aren't for number style or equations, but are just to make your work look a little better. You're welcome to choose any format that you like, but we chose to use the Title option, because that's what this is. Doing this made our new font so big that we had to expand our column widths a little bit to show the full title. That's okay. You can easily make your columns bigger or choose a smaller format (like Heading 1). Next, we want to make our headers look a little more formal.

- *Select the column headers in cells A5 through D5 and apply the Heading 2 style.*

Then select the row headers Units Made, DM, DL, MOH, and Total and apply the Heading 4 style. Now we have a spreadsheet that looks pretty good, but we need to make one more minor change to finish our formatting.

By tradition, the final total or result in an accounting form is shown with a double underline. You probably remember seeing this in the financial statements you studied in your financial accounting classes (Net Income, Total Assets, Total Liabilities and Equity, and ending Cash on the Statement of Cash Flows are typically presented this way). You can find this format using the Borders command that we used earlier, but we've been using the standard formats and you can find it there as well. So, highlight cells A19 through D19, and then choose the Total option in the Cell Styles command. You should get a single border above row 19 and a double underline below row 19. In addition, all of these cells are bolded. You might have to resize column D, but that's an easy fix.

You now have a formal table that presents the total cost information from all of your other spreadsheets in a format that can easily be presented to management. In addition, you have set it up in a way that will allow you to automatically update your work as you move into future weeks or years. Now that's something useful!

Wrapping Up Our Excel Work

That's the end of our Excel lesson for this chapter. As you move into the Wedgewood case below, use the questions asked as an opportunity to practice these Excel skills. Remember, the fundamental goal of managerial accounting is to take raw data and convert it into information that decision-makers can understand and use, so make sure that your spreadsheets look good!

Wedgewood Candle Co.

Basic Production Information

Josey Wedgewood, the company controller, carefully reviewed the paperwork on her desk regarding the new specialty candle division. The executive team had decided to start the line by producing three specialty candles most often requested by Wedgewood's loyal customers. These new candles will still have the distinctive size and coloring of the traditional Wedgewood Candles, but they will feature additional sculpting, imprints, or additives (such as trinkets or small gemstones inside the candles). Overall, the new plans and designs were going well, but she still wasn't ready to support the new division.

"Good morning, Josey," Jordan Leavitt, the new accounting clerk, said from the doorway. "What's up?"

Josey shook her head. "More work, as always. We've got to start getting ready for the new division. Production starts in just ten days, and we have to be ready to track costs, revenues, budgets.... The list just goes on and on." She smiled at her new clerk. "I'm sure glad that you're around to help me deal with all of this fun stuff."

Jordan sighed in mock frustration. "I just knew I should have gone into public accounting."

"What, and miss all this? You've got to be kidding!" Josey laughed. "All joking aside, I have some important things for you to do for me today. First, let me give you a little background.

"As you know from your work these past couple of weeks, our traditional candle division has two production departments: Pouring and Finishing. The Pouring department performs the basic manufacturing of the candles, including melting the wax, adding the color and scent, pouring the candles, inserting the wicks, and removing the candles from their molds.

"Once the candles have been removed and cooled, they move to the Finishing department, where the wicks are trimmed, the candles are examined to ensure that there are no blemishes or rough spots, and then packaged for shipping."

"Right," Jordan agreed. "They walked us through all of this during employee orientation. The Finishing department also performs comprehensive quality control checks by randomly cutting up several finished candles from each batch of wax and examining the scent quality and melting points.

"Good," Josey said. "I'm glad that you were listening. Now we are trying to start up a new division producing specialty candles." Jordan nodded. "The good news is that our development team was careful to plan the new candles in a way that will allow us to fit them into the Pouring and Finishing departments.

"The Pouring department will perform most of the additional steps. For the additive candles, they will add the gems and trinkets during the pouring process. For the imprinted candles, they will remove them from the molds a little early so that the softer wax will hold the shapes and sand. And for the sculpted candle, they will do the actual sculpting after the base candle is set. Once those additional steps are completed, the Pouring department sends the candles to Finishing as usual. The basic treatment in Finishing will be the same, but we will sell all of the specialty candles in batches of a dozen, and we will box each batch separately to streamline the shipping process."

"So," Jordan said, as Josey finished her explanation, "we will need to keep track of the extra wax and coloring for the sculpted candles, the sand for the imprinted candles, and the gems and trinkets for the additive candles in the Pouring department. We'll also need to keep track of shipping boxes and wrapping materials for the Finishing department."

"Right, all of those will increase our DM expenses. In addition, we will be tracking a bunch of extra DL, since all of these new candles are more time intensive than the current candles."

"Which employees will be involved?"

"Well, not the apprentices. They'll continue to perform the basic melting, pouring, and packaging jobs for the new division. Candlemakers will be a little more involved, since they supervise the apprentices, mix the various waxes, prepare the wicks, and help with removing the candles from the molds. However, all of the real specialty work will be done by the Candle Masters, our most senior employees."

Jordan started to laugh. "I always thought that 'Candle Masters' sounded like a title out of an old computer game."

Josey laughed too. "Yeah, I guess it does when you think about it. Pierce Wedgewood, the company founder, actually chose those titles. Back then, things were much more formal and titles were very important in the workplace. He wanted to make it very clear which employees had earned his trust. The names seem silly now, but we keep the traditions. Besides, those who earn the Candle Master title are very proud of it. When we mentioned to some of them that we were thinking of renaming their position it almost came to blows."

"So, the Candle Masters like my dad," Jordan said lightly, "are really supervisors, right? Their wages should be fixed costs, and I think I classified them as variable."

"They are variable costs; we've tested them numerous times to make sure, but the expenses still follow the variable pattern, probably because they know that the work goes up and down based on demand. Anyway, they spend most of their time actually doing production with the candlemakers and apprentices. They teach by doing.

"Anyway," Josey continued. "The executive team has decided that only the Candle Masters will be allowed to work on the specialty candles. So, they will be doing *all* of the sculpting, imprinting, and adding of trinkets. Over time, we hope that we can standardize the processes enough so that candlemakers, and perhaps even apprentices, will be able to help finish the specialty candles."

Jordan nodded. "Okay, so what does all of this have to do with me?"

"I'm so glad you asked!" Josey responded. "I need you to run some numbers for me."

Identifying and Computing the DM and DL Applied to a Job

Josey handed Jordan a purchase order. (All documents required for this chapter are located directly after the assignment pages. You also have a workbook in your downloaded files called **C3 Job-Order Costing** that summarizes all of the expected or standard DM and DL costs we've just talked about. There is one spreadsheet for DM and one for DL.) "This morning we got our first order for a batch of specialty candles. The production departments are using this order as a trial run for the new processes, and I think we need to do the same thing. I want you to calculate the cost of the DM and DL on this job, but then I want you to calculate it for the other two types of specialty candles as well for comparison."

"Okay," Jordan said enthusiastically and headed out of the office. He turned around after a couple of steps. "Um, before I start that, do you mind if I check my thought process with you? I don't want to get done and then find out I was doing it wrong."

Josey smiled. "That's a very good idea. Let's go over this sample Job Cost Sheet together." (The Job Cost Sheets are included in the documents for this chapter, directly after the assignment pages — there are four total, one for this review and three for the related assignment.)

To quickly see the sum of a list of numbers in Excel, use your cursor to highlight those numbers, then look at the bottom-right corner of your spreadsheet. The Average, Count, and Sum are all displayed for you, without having to use any equations.

"This sample Job Cost Sheet is for 120 normal six-inch candles. (You might want to open up the workbook called **C3 Job-Order Costing** and review where the numbers they are talking about are found on the Job Cost Sheet.) From what I remember, there are five direct material costs in the Pouring department. Four of those, wax, wick, coloring, and scent, vary with the number of inches in the candle. The last one, the clip, is one per candle, regardless of height."

"Good," Josey agreed, "And the wax, wick, coloring, and scent all add up to $0.65 per inch. For six-inch candles, that gives you $3.90 in DM per candle plus the $0.01 clip, for a total of $3.91 per candle."

"Okay," Jordan continued. "Then we add the $0.04 per candle from the Finishing department for cellophane and information stickers, plus $0.15 per shipping box for every batch of 12."

Josey nodded. "So, what will be the total direct materials for the 120 candles?" She asked, covering the Job Cost Sheet. "No peeking," she teased.

Jordan whipped out his calculator. "Give me a minute," he said punching buttons, "$475.50?"

"Exactly!" Josey beamed at Jordan and turned the Job Cost Sheet back facing him. "In the cost spreadsheet you'll find the extra materials for the specialty candles immediately below the standard direct materials. Remember that, for each specialty candle, we create a standard candle first and then add the additional materials."

Jordan nodded. "Sounds good. Now, labor is a little different, isn't it? It doesn't vary by candle inches because pouring a small candle and pouring a large candle takes virtually the same amount of time."

"Right, so can you tell me how much labor will cost for our hypothetical job?" asked Josey.

Jordan started thinking out loud. "Well, apprentices are only used in the Pouring department and so the cost per batch would be 0.12 hours times $7 per hour, or $0.84 per batch. Candlemakers are used in both departments, but they get paid the same rate, so we could combine their time into 0.12 hours and multiply that times the rate of $12.25 per hour, or $1.47 per batch. We can do the same thing for Candle Masters. They work a total of 0.05 hours in the two departments. If we take that amount times the $18 per hour wage, we get $0.90 per batch. That's a total of $3.21 per batch times ten batches for total direct labor cost of $32.10."

Josey nodded in approval. "That's the right math. Remember, though, when you fill out a Job Cost Sheet, you need to put down each line item separately. I think you're ready to figure out the direct materials and labor for our specialty candles. We'll worry about the overhead later."

Stop here and answer questions 1 and 2 on assignment page 3-17 before continuing.

Rapid Review:

Job-order costing is a method for tracking production costs that matches costs directly to a job, order, or batch. This means that all direct material (DM) used is traced from raw materials inventory to the specific job that uses it, that the wages of every line worker (direct labor, or DL) are tracked to the jobs they work on, and that overhead is allocated directly based on the actual cost drivers used by the job. Direct tracking like this allows companies to more accurately track production costs since they are mapped directly to the jobs that used them. Downsides to this method include becoming time consuming for large companies and being more easily manipulated by managers wanting to shift costs.

(continued on the following page)

Rapid Review *(continued)*:

On a real job site, a company tracks materials as they move into production and tracks labor costs as employees clock in and out. If you don't have that direct information, then you can estimate it by taking the direct material needed per unit multiplied by the number of units in the job, and adding the direct labor needed per unit multiplied by the number of units in the job. By adding up the cost of each type of direct material and each category of direct labor, you get the total costs for the job.

Calculate the POHR and Apply MOH to a Job

"Josey," Jordan typed in his email. "Here are the numbers you requested about the DM and DL costs for the first job, as well as the alternative totals based on the other two types of specialty candles you asked me calculate." He hit send and leaned back in his chair. He felt good about what he had accomplished, especially since he felt that he wasn't really an Excel guru yet. Now, he could move on to some of the financial accounting tasks for which he felt better prepared.

A couple hours later, he paused and checked his email. "Good work," Josey's reply began. "Now you need to apply MOH so that we have a total estimated cost of the job. Once you have those numbers, I'd like you to calculate per-unit cost as well so that we'll know if we are actually going to make any money on this new line or not. You can refer to the Job Cost Sheet that we used to refresh your memory on to how to apply overhead, but those POHRs are not correct; they are old. I've put a memo in your inbox that has my total overhead estimates for the coming year and estimates from the Pouring and Finishing departments for the drivers they think they will be using (which you can find in the documents for this chapter, directly after the assignment pages).

"After our discussion yesterday, I decided that perhaps we should have a different POHR for each department, so I changed the sample Job Cost Sheet to reflect that. Remember that applying overhead on a department level is the same as using a single plant-wide POHR, except that you apply it in chunks, once for each department.

"Good luck, and keep me advised of your progress."

Jordan sighed. It didn't look like he was going to get a chance to make any journal entries after all.

Stop here and answer questions 3 through 6 on assignment pages 3-19 and 3-21 before continuing.

Rapid Review:

Once you have the DM and DL assigned to each job, the next step in job-order costing is to allocate overhead. In order to allocate overhead, you first need a ***Predetermined Overhead Rate***, more commonly referred to as a ***POHR***. This rate is calculated by taking our best estimate at what we will spend on overhead for the year divided by our best estimate of how many units of our chosen ***cost driver*** we will use during the year. We use estimates for both of these numbers so that we can allocate costs over the year and be consistent in the overhead costs applied. This, in turn, allows consistent prices to be charged to our customers.

Most companies calculate one POHR for the whole company (called the ***plant-wide method***) or one for each department (called the ***departmental method***), like Wedgewood does. Using the plant-wide method makes the process of allocating overhead really simple, but typically leaves you with less accurate production costs. Using the departmental method makes things more accurate, but also requires some extra steps.

Once you have a POHR, you allocate overhead costs to your different jobs. To do this, you multiply the POHR by the actual drivers used by each job. If you use a plant-wide POHR, then you only do one calculation. If you use the departmental method, then you multiply the POHR for the department by the actual drivers used *in that department*. Let's take a look at a quick example.

> Let's say that we have a small business selling candy at a local ball park. Over the course of the year, we estimate that we will spend $10,000 in overhead (utilities, rent, etc.). Of that, we think that $4,000 will be from cooking and preparing food and $6,000 will be from serving customers. We have two ways that we can allocate by costs: we can use an estimated 10,000 DL hours as our driver for the whole business (plant-wide method) or we can use an estimated 5,000 DL hours worked as the driver for the cooking department and 16,000 customers served as the driver for the sales department (departmental method).
>
> In a recent game (one job), our employees worked 500 hours, 300 of which were by the cooking staff, and they served 1,000 customers. How much overhead should we allocate to the game?
>
> Well, under the plant-wide method, we would get a POHR of $1/DL hour ($10,000 estimated total overhead / 10,000 estimated total DL hours). So, we would assign $500 of overhead to the game (500 DL hours × $1 per DL hour).
>
> Under the departmental method, we would get two POHRs: $0.80 per hot dog prepared ($4,000 estimated overhead for the cooking department / 5,000 estimated DL hours for the cooking department) and $0.375 per customer

(continued on the following page)

Rapid Review *(continued)*:

served ($6,000 estimated overhead for the sales department / 16,000 estimated customers served). So, we would assign $615 of overhead to the game (300 DL hours by the cooking staff × $0.80 per cooking class DL hour + 1,000 customers served × $0.375 per customer).

A ***job cost form*** is a company document that summarizes the process we've been describing. You can use this form to keep track of each of the costs (DM, DL, and applied OH), then sum them to get a ***Total Production Cost*** for the order. You can also use this form to get a cost per unit (by dividing the total production costs by the units in the order) and to calculate ***Total Profit*** (the sales price on the job - total production cost of the job).

Creating Forms for Management

Josey looked up as Jordan walked into her office. "Did you get finished?"

Jordan nodded. "I have all the numbers. I put them on the forms you gave me, but wouldn't it work better on the spreadsheet?"

"Yes, but I haven't had time to create a template yet. Do you think you can do that?" Josey asked.

"Well," Jordan replied. "I can certainly try."

"That's a good attitude," Josey replied. "Just make sure that your template is easy to read so that I can show it to the rest of the management team."

Stop here and answer question 7 on assignment page 3-21 before continuing.

Rapid Review:

Different companies use different versions of the job cost forms that you just created. The most effective way to use these forms is to create one in Excel (or a similar program) that automates the process. As you can tell from the rest of your work in this chapter, this process can become very time consuming for a job with many inputs or for companies with many departments. As you think about creating your own job cost sheet in Excel, take the time to think through what would make the form easiest to read and use, since you want to make the process easier on the accountants and the information easier to find for the managers.

Name:

Questions

Note: *For questions and problems that require calculations, attach a copy of your spreadsheet to the related assignment page and hand it in to your instructor.*

Identifying and Computing the DM and DL Applied to a Job

Q-1. Use the information from Josey's spreadsheet and the purchase order for the first specialty candle job to calculate the following amounts. Use your spreadsheet to do the work and just write down the answers here.

a. Total DM costs for the job:

____

____

b. Total DL costs for the job:

____

____

Q-2. Calculate the costs of the DM and DL for the other two types of specialty candles.

a. The total DM + DL (direct costs) for same number of additive candles:

____

____

____

b. The total DM + DL (direct costs) for same number of imprinted candles:

____

____

____

Name:

Calculate the POHR and Apply MOH to a Job

Q-3. Refer to the estimated overhead report Josey provided and calculate the POHR for the:

a. Pouring department.

____

____

b. Finishing department.

____

____

Q-4. Use the POHRs for the two departments you calculated in Question 3 to calculate applied MOH for each department. Remember to apply MOH on the basis of DLH for the Pouring department and on batches completed for the Finishing department.

a. What is the amount of MOH that will be applied to the special order from the Pouring department?

____

____

b. What is the amount of MOH that will be applied to the special order from the Finishing department?

____

____

Name:

Q-5. Complete the job cost forms found in the document section at the end of the chapter. Attach the completed forms to this assignment page.

Q-6. Calculate the following:

a. The total profit for this order.

b. The per-unit profit for this order.

Creating Forms for Management

Q-7. Create a Job Cost Sheet for Wedgewood's specialty candle orders that meets Josey's criteria. Attach a printout of your work to this worksheet.

Name:

Problems

Critical Thinking Issues

Problem #1

In the case, Jordan put together a total cost for the first order of specialty candles by adding up all of the DM, DL, and allocated MOH; in other words, he used *absorption costing*. This is the method most commonly discussed in textbooks because it is also the method required by GAAP for financial reporting purposes. However, there are several other methods for allocating costs to a product or order:

- **Variable Manufacturing Cost.** This method of tracking costs includes only DM, DL, and the variable portion of MOH. No fixed manufacturing costs or selling and administrative (S&A) costs are included.
- **Total Variable Cost.** This method of tracking costs includes DM, DL, variable MOH, and variable S&A. However, fixed costs are still omitted.
- **Full Cost.** This method of tracking costs includes all of the costs of the business, including all S&A costs.

Discuss the pros and cons of each of the four costing methods. Which method do you think Wedgewood should use for its new line of specialty candles? Defend your answer. (Feel free to use the back of this page to continue your answer.)

Name:

Problem #2

One of the primary purposes of calculating a total cost is to evaluate whether or not a company should produce a product. Marketing firms or departments typically do extensive research with potential customers to determine what price they are willing to pay for a new product, like Wedgewood's specialty candles. After the company knows what price customers are willing to pay, it can determine how much it can spend producing each unit while still providing a profit. This process is called *target costing*.

After conducting some market research, Wedgewood has determined that retail customers are willing to pay $15 to $20 for a four-inch sculpted candle. Wedgewood sells to retailers, though, not directly to customers. Retailers mark up their costs 100%—therefore, if they sell something to a customer for $10, they paid $5 to purchase it wholesale. Using your answer to question 6b, and assuming that Wedgewood needs to make a 50% markup on their production costs to cover S&A expenses and achieve their desired profit margin, do you think that Wedgewood should produce the new line of specialty candles?

Write a business letter to Jeremiah Wedgewood, the company CFO, explaining and defending your position on beginning the new line. (You may use the lines provided below and continue on the back of this page, if needed, or attach your own printout to this worksheet.)

Ethical Issues

Jeremiah Wedgewood, the CFO, is adamant that the company needs to move ahead with the new line. While Josey also thinks that the new line is a good idea, she is a little worried about how it is going to affect their financial statements in the short run. After carefully considering what was likely to happen, Josey scheduled an appointment to visit with Jeremiah about her concerns.

"Josey!" Jeremiah said as she came into his office. "How are you doing today?" Josey smiled. Nothing ever seemed to really bother Jeremiah.

"I'm doing well, thanks, Uncle Jerry. Just a little worried about our new line."

"Worried?" Jeremiah asked. "About what?"

"Well, let me just start by saying that I agree that adding these new candles is a great idea. I think we have a really good idea of how much we can charge for them to break into the market and stay competitive in the long run. I also think while our costs will be high while we get the new line started, they will come down over time as we get settled. But I'm a little concerned about what the line will do to our profits for the next couple of years. The profits won't be nearly as good as they are for our traditional candles for at least two years."

"Well, Josey," Jeremiah replied, "Keep in mind that this is a family-owned business, so that's not going to be a big deal. I mean, we don't have investors messing up our stock prices with every little piece of news. However," he paused, looking out his window for a moment as he thought about the changes. "We did just open up a new line of credit with our bank and our interest rate is contingent on maintaining profitability in each segment. Shoot! I didn't think about the new line when I signed that deal. They offered such a low rate that I wanted to make sure I locked it in." He looked at Josey. "We don't have to show a large profit, just a profit. What do you think our chances are of just being above zero with the new line?"

Josey shook her hand back and forth. "About 50-50, I'd say, at least for the first year."

"That's not good enough," Jeremiah said, shaking his head. "What if we adjust the overhead allocation so that both lines show a profit?" Josey frowned. "Now, don't write me off as a bad guy, Josey. This wouldn't be right if we were a public company because we would be misleading investors, but, as I said, we don't have any investors, just the family."

"What about the bank?" Josey asked.

"Well, think about it," Jeremiah said, a smile again forming on his lips. "They really just want to make sure that we pay them back, or that we have the cash to pay them

Name:

back. What I'm talking about won't affect our cash flows at all. We're just shifting overhead from one line to another. Companies do that all time."

Josey looked at Jeremiah and pondered. She was confident that the new line would be profitable soon, probably in just a year or two. And overhead is applied on a somewhat arbitrary basis, especially when using a single, plant-wide rate, or departmental rates. She chose all of those numbers anyway, after all. There was no way to really know if the amount of overhead being applied to any product was the "real" amount. Activity-based costing would get them closer to an actual cost, but she hadn't had time to get into that yet. And Jeremiah was certainly right; the last thing they needed now was for the bank to raise the interest rates over a bookkeeping technicality. Perhaps they could make a change to their overhead allocations....

Problem #3

Make a list of the pros and cons of applying overhead strictly on the basis of specific departmental rates versus "adjusting" the allocations to keep each line profitable.

Name:

Problem #4

Review the four principles and four standards of the IMA's Statement of Ethical Professional Practice (There is likely a copy in your Managerial Accounting or Cost Accounting textbook. However, you can also find this online by Googling "IMA Statement of Ethics.") Based on these principles and standards, do you believe that there are any ethical violations in Jeremiah's proposal? Explain which, if any, of the principles and/or standards Jeremiah's suggestion will violate. Does it matter that this is a family-owned company instead of one with outside investors? If there were no bank loan and Jeremiah wanted to do this just for internal reporting, would it change your answer?

PURCHASE ORDER

Cowboy Specialty Candles

Lighting up the Western World

P.O. # 61375
DATE: JUNE 13, 2016

123 Main Street,
Small Town, CO 80201

VENDOR Wedgewood Candle Company
300 Wedgewood Avenue
Wedgewood, UT 84600

SHIP TO Cowboy Specialty Candles
123 Main Street
Small Town, CO 80201

SHIPPING METHOD	SHIPPING TERMS	DELIVERY DATE
UPS	FOB DESTINATION	JUNE 30, 2016

QTY	ITEM #	DESCRIPTION	JOB	UNIT PRICE	LINE TOTAL
48	SCULPTED - 4	4" TALL SCULPTED CANDLES	S-1	$9.90	$475.20
				SUBTOTAL	$475.20
				SALES TAX	EXEMPT
				TOTAL	$475.20

Wedgewood
Candle Co.

To: Jordan Leavitt

From: Josey Wedgewood

Date: 06/14/2016

Re: Estimated amounts for next year.

Jordan,

Here are my estimates of the number of drivers each department will use next year along with an estimated total overhead for each department. Please use these figures to calculate a POHR for each department, and then use that rate to apply overhead.

Department	Drivers Used	Total Overhead
Pouring (driver: DL hours)	25,000	$400,000
Finishing (driver: batches completed)	125,000	$800,000

JOB COST SHEET

Client Name: Sample

Purchase Order Number: Sample

Item produced and quantity: 120 Normal 6" Candles

DIRECT MATERIALS				
Item	Quantity	Per-unit cost	Extended cost	
Wax	6" x 120	.50	$360.00	
Wick	6" x 120	.05	$36.00	
Coloring	6" x 120	.02	$14.40	
Scent	6" x 120	.08	$57.60	
Clip	120	.01	$1.20	
Cellophane	120	.01	$1.20	
Information Stickers	120	.03	$3.60	
Packing Box	10	.15	$1.50	
			Total Direct Material Cost	$475.50
DIRECT LABOR				
Item	Total Hours	Hourly Rate	Extended cost	
Apprentice Labor	.12 x 10 = 1.20	$7.00	$8.40	
Candlemaker Labor	(.06 + .06) x 10 = 1.20	$12.25	$14.70	
Candle Master Labor	(.02 + .03) x 10 = .5	$18.00	$9.00	
			Total Direct Labor Cost	$32.10
APPLIED MANUFACTURING OVERHEAD				
Driver/Department	Quantity	POHR	Extended cost	
Pouring (DLH)	1.20+1.20+.5=2.90	$75.00	$217.50	
Finishing (Batches)	10	$25.00	$250.00	
			Total Applied Manufacturing Overhead	$467.50
			TOTAL COST	**$975.10**
			Per-Unit Cost	$8.13

JOB COST SHEET

Client Name: Purchase Order Number:

Item produced and quantity:

DIRECT MATERIALS				
Item	Quantity	Per-unit cost	Extended cost	
Wax				
Wick				
Coloring				
Scent				
Clip				
Cellophane				
Information Stickers				
Packing Box				
			Total Direct Material Cost	
DIRECT LABOR				
Item	Total Hours	Hourly Rate	Extended cost	
Apprentice Labor				
Candlemaker Labor				
Candle Master Labor				
			Total Direct Labor Cost	
APPLIED MANUFACTURING OVERHEAD				
Driver/Department	Quantity	POHR	Extended cost	
Pouring (DLH)				
Finishing (Batches)				
			Total Applied Manufacturing Overhead	
			TOTAL COST	
			Per-Unit Cost	

JOB COST SHEET

Client Name: Purchase Order Number:

Item produced and quantity:

DIRECT MATERIALS				
Item	Quantity	Per-unit cost	Extended cost	
Wax				
Wick				
Coloring				
Scent				
Clip				
Cellophane				
Information Stickers				
Packing Box				
			Total Direct Material Cost	
DIRECT LABOR				
Item	Total Hours	Hourly Rate	Extended cost	
Apprentice Labor				
Candlemaker Labor				
Candle Master Labor				
			Total Direct Labor Cost	
APPLIED MANUFACTURING OVERHEAD				
Driver/Department	Quantity	POHR	Extended cost	
Pouring (DLH)				
Finishing (Batches)				
			Total Applied Manufacturing Overhead	
			TOTAL COST	
			Per-Unit Cost	

JOB COST SHEET

Client Name:

Purchase Order Number:

Item produced and quantity:

DIRECT MATERIALS				
Item	Quantity	Per-unit cost	Extended cost	
Wax				
Wick				
Coloring				
Scent				
Clip				
Cellophane				
Information Stickers				
Packing Box				
			Total Direct Material Cost	
DIRECT LABOR				
Item	Total Hours	Hourly Rate	Extended cost	
Apprentice Labor				
Candlemaker Labor				
Candle Master Labor				
			Total Direct Labor Cost	
APPLIED MANUFACTURING OVERHEAD				
Driver/Department	Quantity	POHR	Extended cost	
Pouring (DLH)				
Finishing (Batches)				
			Total Applied Manufacturing Overhead	
			TOTAL COST	
			Per-Unit Cost	

USING PROCESS COSTING

This page is intentionally blank.

CHAPTER 4

Using Process Costing

Objectives

Excel Skills

- Set up a template for common projects
- Save the template as backup for monthly journal entries

Accounting Skills

- Perform process costing calculations using both the Weighted Average and FIFO methods
- Determine equivalent units (EU) of production and cost per EU
- Calculate transferred-in costs, direct material costs (DM), and conversion costs (CC)
- Make journal entries to record the transfer of goods between departments or into finished goods inventory

Mastering Excel

Introducing Templates

As we've already seen, Excel can greatly speed up our processes and calculations. It also allows you to create easy-to-follow and easy-to-read forms that you can use to share those calculations with others. In this chapter, we combine those two processes to create a special kind of template that not only allows the rapid performance of multiple calculations each period, but also provides a specialized form that makes it easy to follow, present to management, or turn over to a less-experienced employee. These special tools are called *templates*.

A template, in a nutshell, is a workbook saved in a raw format. In a template, you create the basic equations and formatting, but don't add any of the data. When you double-click on a template file, Excel doesn't actually open the template. Instead, it opens up a copy. All you have to do is type in the data, click Save, and you have a brand new file ready to go. And the best news is that the template file, still clear and clean and without any changes, is ready for the next set of data.

While the process of creating a template is simply saving your file in a special way, we're going to walk through an example that will allow you to not only learn this new skill, but also practice the skills we've been learning in this book and in your management accounting class. We're going to create a template for a process costing system. Let's get started!

Creating and Formatting a Weighted Average Process Costing Table for the First Step in the Production Process

First, open the workbook from your downloaded files called **C4 Excel Practice Sets** to the first spreadsheet and let's review the information on it. We've provided you with some raw data for a sample company that has two departments: Cooking and Packaging. In this company, the units are started in the Cooking department, and then moved to Packaging where they are completed and then transferred to finished goods inventory. For this example, we'll assume that the company uses the weighted average method of process costing. You'll also see that all of the materials used by the Cooking department are added at the beginning of the production process, and all the materials are added at the end of the process in the Packaging department.

We have also provided the number of units in beginning work-in-process (WIP) in each department for the current month, the number of units added to processing during the month, and the number of units left in ending WIP at the end of the month. Why doesn't it tell you how many units were added to packaging during the month? Think about that while we work through the rest of the problem and you shouldn't have any trouble coming up with the answer.

We've provided you with some percentages with column headers "CC." CC stands for *conversion costs*: the DL and MOH that we add to convert the raw material into the finished product in each department. So, for example, the Packaging department had 32,500 units in beginning inventory that were 25% complete with respect to conversion.

Finally, in columns G through K are the costs assigned to beginning inventory and those added during production this period. To help with the process costing calculations, we've already broken out how much of those costs are direct materials and how much are conversion costs for each department.

Now that we've looked at the data, let's get started creating our process costing template.

Basic Spreadsheet Preparation

- *Rename the first spreadsheet* Production Data *to make it easy to reference to the basic data.*
- *Create a second spreadsheet named* Cooking Department *for the calculations that we will be making.*

In the new Cooking Department worksheet, create a table for your calculations.

- *Type a title such as* Weighted Average Process Costing *and subtitle* Cooking Department. *Center your titles over columns A through E.*
- *Type the following column titles, starting in column B:* Units, Materials Costs, Conversion Costs, *and* Total Costs.
- *Wrap text and/or resize the columns so that you can read the titles.*
- *Format your titles to distinguish them from the rest of your work (centering, underlining, different fonts, etc.). The exact formatting does not matter as long as it looks professional.*

When you are done with these steps, the spreadsheet should look something like this:

	A	B	C	D	E
1	**Weighted Average Process Costing**				
2	**Cooking Department**				
3		**Units**	**Materials cost**	**Conversion Costs**	**Total Costs**

Weighted Average Calculations

Now that we have the basic format set up, we can calculate the flow of units in and out of the WIP inventory accounts and calculate the total costs. Let's start with the unit flow.

- *In row 4, the first blank row, type the title* Beginning *in column A. (As you go, be sure to think about formatting.)*
- *Link cell B4 to the beginning inventory number on the Production data worksheet (cell B7).*
- *Type the title* Added this Period *into row 5, column A.*
- *Link cell B5 to the units added during the month on the Production data worksheet (cell B8).*
- *Type the title* Total to Account For *into row 6 and sum up the total units in column B.*

- *In row 7, type the title* Ending Inventory *and link cell B7 to the number of units left in the Cooking department on the Production data worksheet (cell B9).*
- *Type the title* Transferred to Packaging *into row 8.*
- *Subtract the units in Ending Inventory from total units to get the Transferred to Packaging value.*

Here's what it should look like so far. Notice that we included a double underline at the bottom of our first column to show that we are done with that calculation.

	A	B	C	D	E
1	**Weighted Average Process Costing**				
2	**Cooking Department**				
3		**Units**	**Materials cost**	**Conversion Costs**	**Total Costs**
4	Beginning	32,500			
5	Added this Period	184,000			
6	Total to Account for	216,500			
7	Ending Inventory	17,900			
8	Transferred to Finishing	198,600			
9					

Now that we have the unit information needed, let's start calculating the costs. We'll go through the process step-by-step.

Tip:

Because the cells from which these numbers come are in a two by two cell format, and the place to which you are transferring them is also two-by-two, the quickest way to do this is to pull the data from "Production Data" cell H7 to "Packaging Department" cell C4 and then copy down and over by pulling on the bottom-right corner of cell C4.

- *Link cells C4 and D4 to the beginning DM and conversion costs values provided in the Production Data worksheet (cells H7 and I7).*
- *Link cells C5 and D5 to the costs added during the month provided in the Production Data worksheet cells H8 and I8.*
- ***Optional:*** *To keep track of units vs. costs, you may want to format the unit cells in column B as numbers and your cost values in cells C4 through E9 as currency or accounting numbers. We chose the latter.*
- *Sum the total material costs and conversion costs in row 6.*

- *Calculate the total column as the sum of the materials and conversion costs.*

> **Tip:**
>
> Be careful if you use the AutoSum feature here – it will try to include the units in the total, but this total should only be the dollars.

To get the ending inventory values, we first need to calculate the Cost per Unit. To do this, we need to set up a new equivalent unit table.

- *Create a new heading in row 11,* Equivalent Units, *and center it over columns A through D.*
- *Type the headings* Materials *and* Conversion Costs *into C12 and D12. This way they will line up with the DM Costs and Conversion Costs in our first table.*
- *Label row 13 as* Transferred to Packaging, *row 14 as* Ending Inventory, *row 15 as* % Completed this Period, *row 16 as* Total Equivalent Units, *and row 18 as* Cost per Equivalent Unit. *Leave row 17 blank.*
- ***Optional:*** *To set apart cell A15 from the actual unit values, highlight the cell and click the Center and Italic format commands.*
- *Link both C13 and D13 to the units transferred to Packaging in cell B8.*
- *Because this department always adds materials at the beginning of the process, type* 100% *in cell C15. If a department had a different policy, or if materials were added at different times, this cell would need to be linked to the information tab.*
- *For cell D15, the percentage for Conversion Costs, link to the ending WIP CC percentage (cell C9) on the Production Data spreadsheet.*
- *In cells C14 and D14, calculate the equivalent units in ending inventory for both materials and conversion costs by taking the % completed multiplied by the units in ending inventory (for materials, this will be* =B7*C15*).*
- *Sum the total Equivalent Units for DM and CC in row 16.*
- *Skip a row and then calculate the Cost per Unit in row 18. To do this, divide the Total costs reported in row 6 by the total equivalent units in row 16.*

> Show the equivalent units and the dollars to account for as whole numbers for ease of reading; however, format the cost per EU as dollars and cents to still account for all the monetary costs.

Now that we have costs per unit, we can now go back and finish our costing table.

Tip:

Be sure to use the units calculated in the equivalent units table for these calculations, and not from the main table.

- *Calculate the ending inventory value as the cost per EU multiplied by the equivalent units in ending inventory. For materials, this will be* =C18*C14. *Use the same basic equation for conversion costs.*
- *Sum up the ending inventory from materials and conversion costs to get the total ending inventory value in E7.* Be careful not to include column B.
- *Calculate the value of the inventory transferred out as the total cost less ending inventory. Use the same basic equations for conversion costs.*
- **Optional:** *Highlight the two key numbers in your spreadsheet: total cost of ending inventory and total cost transferred to packaging. The easy way to do this is to select the two cells, then click on the Cell Styles command in the Styles menu of the command ribbon, then select a highlight option. We chose green for our example, but Excel provides many other automatic formatting options.*

Here's what your finished product should look like:

	A	B	C	D	E
1		**Weighted Average Process Costing**			
2		**Cooking Department**			
3		**Units**	**Materials cost**	**Conversion Costs**	**Total Costs**
4	Beginning	32,500	$ 7,960	$ 21,675	$ 29,635
5	Added this Period	184,000	$ 197,715	$ 630,488	$ 828,203
6	Total to Account for	216,500	$ 205,675	$ 652,163	$ 857,838
7	Ending Inventory	17,900	$ 17,005	$ 8,699	$ 25,704
8	Transferred to Packaging	198,600	$ 188,670	$ 643,464	$ 832,134
9					
10					
11		**Equivalent Units**			
12			**Materials**	**Conversion costs**	
13	Transferred to Packaging		198,600	198,600	
14	Ending Inventory		17,900	2,685	
15	*% Completed this Period*		100%	15%	
16	Total Equivalent Units		216,500	201,285	
17					
18	Cost per Equivalent Unit		$0.95	$3.24	

Creating and Formatting a Weighted Average Process Costing Table for the Following Steps in the Production Process

Next, we need to create a form for the Packaging department. The basic format is the same, as are the basic equations, for any additional departments. The only real difference is the need to add a column, usually right after units, for the Transferred-In Costs. Then link that value to the total transferred out costs from the previous table (highlighted, if you chose to do so, in green). Here are the steps for creating a new worksheet for the Packaging department for this example:

- *Create another spreadsheet and change its name to* Packaging Department.
- *Highlight all of your work in the Cooking Department worksheet by clicking and dragging, using the [Ctrl] [A] command, or by clicking in the gray box in the top-left corner of the spreadsheet between A and 1 (the column and row headers).*
- *Copy the cells using the [Ctrl] [C] command or the Copy option in the Clipboard section of the ribbon.*
- *Click on worksheet tab Packaging Department, click in cell A1, and paste your work.*
- *Change the title in row B to* Packaging Department *and the row header in rows 8 and 13 to* Transferred to Finished Goods. *Adjust the column widths.*
- *Update the links to the Production Data tab to use the Packaging Numbers.* Added this Period *(cell B5) will come from the Cooking Department worksheet (Transferred to Packaging, B8). The other data will all come from the Production Data worksheet.*
- *Change the 100% in cell C15 to* 0%, *because all of the raw materials are added at the end of the process in Packaging.*

	A	B	C	D	E
1	**Weighted Average Process Costing**				
2	**Packaging Department**				
3		**Units**	**Materials cost**	**Conversion Costs**	**Total Costs**
4	Beginning	14,600	$ 18,250	$ 54,750	$ 73,000
5	Added this Period	198,600	$250,382	$ 790,728	$1,041,110
6	Total to Account for	213,200	$268,632	$ 845,478	$1,114,110
7	Ending Inventory	27,300	$ -	$ 88,886	$ 88,886
8	Transferred to Finished Goods	185,900	$268,632	$ 756,592	$1,025,224
9					

(continued on the following page)

(continued from the previous page)

11	**Equivalent Units**		
12		**Materials**	**Conversion costs**
13	Transferred to Finished Goods	185,900	185,900
14	Ending Inventory	-	21,840
15	*% Completed this Period*	0%	80%
16	Total Equivalent Units	185,900	207,740
17			
18	Cost per Equivalent Unit	$1.45	$4.07
19			

You should have a spreadsheet that looks like the one pictured above and on the previous page, but we aren't done quite yet. Take a minute to examine each number carefully, and if any of yours don't match ours, review your formulas carefully. Here's another picture shown below to show you what your formulas should look like.

	A	B	C	D	E
1			**Weighted Average Process Costing**		
2			**Packaging Department**		
3		**Units**	**Materials cost**	**Conversion Costs**	**Total Costs**
4	Beginning	=+'Production Data'!D7	=+'Production Data'!L7	=+'Production Data'!M7	=SUM(C4:D4)
5	Added this Period	=+'Cooking Department'!B8	=+'Production Data'!L8	=+'Production Data'!M8	=SUM(C5:D5)
6	Total to Account for	=SUM(B4:B5)	=SUM(C4:C5)	=SUM(D4:D5)	=SUM(E4:E5)
7	Ending Inventory	=+'Production Data'!D9	=C18*C14	=D18*D14	=SUM(C7:D7)
8	Transferred to Finished Goods	=B6-B7	=C13*C18	=D13*D18	=E6-E7
9					
10					
11			**Equivalent Units**		
12			**Materials**	**Conversion costs**	
13	=A8		=$B$8	=$B$8	
14	=A7		=B7*C15	=B7*D15	
15	*% Completed this Period*		0	=+'Production Data'!E9	
16	Total Equivalent Units		=C13+C14	=D13+D14	
17					
18	Cost per Equivalent Unit		=C6/C16	=D6/D16	

Now we need to add in the costs transferred in from the Cooking department.

- *Insert a column between the current columns B and C.*
- *Type the header* Transferred-In Costs *into cell C3 and* Transferred-In *into cell C12.*

- *Link the beginning transferred-in costs (cell C4) to the Production Data spreadsheet (cell K7 on that tab).*
- *Link the* Added this Period *value (cell C5) from the Cooking Department tab (E8, highlighted in green if you used the optional formatting suggestion).*
- *Calculate the Equivalent Units for Transferred-In Costs, keeping in mind that all of the units are 100% done with respect to transferred-in costs.*
- *Update the equations in the total costs column to include the transferred-in costs.*

	A	B	C	D	E	F	G
1		Weighted Average Process Costing					
2		Packaging Department					
3		Units	Transferred-In Costs	Materials Cost	Conversion Costs	Total Costs	
4	Beginning	14,600	58,500	$ 18,250	$ 54,750	$ 131,500	
5	Added this Period	198,600	832,134	$ 250,382	$ 790,728	$ 1,873,244	
6	Total to Account for	213,200	$ 890,634	$ 268,632	$ 845,478	$ 2,004,744	
7	Ending Inventory	27,300	$ 114,045	$ -	$ 88,886	$ 202,931	
8	Transferred to Finished Goods	185,900	$ 776,589	$ 268,632	$ 756,592	$ 1,801,813	
9							
10							
11		Equivalent Units					
12			Transferred-In	Materials	Conversion Costs		
13	Transferred to Finished Goods		185,900	185,900	185,900		
14	Ending Inventory		27,300	-	21,840		
15	*% Completed this Period*		100%	0%	80%		
16	Total Equivalent Units		213,200	185,900	207,740		
17							
18	Cost per Equivalent Unit		$4.18	$1.45	$4.07		

Again, take a minute to compare your solution to the one pictured. If there are any differences, review each step carefully.

Creating a Template

Now that we have the tables ready to go, creating the template is simple. Here's the process:

- *Click on the File tab in the top-right of the screen.*
- *Choose the Save As option.*

- *In the Save as Type box at the bottom of the Save As menu screen, choose "Excel Template (*.xltx)."* (In Excel 2013, you need to choose a folder before you get the command screen to choose your file format.)
- *Change the file location from the Excel default to the place where you would like to save your file.*
- *Name the template. A good example might be:* Production Costs – 20XX.
- *Click Save.*

Next month, all you need to do is double-click on the template to open up a brand new file for your process costing. After you change your data in the Production Data to the new values (on the Production Data spreadsheet), save your file. Excel won't save over the original. Instead, it will bring up the "Save As" menu screen and you can change the file name to the current year and month. You get an updated version, and you still have your template.

If you do need to update your template (for example, if you find a mistake), just use the Open file command through Excel instead of double-clicking on the template. This will open up the template itself, and you can make fundamental changes that will affect all future months.

Now you are ready to make your monthly calculations without having to reinvent the wheel or worry about losing earlier data.

Wrapping Up Our Excel Work

Okay, now that you've worked through weighted average process costing in your practice set, it's time to head back to Wedgewood. Pay attention to what Josey has to say, though. Wedgewood doesn't use the weighted average method for process costing!

Wedgewood Candle Co.

Starting Up a Process Costing System

"Josey!" Jeremiah's boisterous voice echoed around Josey's small office. "I just got back into town and found the numbers from last year on my desk. Are these really accurate?"

Josey gave him an exaggerated grin. "No, Uncle Jerry, I just made them up. I do that a lot, because I have so much free time."

Jeremiah laughed. "Okay, okay. I'm sorry I suggested it! I just can't believe we've been missing out on this much profit for so long."

"It is impressive. The specialty candles have done better than we could have imagined, especially the imprinted ones."

Jeremiah nodded. "We're already moving ahead with full production of the imprinted line. I guess operations started full production last quarter without really telling us about it."

"That's what I heard, so I've already started getting things ready on our end to switch to a process costing system for the new imprinting line."

Jeremiah nodded. "How soon?"

"Well, I have a standard worksheet for process costing here. I started filling it out for Pouring, but I'll have our staff accountant, Jordan, finish filling it out for the end of the first quarter, then I'll have him create a form for the Finishing department. After that, we'll be all set up and ready for the next quarter."

"Good. I'll look forward to seeing the new system."

As Jeremiah left, Josey buzzed Jordan to come to her office. "You've heard the news about the new line?" she asked as he got settled. Jordan nodded. "Good. Now that we are moving into full production we have to switch from a job-order costing system to a process costing system, at least for this first line. We'll still use the job-order costing system for the sculpted and additive lines, at least until demand picks up enough for us to start full-time production of those lines as well.

"For now, I need you to start the transition to the process costing system for the new imprinted candle line. Here's a copy of the standard form I want you to use." Josey handed Jordan a blank process cost Production Report (which you have at the end of the chapter, directly after the assignment pages. "Get it filled out ASAP for the Pouring department, and then we'll talk about the other departments. I emailed you the data you'll need." (This data file is labeled **C4 Excel Process Costing.** The first spreadsheet in this workbook is called Josey's Email.)

Jordan nodded. "Just so I know, which method do we use for our process costing? We learned two or three methods in school."

Josey smiled. "We use FIFO, just like it says at the top of that form I just gave you. Do you remember how to do process costing using FIFO?"

"Not really, but I bet I can find it in my old managerial accounting book." Jordan blushed. "I'll get right on it," he said quickly and left Josey's office.

Tip:

When you start your questions, don't forget that Wedgewood uses FIFO, not the Weighted Average method!

Jordan examined the form Josey handed him and sighed. It was horrible. There wasn't any place to do the calculations, and the flow didn't make any sense at all. He'd have to do the work on the computer anyway. He decided that he'd fill this one out for Josey, just this once, but then he was going to create a template on the computer to use next time.

Stop here and answer questions 1 and 2 on assignment page 4-17 before continuing.

Rapid Review:

Process costing is a method for tracking production costs directly to a process or department. Tracking costs by process allows companies to allocate costs to large numbers of similar units manufactured in a continuous process. For example, you can't track each individual gallon of gasoline that is being produced in a refinery—you have to use process costing. At the end of the period, you add up the total costs assigned to each process and divide by the ***equivalent units*** produced to get the assigned production costs per unit for that process.

Equivalent unit (EU) is a special term used in process costing. EUs are the number of units we could have made if we had made one unit at a time instead of partially finishing several units. For example, imagine that you work for a company that produces cakes. One option would be to bake each cake, frost it, and then wrap it for delivery. This method would probably use job-order costing. Another option would be to have one group baking all of the cakes, another group frosting them, and then another group doing the packaging. This method would use process costing. So in our pretend company, the baking department finished baking 800 cakes, and has another 150 mixed and ready to go into the ovens (50% done). You need to know how much you've spent on both finished cakes and on the cakes that are partially complete, so, you come up with the ***equivalent units***:

	Started	% Complete	Equivalent Units
Finished	800	100%	800
Ready to Bake	150	50%	75
Equivalent Units			875

To get your production cost per unit for the Baking Department, you would take the total costs assigned and divide by 875.

(continued on the following page)

Rapid Review *(continued)*:

Many companies break down their EU calculations into two costs: DM and Conversion (DL + MOH). Because most ingredients are added at the beginning of the baking process, you would get a table that looks like this:

	Materials	Conversion costs
Beginning Inventory	0	0
% Completed this Period	0%	0%
Started and Completed	800	800
Ready to Bake	150	75
% Completed this Period	100%	50%
Total Equivalent Units	950	875

Since DM and Conversion Costs will always have a different number of EUs (unless materials are added evenly throughout the process), most companies choose to track the costs separately and calculate a cost per EU for DM and for Conversion separately.

At the end of the period, the company calculates DM and Conversion costs per EU and multiplies it by the number of units finished and transferred. This is the amount that is moved to the next department with journal entries. In our example, you would multiply the costs per equivalent unit multiplied by the 800 units finished and record an entry crediting WIP Inv. (Baking) and debiting WIP Inv. (Icing). The costs remaining in WIP inventory are what have been spent so far to create the partially completed units.

Creating a Production Report

"Jordan," Josey said coming into his office. "Great work on this first Production Report!"

"Thanks, Josey, but somehow I doubt that you came by just to tell me that."

Josey laughed. "You're really starting to get the hang of this, aren't you? You're right. Now that you've finished filling out this first form, I need you to create the report for the Finishing department."

"Create it?"

"Yep. You can do it. Just use the first report as a template and create a new one. Just remember that this is the second department in the process, so you will need to add in the transfer costs from the Pouring department."

"I wanted to talk to you about that the form, actually. It isn't very . . . umm . . . intuitive . . . and. . . ."

Josey interrupted with a laugh, "You're trying very hard to be diplomatic, and you don't have to be. I hate that form too. It was passed on to me by my former boss, and I just haven't had time to redo it. Do you think you can whip up something in Excel that will work better?" She grinned as he nodded. "Well, then, go for it!"

"Okay, I'll get right on it." Jordan was already visualizing how he'd need to set up the rows and columns in a template that would record the quarterly production data and generate a journal entry for transferring the goods each quarter.

"Good. I think the information you need is on the same email I sent you earlier." She smiled at Jordan and then left the office.

Stop here and answer questions 3 and 4 on assignment page 4-19 before continuing.

Rapid Review:

As the units are moved from process to process in this system, the costs of earlier processes are also transferred. So, the first process in the production cycle will have only two costs: DM and Conversion costs. Processes later in the system will have three costs: DM, conversion costs, and transferred-in costs. This leads to the next version of our equivalent units table (this time for the frosting division):

	Transferred-In Costs	Materials	Conversion costs
Beginning Inventory	0	0	0
% Completed this Period	0%	0%	0%
Started and Completed	700	700	700
Almost Done	100	75	45
% Completed this Period	100%	75%	45%
Total Equivalent Units	800	775	745

Using a Process Cost System

"Josey?" Jordan asked as he stepped into her office. "Do you have a minute?"

"Sure, Jordan. What do you need?"

"Well, I just received a call from operations giving me a ton of data about their production costs during the second quarter. I wrote it all down for you." He waved a paper in her direction. (You have a copy of this document at the end of the chapter, directly after the assignment pages.)

Josey waited, but Jordan didn't say anything else. "Is that a problem?"

"Well, they usually report numbers to you, not to me."

Josey smiled. "Well, you did such a good job creating our process costing system that I decided to let you take over. You'll be running the numbers for the new division. Check in with me if you have questions, and make sure that you have your numbers in for each quarter quickly so that I can create the quarterly reports. Other than that, take care of things."

Jordan smiled. "Really?"

"Really. Consider yourself the divisional controller for the specialty division. It would mean a lot more if you had some staff, but I guess that will come with time. But I'm pleased with the work you've done and look forward to having you take some of this work off of my plate."

Jordan's face beamed as he left her office. Josey let him get part way down the hall before she yelled after him. "Hey! Don't forget to finish up the production reports for the second quarter. I need those numbers for finished goods and work-in-process inventory ASAP."

Stop here and answer questions 5 and 6 on assignment page 4-21 before continuing.

Rapid Review:

By the end of production, all of the process costs have been transferred to the last process in the line. After this final process is complete, then we calculate a total production cost per unit and multiply that value by the units completed. We then debit Finished Goods Inventory for that amount and credit the last WIP Inventory account (Packaging in our cake example earlier in this chapter).

Each of the processes will now have an ending balance, which is the amount spent on the units that are still being processed. That value will stay in the WIP accounts and will become the beginning inventory for the next period.

This page is intentionally blank.

Name:

Questions

Note: *For questions and problems that require calculations, attach a copy of your spreadsheet to the related assignment page and hand it in to your instructor.*

Starting up a Process Costing System

Q-1. Using the information from Josey's email, complete the Pouring Department Production Report for the imprinted line of candles (be sure to hand it in with this worksheet), then answer the following questions for the Pouring department:

a. How many units need to be accounted for?

____

b. What are the equivalent units for 1) materials and 2) conversion?

1) ____

2) ____

c. What are the total conversion costs added during the period?

____

d. What is the total cost per equivalent unit?

____

Q-2. Complete Josey's process cost Production Report for the Pouring department, then answer the following questions:

a. How much cost was transferred from the Pouring department to the Finishing department?

____

b. How much ending inventory cost remains in the Pouring department?

____

Name:

Creating a Production Report

Q-3. Using the information from Josey's email, create a Production Report Template for the Pouring and the Finishing departments for the imprinted line. Attach a printout of your work to this worksheet, then answer the following questions for the Finishing department:

a. How many units need to be accounted for?

____

b. What are the equivalent units for 1) transferred-in costs; 2) materials; and 3) conversion?

1) ______________________________

2) ______________________________

3) ______________________________

c. What are the conversion costs added during the period?

____

d. What is the total cost per equivalent unit for DM?

____

Q-4. Complete the template you created for the Finishing department, then answer the following questions:

a. How much cost was transferred from the Finishing department to Finished Goods Inventory? Create the journal entry summarizing the transfer.

____

____

____

____

b. How much ending inventory cost remains in the Finishing department?

____

Name:

Using a Process Cost System

Q-5. Using the information from Jordan's table and your new Excel template, create the Production Reports for both departments for the imprinted line for Quarter 2. Attach a printout of your work to this worksheet, then answer the following questions:

a. What is the total cost per equivalent unit for the Pouring department?

____

b. What is the total cost per equivalent unit for the Finishing department?

____

Q-6. Complete the Cost Reconciliation for both departments, then answer the following questions:

a. How much cost was transferred from the Finishing department to Finished Goods Inventory? Create the journal entry summarizing the transfer.

____

____

____

____

b. How much ending inventory cost will be reported in Wedgewood's second quarter WIP inventory for the Imprinted product line?

____

Name:

Problems

Critical Thinking Issues

Problem #1

In Chapter 3, you calculated the cost per batch of a dozen candles using the job-order costing method. In this chapter, you calculated the cost per batch using the process costing method. What are the pros and cons of each method? Which method do you believe provides the most accurate estimate of the actual cost of producing a unit? Which method do you think is the easiest to use? Which method do you believe Wedgewood should be using for its new line of imprinted candles?

Name:

Assume that Josey Wedgewood is still considering the best method for tracking the costs of the new line of imprinted candles. Use your answers to these questions to write a memo to Josey explaining which method she should use. Remember that Josey is a member of senior management, so your memo should be formal, include strong logic supporting your arguments, and should be written clearly.

Name:

Problem #2

One of the primary purposes of calculating a total cost is to evaluate whether or not a company should produce a product. Marketing firms or departments typically do extensive research with potential customers to determine what price they are willing to pay for a new product, like Wedgewood's specialty candles. After the company knows what price customers are willing to pay and how much it costs to produce each product, they can determine whether or not it makes sense to introduce the new line. This process is called *Target Pricing.*

Using your answer to Q-3.d., decide if Wedgewood should continue to produce the imprinted candle line. Assume that Wedgewood needs to make a 150% markup on their production costs to cover S&A costs and to achieve their desired profit margin. A high quality, four-inch sculpted candle can sell for $10.00 to $10.50 in the current market.

Write a business letter to Jeremiah Wedgewood, the company CFO, explaining and defending your position on beginning the new line. In doing so, don't forget that a CFO will want to see the cost and revenue numbers.

Tip:

Microsoft Word has many templates, including some for formal business letters. If you aren't comfortable writing a business letter from scratch, start with one of these templates. In Word, click on **File**, then **New**, scroll down and you will see the templates. Look under **Letters** to find one you like.

Ethical Issues

"Maria, do you have a minute?" Josey asked the COO after stopping her in the hall.

"If it's quick, I do. I'm on my way to a meeting in a few minutes with the rest of the executive team."

"I'll only take a minute. I've been going through the numbers your team gave me about the new line," Josey said as they slipped into an alcove in the lobby, out of the foot traffic of Wedgewood's main offices.

"Is there a problem?" Maria asked, a little concerned.

"I don't know. That's why I thought I'd ask. I went down to the floor the other day to do a spot check on some inventory. I noticed that the ending inventory is still pretty rough."

Maria smiled. "Well, we're moving as fast as we can, but we can't work miracles, even with a new line that is making TONS of money."

"That's not it. How fast you move is none of my business. My concern is that it was reported as being 74% completed for DM and 26% completed for conversion costs. But it doesn't look like it's that far along. I mean, to me it looked only about 50% done with materials and 5 or 6% done with conversion. Am I missing something?"

"Probably, but I see your point." Maria glanced up and down the hall. "Look, sometimes line managers are a little ... generous with their estimates of how far along they are in production. It makes them look better, and it gives us better numbers. Because none of them really exaggerate too much, I usually look the other way. I mean, the effects, as far as I can tell, are minimal on the financial statements. Because it doesn't really change anything, I just let it go."

"But...."

"Josey, I already know about it, and I don't think that it's a big deal, okay? These are my managers, my area. You need to let me handle it. It's my call. Now," Maria continued before Josey could say anything else. "I have to get to my meeting, or I'll be late. Call me sometime, and we'll do lunch."

Name:

Problem #3

What effect will the line managers' generous estimates have on Wedgewood's financial statements? What effects might they have on the company's taxes?

Name:

Problem #4

Josey walked away from this short interview feeling very uncomfortable with Maria's answers. Knowing GAAP as well as she does, Josey feels that this is an inappropriate decision that will skew the company's financial numbers and misrepresent their position. What can Josey do to change this company policy?

Process Cost Production Report

(Pouring Department)

Period:______________________

Units to account for:

Starting WIP: ______________________
Units started during the period: ______________________
Ending WIP: ______________________
Units Transferred to Finishing: ______________________

Material Costs to account for:

Starting WIP: ______________________
Material costs added during period: ______________________
Ending WIP: ______________________
Costs Transferred to Finishing: ______________________

Conversion Costs to account for:

Starting WIP: ______________________
Conversion Costs added during the period: ______________________
Ending WIP: ______________________
Costs Transferred to Finishing: ______________________

Journal Entry:

Finishing Department ______________________
    Pouring Department ______________________

Jordan's Notes regarding the 2nd Quarter:

1. Beginning inventory and values come from the 1st Quarter's ending values.

2. An additional 32,800 units were started in Pouring during the 2nd Quarter.

3. Pouring added $19,800 worth of direct materials and $6,560 in conversion costs during the 2nd Quarter. Finishing added $3,000 in direct materials and $3,800 in conversion costs during the 2nd Quarter.

4. Units totaling 31,900 were transferred from Pouring to Finishing, and the ending WIP in Finishing showed only 300 units. Ending conversion was 90% complete in Pouring and 40% complete in Finishing.

USING ACTIVITY-BASED COSTING

This page is

intentionally blank.

CHAPTER 5

Using Activity-Based Costing

Objectives

Excel Skills

- Use advanced formatting tools
- Prepare Excel files for printing
- Embed Excel output in Word or PowerPoint

Accounting Skills

- Assign costs to activities in an ABC environment
- Calculate Activity Rates
- Assign overhead to products using Activity Rates

Mastering Excel

Using Advanced Formatting Tools

We've already learned a lot of terrific formatting tools, but we have just seen the tip of the iceberg. One of the real powers of Excel is in the many ways you can format various reports. Let us show you what we mean. Open up the Excel Practice Set for this chapter and take a look at the ABC information on the ABC Info spreadsheet. As you can see, we haven't changed column widths, put in any kind of underlines, or added any color. In fact, the only formatting we did was to choose the Percentage format and the Currency format for columns B, C, and D.

Once you get the hang of the Excel basics, you can play around with all types of formatting and color while you work on your spreadsheets. Be creative, but keep it professional. Your spreadsheets will eventually become part of reports and presentations that will be shown to many people. Remember that the first rule of managerial accounting is to make the information easily understandable to those who need it.

As your first step in fixing this hard-to-read spreadsheet, set your column widths, wrap the text, and use lines and/or boxes to make all the information legible. You can do this however you want to; there aren't any rules. If the headings are too tall after wrapping the text, you can adjust the row height. We've included our example here to give you some ideas.

	A	B	C	D	E
1	Cost	Cost Pool A	Cost Pool B		Total Annual Cost
2	Painting Costs	10%	90%		$700,000
3	Priming Costs	75%	25%		$350,000
4	Purchasing Costs	50%	50%		$225,000
5	Sanding Costs	100%			$125,000
6	Inventory Costs		100%		$115,000

Notice that we chose to keep narrower column widths by wrapping the text in the column headers. Also, we inserted a column (column D) to separate two different sets of information from each other. To keep from wasting any space or making it difficult for readers to follow along the rows, we made column D very narrow.

Now we've made our table much more legible, but it's still rather bland. If this set of information were a lot larger, it would still be difficult to read, not because the formatting is poor, but because it is monotonous. So let's fix that with an easy Excel tool—the Table format.

- *Click on cell A1 and then, holding down the left mouse button, move to cell E6, selecting all the active cells (i.e., the cells with something in them).*
- *Click on the Insert tab on the Excel ribbon, then on Table.*
- *Verify you have all the cells selected in the dialog box that pops up.*
- *Check the box next to "My table has headers" if it is not already checked.*
- *Click OK.*

You should notice two things immediately. First, Excel has added colors that set off the headers and related colors that highlight the rows, making them much easier to follow across the page. (Imagine how that would help in a table with 200 columns!) Second, Excel added some drop-down menus to the right of each header. We'll talk about those in a minute. For now, your information is in a table and ready for easy formatting.

In addition to the obvious changes we just talked about, Excel also automatically made the column widths wide enough to contain the titles and added "Column1" to the column that didn't have a title. Before we talk a little bit more about the tools available in a table, let's clean up this table a little bit.

 *Delete any unnecessary columns.*

As we've just seen, creating a table in Excel is very easy. Using a table is also easy. If you would like these costs to be sorted alphabetically, just click on the arrow next to "Cost" at the top of column A and select "Sort A to Z." Or suppose you want the table sorted by highest to lowest cost. Try that. Next try sorting by Cost Pool A.

Tip:

If you make the columns too narrow, part of the column header might get hidden under the drop-down arrow. You can change it if it bothers you, but it isn't necessary because the arrows won't print.

You can also filter your table to show only those data points that you need for a specific decision or search.

 *To apply a filter, click on the drop-down menu arrow.*

Down at the bottom of the menu is a large white field that contains all of the unique titles in our table. By selecting the values or titles that we want, we can omit them or highlight them in our table. Let's say that we really aren't interested in seeing the painting costs right now.

Click on the arrow next to our Cost title, then click on the small box in front of the Painting Cost. When the check mark disappears, click OK.

Notice that the table is now much smaller because the painting cost row has been removed.

Tip:

When you hide rows in a table, Excel will hide the full row on the spreadsheet. If you aren't careful you will suddenly find that you don't have access to necessary data. To avoid this problem, you might want to move any other data to show above or below the rows of a table.

When you want the full table to appear again, click on the arrow near the header again and check the box in front of the Select All option.

Now all of your data is back, ready to go!

In addition to sorting and filtering options, the Table format in Excel also makes it easy to change the formatting in a table of data. When we created our table, our spreadsheet defaulted to Excel's favorite shade of blue. But you can use almost any color you like. To change the color:

- *Select any cell in the table.*
- *Click on the Page Layout tab of the Excel ribbon.*
- *Click on Themes.*

You'll notice that Excel has a lot of preset themes for you to choose from. You can see the primary colors of a particular theme in the boxes under the name of the theme. If you hover your mouse pointer over a theme, Excel previews it for you. If you can't see the preview, you can move the table by inserting columns to the left until it isn't blocked by the drop-down menu. Watch out, though—changing themes will change not only the color scheme, but the fonts as well.

If you want to change colors without risking a change in your fonts (which can be important in a formal document), you can use the Colors option instead of Themes. Again, you can preview the changes by hovering your mouse over the options. You can also use the Table Tools Design tab on the Excel ribbon to quickly format your table. There are many options, including a "Total Row" option that will instantly add a set of totals to your data and many different formatting styles that go beyond the Colors and Themes options. Again, Excel will demonstrate each option for you if you hover over the design. Just left-click to apply your final choice.

Tip:

Another way to change the Number format is to highlight the cells, then right-click and bring up the menu. Toward the bottom of this menu is a Format Cells option. If you click on that option, you will see the same list of formats as seen in the drop-down menu, but you will have more control over those formats. For example, you can click on Number and have the choice to add a comma in the thousands place as well as how many decimal places you would like to add. This can really speed things up, because you can play around with several options at the same time until you find the one you want.

The last formatting tool we'd like to discuss is Number formats. Up to now, we've kept that discussion very simple, but there are some options that you should know about. Excel lets you choose how it displays the numbers that you report. Most new Excel users just type in their numbers and leave them in the default format. Unfortunately, that default format is usually hard to read. It doesn't use commas to separate out thousands or provide uniform decimal places. For one or two numbers, that's not a problem. For several thousand numbers, it can make your work impossible to understand. So, let's take a look at the number options available.

The easiest way to change formats is to:

- *Click on the cell or cells you want to change. (For now, let's select the numbers Cost Pool A, column B.)*

- *Return to the Home tab of the Excel ribbon.*
- *Click on the arrow next to the word Percentage in the Number section of the Home tab.*
- *Change the numbers under Cost Pool A to General.*

You'll notice that the cells currently have no formatting at all. They don't look bad but they aren't uniform and easy to read either. That's the problem we were trying to avoid. The General number option is basically the same as no formatting. The drop-down menu that we just used has a lot of options, and the best way to get the feel for what they do is to experiment with them. Most of the time you will probably end up using the Number format, the Currency format, the Accounting format, and the Percentage format. It's fun to see what the others do as well, but they aren't as commonly used in accounting.

Now that we have looked at the options, let's play around with some of them.

- *Keep the Cost Pool A numbers in the General format.*
- *Change the numbers under Cost Pool B from Percentage to Fraction.*
- *Change the first two numbers under Total Annual Cost from Currency to Accounting.*
- *Change the last two numbers under the Total Annual Cost from Currency to Number.*

So here's what our example looks like now. Hopefully, yours looks about the same (although you may have chosen a different set of colors).

Tip:

When you change to the Accounting format, you'll get ##### in your column — remember that's because the column isn't wide enough to display the contents. Resize it. The problem is the decimals. Using the tools we have already discussed, reformat these cells to remove the decimals and resize the column.

	A	B	C	D
1	Cost	Cost Pool A	Cost Pool B	Total Annual Cost
2	Painting Costs	0.1	8/9	$ 700,000
3	Priming Costs	0.75	1/4	$ 350,000
4	Purchasing Costs	0.5	1/2	$225,000
5	Sanding Costs	1		125000
6	Inventory Costs		1	115000

Notice that in the general formatting (under Cost Pool A), Excel used as many decimals as it needed to report the answer, but it isn't consistent from row to row. Usually when we want to show our work to others, we don't use this format, because it's easier to read a column if all of the numbers in it have a consistent number of decimals and the commas and periods all line up. In the next column, fractions are displayed. On the sixth line, there isn't a fraction because the value in that cell is a whole number. You can format fractions in a variety of ways, including reporting only single-number denominators, two-digit denominators, etc. Sometimes fractions are easier to use and understand than decimals, but be careful using them. Most individuals prefer decimal places in business documents, but you have the option of using fractions if you think it will be easier for users to understand your calculations (such as if you are reporting a Sum-of-the-Years'-Digits depreciation table). In the last column, we have a combination of formats, so you can see the difference between the Accounting, Currency, and Number options. We don't use the Number format often, unless we take time to add the commas. Most of the time, the numbers are too hard to read without commas. (Note that in Excel 2013, the Number format option defaults to two decimal places.) The Currency format works best when you want to copy your table into Word or PowerPoint. But the Accounting format is beautiful, isn't it? It shows that we are talking about money, but that dollar sign is off to the left, staying out of trouble. That's our favorite format. Do you have a favorite yet?

Preparing Excel Files for Printing

Now that you have a beautifully formatted document, you need to prepare it for printing. Realistically, most of us don't worry about printing when we are working in Excel. We think about the formats of our tables, the colors and highlighting we choose, and the equations and structure of our calculations. As long as you and your colleagues will only be looking at your work on the computer, then that's all you need to think about. However, if you intend to print out your report, a few simple steps will make sure that your document looks as good on paper as it looks on the computer screen.

The good news is that getting ready to print in Excel is just as easy as the other formatting techniques we've looked at. To help us get started, we've created a more detailed spreadsheet for us to use for practice. Please go to the second worksheet in your workbook (called **Printing Info**), and you will see an example that walks all the way through an ABC problem. The numbers are accurate, but it's not a very pretty worksheet, and it's even worse on paper!

The first step in improving printability is to see what the document will currently look like if printed. Here's how:

- *Click on the File tab of the Excel ribbon.*
- *Click on Print, but don't print it yet.*
- *Look at the preview on the right side of the screen.*

Notice that our preview shows that our worksheet is more than one page long and more than one page wide. Worse than that, the "white space"—or space that lets the reader/user know that one thought is done and another one is starting—is uneven. Sentences, even words, are cut off at the right edge of the page, and one table is cut off at the bottom of the page. Can you image how frustrating it would be to be handed this report?

The second step is to try different orientations. To do this:

- *Click on the drop-down arrow to the right of Portrait Orientation.*

- *Select Landscape Orientation.*

Does this look any better? Not really. You could probably say that it is even worse!

If you can't fix the appearance of your report by changing the orientation, you can move on to step 3—*making* it fit.

- *Change the orientation back to Portrait.*
- *Click on the drop-down arrow next to No Scaling.*
- *Select Fit Sheet on One Page.*

How does that look? You have to admit, it does fit now, but your teacher (or boss or client) might need a magnifying glass to read it!

The fourth step is to go back to the work view, delete extra rows (leaving only one blank row in between tables), format the tables, add colors and use bold or italics to make important numbers "pop," use merge cells and wrap text options to make the notes narrower but take up more lines, and change the font size of the notes to a smaller size so that they take up less room. You can also change column widths. Do whatever you can to improve the layout and readability of this page and make it fit in a standard print layout. You can

Tip:

If your printout is going to be added to something like a board report or client report that might be photocopied, be sure to choose grayscale when printing. Alternatively, you can use only black, white, and shades of gray when formatting. Many of our students have turned in reports electronically that are not legible when printed on a black and white printer. Remember to always think about your audience and how they will use your materials.

check back with the print preview every once in a while to be sure that what you are doing is helping. This is your chance to play with formatting, so use everything you've learned so far to make this page shine. Finally, keep in mind that you can still choose to force your output to one page if necessary, but always make sure that it will still be legible. Take a few minutes to see what you can do with this format. The printed version of our solution is shown below.

Cost	Cost Pool A	Cost Pool B	Total Budgeted Cost
Painting Costs	10%	90%	$ 700,000
Priming Costs	75%	25%	$ 350,000
Purchasing Costs	50%	50%	$ 225,000
Sanding Costs	100%		$ 125,000
Inventory Costs		100%	$ 115,000

Note: These are the allocations between cost pools for each of the budgeted costs this year.

Cost Allocations:	Cost Pool A	Cost Pool B	Cost
Painting Costs	$ 70,000	$ 630,000	$ 700,000
Priming Costs	$ 262,500	$ 87,500	$ 350,000
Purchasing Costs	$ 112,500	$ 112,500	$ 225,000
Sanding Costs	$ 125,000	$ -	$ 125,000
Inventory Costs	$ -	$ 115,000	$ 115,000
Total	**$ 570,000**	**$ 945,000**	**$ 1,515,000**

Note: These are the amount of each cost listed in the first table allocated between the two cost pools.

Allocation Bases:	Hours	Square Feet

Note: Cost Pool A is allocated on the basis of Machine Hours and Cost Pool B is allocated by square feet.

Allocation Bases	Product 1	Product 2	Total Base
Machine Hours	760,000	1,520,000	2,280,000
Square Feet	7,600	1,900	9,500

Note: This is the budgeted machine hours for this year and the actual square feet of the production facility broken down by useage of each product.

	Hours	Square Feet
Activity Rates	$ 0.25	$ 99.47

Note: These are the activity rates.

Actual Usage	Product 1	Product 2	Total
Machine Hours	775,000	1,500,000	2,275,000
Square Feet	7,600	1,900	9,500

Note: These are the actual quantities of the driver units consumed during the year.

Cost Allocations:	Product 1	Product 2	Total
Cost Pool A	$ 193,750	$ 375,000	$ 568,750
Cost Pool B	$ 756,000	$ 189,000	$ 945,000
Total	**$ 949,750**	**$ 564,000**	**$ 1,513,750**

Note: Here are the actual amounts of overhead to be allocated.

Total Actual Costs:	
Painting Costs	$ 703,250
Priming Costs	$ 345,000
Purchasing Costs	$ 227,900
Sanding Costs	$ 130,500
Inventory Costs	$ 114,500
Total	**$ 1,521,150**

Note: Here are the actual costs incurred during the year.

Over(under)allocated Overhead:	$ (7,400)

Note: This amount should be adjusted for over[under]allocated overhead.

Embedding Tables into Word or PowerPoint

Now that you know how to clean up your Excel work so that it can be printed and added to a professional report, you need to make a final decision. Do you leave your work in Excel or move it into a report? While there are many times when you can just leave your work in Excel and print out forms as necessary, there will be times when your work is part of a larger report or business letter. In a formal situation, you can't just email your boss or client (or instructor) two files and expect him or her to flip back and forth and sort through all of your work. Instead, you need to put your Excel work into a formal report in Word or PowerPoint. The good news is that these programs work well together, so it is pretty easy to merge everything into one place.

The basic methods for copying are the same for both Word and PowerPoint, so we'll go through them once in Word and you should be good to go.

- *Open a blank Word document.*
- *Type a one- or two-sentence introduction explaining that the first table describes how the various overhead costs are allocated between Cost Pools A and B.*
- *Then type* Table 1–Cost Pool Allocation *on the next line.*
- *Select that line, and then on the Home tab of the Word ribbon (just like the Excel ribbon); select Heading 1.*
- *Center the header.*
- *Go to your Excel workbook and select the first table.*
- *Right-click and copy.*
- *Return to Word.*
- *Right-click and paste.*

That's all there is to it. If you need to, in both programs, you can double-click on the right edge of any column to resize it so all of the information fits on one line, and you can use the formatting tools in either program if you don't like how something has copied.

Tip:

Word and PowerPoint both have a hard time with the Accounting format for numbers. They add spaces between the dollar sign and the numbers, making it very difficult to format the cells or even keep the numbers lined up from row to row in one column. Rather than deal with this frustration, you might want to change all of your Accounting formats to Currency before copying the table into Word or PowerPoint.

Because of this extra help, you'll almost always want to use the formatting tools in PowerPoint to simplify your table or at least clean up some of the colors you never intended your work to have. Luckily, PowerPoint provides two new tabs on its ribbon when you click on your table to allow you to quickly change the formatting of your work. You'll find them at the very end of the ribbon, typically highlighted in yellow or green. Your other option in PowerPoint is to right-click and choose the "Keep Source Formatting" option under the Paste Options command. That will paste your work without any help from PowerPoint at all.

Wrapping Up Our Excel Work

And that's the end of our Excel lesson for this chapter. As you move into the Wedgewood case, use the questions asked as an opportunity to practice your formatting skills, especially the use of tables. Since ABC Costing required several different tables and calculations, these formatting tools can be very helpful. In addition, you should also practice printing and embedding your tables in other programs. You'll often need to do that in order to present your work to senior management, so you might as well get the hang of it now.

Wedgewood Candle Co.

Assigning Costs to Activities in an ABC System

"Josey," Jeremiah Wedgewood, Wedgewood's CFO, said happily as he walked into the controller's office. "How are you doing?"

"Well," Josey said carefully. "I *was* doing okay."

"What do you mean you *were* doing okay?" Jeremiah said, frowning.

"Every time you walk in here with that kind of energy it means that you are going to ask me to do something."

Jeremiah laughed. "I guess I'm getting a little predictable, huh?"

"I'm afraid so. So, what do you want?"

"Well, I have an idea for improving our cost accounting process."

"Uh, huh. Just came back from a conference, didn't you?"

"As a matter of fact, I did. How did you know?"

"Because you only come up with accounting ideas when you've been to a conference. So, what is it this time?" Josey asked.

"Have you ever thought about switching to an ABC costing system?"

Josey shuddered. "Do you have any idea how much work is involved in creating one of those systems, not to mention maintaining the system after it is supposedly done? Believe me, Uncle Jerry, we don't want to go there, not without a much larger accounting staff than we currently have."

"I know it's a lot of work, Josey," Jeremiah said after a moment. "But I think we need to look into it anyway. The numbers are more accurate and they allow for better decision making. With the new system coming online, I think that we are going to need a solid ABC system in order to really determine which of our new products, if any, are making money."

"But . . ." Josey started to protest.

"No 'buts,' Josey. I want you to do it. I'll talk to Sam in HR about hiring another staff member to free up some resources."

Josey sighed. "Alright, if that's your decision. When do you want to hold the first meeting?"

"First meeting?" Jeremiah frowned.

"To determine the cost centers and other components of the ABC system. We'll all have to agree on what they are if this is going to work. That means that you'll have to be part of the process in creating this system."

"Oh, that. I did that on the plane. Here's what I came up with." He handed Josey a set of notes. (This document is at the end of this chapter after the assignment pages and is called Notes about ABC.) "I started with the questions the presenter at the conference asked us, and realized that I already had a lot of those answers that I could pull from the information I had with me. What do you think?"

Josey spent a moment going over the notes, nodding to herself as she went. "I have to hand it to you, Uncle Jerry. These look really good. When did you learn about accounting?" While she was talking to Jeremiah, she quickly added the actual overhead costs to a spreadsheet that she named **C5 Activity-Based Costing** (which you can find in your data files).

"Ha, ha. That's very funny," Jeremiah said with mock indignation. "Just because I don't flaunt my knowledge, doesn't mean that it isn't there. Now, what else do we need?"

"Well, we just need to figure out what activities are consuming the various types of overhead expenses. After I have that information, the rest of the process is long, but pretty straightforward."

"Okay," Jeremiah nodded as he looked again at the list of costs and activities. "So, the biggest overhead expenses are the indirect salaries. I would think that 30% of those salaries are paid to the workers who help set up the production runs, 50% are paid to the experts in quality control, 15% are paid to the maintenance staff, and the remainder are paid to those who help with transporting materials and goods around the factory and receiving merchandise from vendors."

Josey nodded. "That sounds about right; so that pool of overhead money needs to be split up between four activities. Let's call those activities "setups," "quality control," "maintenance," and "transportation/receiving." She continued examining the document. "The cleaning supplies and depreciation are both part of maintaining the equipment. Shipping costs are all part of transportation and receiving."

"That sounds right," Jeremiah agreed. "Let's see. Well, most of the rent on the warehouse, probably 75%, is part of the transportation and receiving, wouldn't you say?" Josey nodded. "The rest is for holding merchandise waiting for quality control inspections."

"Right. And maintenance and setup of production runs each account for 45% of the utility costs. The remainder is pretty evenly split between transportation and quality control. The parts and repair costs are evenly split between maintenance and setups." She pondered a minute more. "Finally, the insurance costs are evenly distributed among all four of these activities."

"Perfect," Jeremiah said. "That didn't take long at all."

"No, it didn't, which surprises me. But then, we still have all of the numbers to crunch and drivers to choose. And don't forget that we have to maintain this system. It's still a lot of work."

"Agreed, but I still think that it will be worth the effort."

"Well, you're the boss!" Josey said with a grin.

"And don't you ever forget it!" With a return grin, Jeremiah headed out the door.

Stop here and answer question 1 on assignment page 5-17 before continuing.

Rapid Review:

Activity-Based Costing (or ABC, as it is more commonly called) is a method for allocating overhead, not a method for tracking production costs. Companies have three options for assigning overhead costs to jobs or processes. The first two (plant-wide and departmental) were discussed in Chapter 3 and are probably the most commonly used methods. ABC is a more advanced method. Instead of lumping together all of the costs (like plant-wide) or allocating costs to specific processes or departments (like departmental), the ABC method breaks the company's overhead into activities, assigns the overhead costs to those activities, chooses a cost driver for each activity, then calculates a predetermined overhead rate (POHR) for each activity. As each job or process uses the different activities, overhead is assigned to that job or process using the POHR multiplied by the drivers actually used.

Let's say, for example, that you work for an accounting firm. Your firm will have very little in DM costs, but will have lot of DL costs (like you) and overhead costs. In order to keep the doors open, your company needs to pay for clerical staff, photocopying, rent, janitorial services, and computer support. These are the overhead costs that the company accrues. In order to use the ABC method, your company would then have to define the other activities performed to help the auditors do their job. Let's say that this company has chosen office support and technical support as their two activities.

The first step in using the ABC method is to allocate the overhead costs into ***cost pools***. Each cost pool is made up of the costs incurred by or related to one of your defined activities. So, you might decide that all of the clerical staff costs are part of the office support activity and put them in the office support cost pool, while all of the computer support costs are part of the technical support activity and are part of the computer support pool. However, the rent on the building gets split: 80% to office support and 20% to technical support. Similarly, the janitorial costs get split: 60% to office support and 40% to technical support.

Calculating Activity Rates for an ABC System

"Jordan," Josey looked up as he knocked on her open door. "Come in and meet Fong Li." Jordan shook the hand of the young Asian woman. "We just hired Li this morning as another member of our accounting staff. She's from Beijing, China, and has just completed her accounting degree at the University of Idaho."

"I'm pleased to meet you, Li" Jordan said as he took a seat. "How long have you been in the U.S.?"

"Almost ten years," Li answered. "My family moved to Idaho when my father got a job as an engineer for Coeur d'Alene Mines."

"Great. I'm excited to work with you." Jordan replied.

Li nodded. "So, Josey, what do you need?"

"Now that we have some extra help, we are going to move forward on one of Jeremiah's pet projects."

Jordan frowned. "Why does that not make me feel very excited?"

Josey laughed. "Because of the amount of work his projects usually cause. This one is no exception to that rule, although it might give us some good data." She looked at her two young staff members. "We're going to create an ABC costing system."

Li nodded. "Those do provide the best data."

Jordan added. "And they can be difficult to create."

"Well, in this case we have most of the basics done. We are going to have four activities: setups, quality control, maintenance, and transportation/receiving. After some careful analysis, we will be using the number of set-up hours as the driver for setups, number of batches checked for the quality control activity, machine hours for maintenance, and items transported as the driver for transportation and receiving activity.

"Li," she continued after a moment. "I'm going to have you start the process by determining the various activity rates. Here are my estimates of next year's driver usage." She handed a list to Li (which is called Driver Activity, Past and Present and is included in the documents for this chapter, directly after the assignment pages). "For right now, you'll only need to use the first table on this list. Later, when you are actually allocating costs to the different products, you'll need the second table."

"Okay," she said as she took the paper. "I'll get it done right away."

Stop here and answer question 2 on assignment page 5-19 before continuing.

Rapid Review:

Once the costs are assigned to the activities' cost pools, the ABC system starts to look like the departmental method. Each activity is treated like a department, with its own driver and its own POHR. The POHR is calculated in the same way it was for the plant-wide and departmental methods we discussed in Chapter 3: Total estimated costs (for the activity in this case) divided by the total estimated drivers for that activity.

Assigning Overhead in an ABC System

"Li?" Li looked up as Jordan stepped into her office.

"Can I help you?" she asked politely.

Jordan smiled. "I'm not the boss. You don't have to be nervous when I stop by. I only graduated a few months ago myself."

Li smiled. "This is my first real job; I want to do everything correctly."

"I know the feeling, which is why I stopped by." Jordan pulled a form out of his pocket. "I thought you might want to take the next step on that ABC project assigned from earlier in the quarter without waiting to be asked."

"What do you mean?"

"Well," Jordan put the paper on her desk. "I just compiled my end-of-quarter reports for the new special candle division, including my estimates of the drivers they used. Why don't we go ahead and run the numbers and see just how much overhead will be applied to each kind of candle?"

Li smiled. "And surprise Josey with the numbers all ready to go!"

"Exactly."

Stop here and answer questions 3 and 4 on assignment page 5-21 before continuing.

Rapid Review:

The final steps in the ABC method are to allocate costs as jobs or processes use the drivers. So, in our audit firm example, let's assume that the technical support driver was server hours used. As you and your colleagues use the company's server, costs are allocated to the audit on which you are working. When you switch from one audit to the next, the system keeps track and starts to allocate costs to the new audit instead of the old one.

The biggest challenges with an ABC system are deciding on the appropriate activities and then tracking the use of drivers within each job or process. After that, the allocation is fairly straightforward, but a little labor intensive. At the end of the period, you would add up all of the drivers used and multiply by the POHR to see how much overhead should be allocated to each job or process. You then divide by the number of units produced within the job or the equivalent units produced in the process to find the overhead allocated to each unit.

This page is intentionally blank.

Name:

Questions

Note: *For questions and problems that require calculations, attach a copy of your spreadsheet to the related assignment page and hand it in to your instructor.*

Assigning Costs to Activities in an ABC System

Q-1. Using the information from Jeremiah's notes and his discussion with Josey, set up a table showing the percentage of each overhead cost account that should be allocated to each of the four activities. Use a total (also known as a *proof*) column to be sure you are allocating 100% of each cost.

Create another table and determine the amount of overhead that should be allocated to each of the four ABC activities (setups, quality control, maintenance, and transportation/receiving). Again, use a total (or proof) column and a totals row to summarize your results.

Attach a copy of both tables to this worksheet.

Name:

Calculating Activity Rates for an ABC System

Q-2. Using the information provided by Josey about estimated cost driver usage and your answer to Q-1, determine the activity rate for each activity in the new ABC system.

Name:

Assigning Overhead in an ABC System

Q-3. Using the information compiled by Jordan about the drivers used by each specialty candle line, determine the amount of overhead that will be allocated to each line.

Q-4. Assuming that Wedgewood produced 180,000 sculpted candles; 202,500 imprinted candles; and 67,500 additive candles, how much MOH will be assigned to each candle under the ABC system?

Name:

Problems

Critical Thinking Issues

Problem #1

a. Assume that Wedgewood spends $3.38 in DM and $0.63 in DL for each sculpted candle. What is the total cost to produce one sculpted candle under the ABC system?

b. Now do the same calculation under the departmental MOH allocation method used in Chapter 3.

c. Which estimate do you believe is the most accurate? Defend your answer.

Name:

Problem #2

Refer back to Jeremiah and Josey's argument about ABC costing systems. Now that you have spent the time creating an ABC system, do you agree with Josey or Jeremiah? Do you think that the improved information is really worth the additional work involved with creating and maintaining the system? Defend your position in a business memo written to either Jeremiah or Josey. You should write to Josey if you chose to support the use of the ABC system to convince her that it is a good decision; you should write to Jeremiah if you chose to support using Wedgewood's old method of allocating overhead using departmental overhead rates. Use the space below to create an outline of your memo before you create it in Word. When you have completed the memo, attach a copy of it to this sheet and hand it in to your instructor.

Ethical Issues

Jordan moved slowly down the hall, reading back over his report as he neared Josey's office. He was pleased with his work, but he needed to ask a few clarifying questions before he went on. As he started to knock, though, he stopped cold, one hand raised. He leaned forward slightly, listening for just a moment before he moved quickly back to his office, deeply troubled.

He had clearly heard Jeremiah and Josey arguing through the door about the new ABC system. Josey was completely against the waste of resources, especially the time that she would have to spend making sure that it was done correctly. Jeremiah had sounded defensive in his insistence. If he lost....

Jordan shut his door and sat down at his desk. The company had hired Li specifically to help with the ABC system. If they dropped the system, they would have to let her go, and that was very depressing. He enjoyed working with Li. She was a great colleague who worked extremely hard and did excellent work.

He paused again. Would they really let Li go? The company was family-owned and operated, but they were still trying to diversify their employee base. He only had about six months seniority, not really enough to be sure that they would keep him if they downsized the department. With political pressures, the company might choose to downsize him instead.

He tried to push his worries away and get back to work, but he couldn't. The possibility that he might lose Li as a colleague had been troubling; the possibility that he might lose his own job in this economy was far more than troubling. He was now downright scared.

Name:

Problem #3

Answer each of the following questions about Jordan's situation:

a. Based on your opinion of ABC costing, do you think that Jordan's fear that the company will drop the ABC system is justified? Defend your answer.

b. If the company does choose to downsize the accounting department, do you think that gender and/or ethnicity will play a part in the decision of who will be let go? Should these factors be considered? Why or why not?

Name:

c. Should Jordan discuss his fears with Li? With Josey? What should Jordan do in this situation?

Notes about ABC

The conference I attended gave a list of steps to follow to implement ABC:

1. Identify the cost objects
2. Identify the direct cost of the cost objects
3. Select allocation bases for assigning indirect costs to the cost objects
4. Identify the indirect costs
5. Compute an activity rate for each allocation base
6. Compute the amount of indirect costs assigned to each cost object
7. Determine total cost of the cost object by summing direct costs and assigned indirect costs

I can't do all of that here, but I can start it and then Josey can have an accounting clerk finish the job. So, what are the cost objects? Well, the different types of candles, of course. The direct costs of the candles are the direct materials and the direct labor, and we do a pretty good job of tracking those, so I won't deal with them in these notes.

What allocation bases should we use? Well, I can't figure that out until I know what the overhead is and how we can break it down. Let's see. We have two departments. Last year's data are as follows:

Department	Drivers Used	Total Overhead
Pouring (driver: DL hours)	25,000	$400,000
Finishing (driver: batches completed)	125,000	$800,000

We will need the overhead amount of $1,200,000 from this table broken down more into actual activities and categories. Digging through the accounting records from last year, I was able to categorize the overhead costs as follows:

Actual OH Costs	
Indirect salaries	$474,000
Cleaning supplies	$24,000
Shipping costs	$180,000
Rent on warehouse	$72,000
Depreciation	$360,000
Utilities	$60,000
Parts and repairs	$18,000
Insurance	$12,000

Driver Activity, Past and Present

The following table presents the drivers used by the company last year:

Overhead Activities	Driver	Budgeted Drivers
Setups	Setups	15,100
Quality Control	Batches checked	2,500
Maintenance	Machine hours	5,490
Shipping and Receiving	Items transported	351,600

During the first quarter of this year, production dramatically increased in all three of the product lines. The following table shows the drivers used by the three specialty lines during that quarter:

Products (Outputs)	Setups	Batches Checked	Machine Hours	Items Transported	Batches Produced
Sculpted	563	300	750	60,938	15,000
Imprinted	1,406	338	500	158,438	16,875
Additive	844	113	1,250	24,375	5,625

CHAPTER 6

JOINT AND BY-PRODUCTS

This page is intentionally blank.

CHAPTER 6

Joint and By-Products

Objectives

Excel Skills

- Using the Max and Min functions
- Using Conditional Formatting
- Using the If function

Accounting Skills

- Determining joint versus by-products
- Allocating joint costs
- Mastering Excel

Mastering Excel

In these next few chapters, our discussion of Excel will change a little bit. By now, you should have a good grasp of the basics, which means that we can turn our attention to the more powerful (and exciting) tools in Excel. The good news is that we have several chapters to cover these fun new techniques. The bad news is that we still won't have time to discover them all. We're going to focus our attention on the most commonly used tools, and with this background you'll be familiar enough with Excel that you can discover the others as you need them. Let's get started!

Using Max and Min Functions

Some of the most powerful tools in Excel are functions: preprogrammed equations that do basic arithmetic and more advanced calculations quickly. These functions start out as simple as the standard AutoSum command that we have already discussed, to more advanced features such as time value calculations, and become as complicated as complete statistical analysis programs. There are hundreds of functions that we wish we had time to discuss, but we'll have to focus our discussion on just those most commonly used in managerial accounting. Let's start with the Max and Min functions.

Frequently in accounting we are asked to report the highest or lowest values in a list of numbers. Or sometimes we need to use the item, method, or accounting procedure that yields the highest or lowest value. While you can always use the Sort function to find these values (see Chapter 2 for a discussion of how to sort data), it is typically easier to let the spreadsheet automatically choose these values for you based on a set of predetermined rules. To show you how this works, let's take a look at the Max function, with the understanding that the Min function works the same way.

To get started, open the Excel Practice Set for this chapter that contains a joint cost allocation worksheet. Let's assume that we have been assigned to allocate the joint costs using the net realizable value (NRV) as the allocation base. Unfortunately, this table doesn't give us NRV, but we know that we have two choices: sell the units as they are or process them further. At the bottom of the spreadsheet you can see that we have already provided you with the values for each of those choices, so you just need to pick the best option for the company, the one that will maximize company profits. Now in this case, it is pretty simple to look at the two numbers and decide which to choose, but let's automate the process so that we can practice using the Max function. Here's how:

- *Click on cell B18.*
- *Click on the drop-down arrow to the right of AutoSum (found in the Editing group of the Home tab in the Excel ribbon).*
- *Click on Max.* Notice that Excel has already "guessed" that you wanted to choose the maximum value between B16 and B17.
- *Press [Enter] and the correct answer, $121,875, should appear in B18.*
- *Click on cell B18 again.*
- *Move your mouse pointer to the lower-right corner, click on the small black box, and copy the formula over to cells C18 and D18.*

Tip:

If Max isn't a choice that is shown, you can still access it by clicking on More Functions and typing Max into the search box.

Tip:

Even though Excel will guess the range of cells you want to search for a maximum value, it won't always guess correctly. You might want to make it a habit to check the range every time and adjust it when necessary by using the blue boxes in the corners of Excel's guess range to expand or contract the selection.

With our new equations, you can see that this company should process Doodads further, sell Whatchamacallits as-is, and can choose either option for the Thingamabobs, because they provide the same profit either way. Now that our spreadsheet automatically chooses the profit maximizing option for each product, let's see if we can make it a bit easier to read, especially for nonaccountants.

Using Conditional Formatting

To help make our spreadsheet easier to read, let's add some color by highlighting which items should be processed further and which should be sold as-is. We could easily do this by just clicking on the cells and highlighting those that should be processed further, but what we really want is for Excel to automatically add color to the right cells any time we update those input figures. Luckily, Excel provides a great tool to do this called *conditional formatting*. Let's try it.

- *Select cells B16 and B17.*
- *Click on the drop-down arrow to the right of Conditional Formatting in the Styles group of the Home tab of the ribbon.*
- *Select Highlight Cells Rules and then slide your mouse to the right to open the options.*
- *Click on Equal To.*
- *Click on the red arrow in the cell selector box and then click on cell B18.* (In Excel 2013, you may need to press [Enter] to get back to the Equal To box.)
- *Click on the red drop-down arrow next to the rule box and select Green Fill with Dark Green Text.*
- *Click OK.*

Tip:

Unfortunately, you can't just use the Format Painter option with conditional formatting. The equations use permanent references (discussed in more detail later) that would try to compare the values in columns C and D to B18, which is not what we want at all. Instead, you have to recreate the formatting for each new comparison value (C18 and D18, in this case). The other option is to compare to a set value that you want to stay the same from column to column, such as 0 or net income for the period.

12	Joint Cost Allocation Ratio	43%
13		
14	Joint Cost Allocation	$ 65,000
15		
16	Revenue w/o further processing	$ 113,750
17	Net Realized Margin w/further processing	$ 121,875
18	Net Realizable Value	$ 121,875

Your worksheet should now look like the one pictured here. Go ahead and complete these steps again for columns C and D. After you're finished, cell 16 should be highlighted in column C and both cells 16 and 17 should be highlighted in column D. Anyone glancing at this spreadsheet can now easily see that the company should process Doodads further, sell Whatchamacallits as-is, and be indifferent toward Thingamabobs. Management will need to make a determination as to whether they should process Thingamabobs further or not, based on nonfinancial information such as customer relations or market demand for as-is versus processed units.

Let's be sure that your formatting will change if the company's numbers change. To do this, you'll need to replace the raw values currently in your file with actual equations. Here's how:

Tip:

One of the authors uses the [=] at the beginning of equations and the other uses [+] instead. It doesn't matter which, but if you use the numeric keypad a lot, you may find [+] is easier to find. Try both and develop your own preference!

- *Replace the 43% in B12 with the following equation:* =+B8/sum(B8:D8).
- *Replace the $65,000 in B14 with:* =B10*B12.
- *Replace the $113,750 in B16 with:* =B8*B5.
- *Replace the $121,875 in B17 with:* =(B7-B6)*B8.

Now that your calculations for Doodads are equations, we can test our formatting. Let's assume that the cost of additional processing for Doodads was actually $2.00 instead of $1.25. Go ahead and change that number in B6. The net realizable value (B18) should have changed to $113,750 and the highlighting should have moved up to indicate the company would be better off selling this product without further processing. Now, go ahead and change the amount back to $1.25 and let's move on to another powerful tool.

Using the If Function

Being able to pick between options is one of the most useful tools in Excel. Excel's If function, after you get the hang of it, can be used in many different situations and problems. The basic idea of this function is to set up a condition. For example: if net income is positive, then pay a dividend. In Excel, we go one step further. Using the If function, we set up the conditions for both a true and a false result, such as: if net income is positive, then pay a dividend; if not, then draw on the company's line of credit. These statements can be just that simple or they can be expanded to house multiple If functions within one command. This is a tool that you'll really want to know, especially as you start working with more involved spreadsheets.

So, let's use our current example to provide some practice using the If function. Let's say that we want to expand our table to not only automatically highlight the option that the company should choose, but to also automatically calculate our gross margin. Normally this would be an easy subtraction problem, but when you have joint (main) and by-products some months you may choose to process further and some months you may not. You don't want to have to recreate your table each time a decision changes, and yet the revenue, additional cost of processing, etc., will all change with that decision.

To fix this problem, we'll use the If function to get the spreadsheet to know which option to pick: the one without further processing or the one with further processing. Here's how to set it up:

- *Insert a row above "Gross Revenue" (which is in row 20). Label the new row* Sales Price (each).
- *Click on the cell in the new row in the Doodads column.*
- *Click on the drop-down arrow to the right of AutoSum in the Editing group of the ribbon.*
- *Click on More Functions and then scroll down and select If.*
- *Click OK.*

Tip:

You can always find functions using this drop-down menu, but you can also type them in after you are familiar with the Excel commands. For example, you can simply type =SUM(and then select the cells you want to add up or you can type =IF(to get started with an if/then statement. Just make sure to type the final) after you are done.

This brings up a window entitled Function Arguments. All of the functions built into Excel will give you a window like the one below if you use the drop-down menu to select them.

Function Arguments

IF

Logical_test B16=B18 = FALSE

Value_if_true B5 = 3.5

Value_if_false B7 = 5

= 5

Checks whether a condition is met, and returns one value if TRUE, and another value if FALSE.

Logical_test is any value or expression that can be evaluated to TRUE or FALSE.

Formula result = $ 5.00

Help on this function

OK Cancel

You may remember using one like it when we did regression analysis. In the first box you put the logical test you want Excel to perform, in the second box you put what Excel should do if that test is true, and in the third box what to do if it is false. Let's give it a shot.

- *Click in the first box.*
- *Click on cell B16.*
- *Type an equal sign* [=].
- *Click on cell B18.*
- *Click inside the second box.*
- *Click on cell B5.*
- *Click inside the third box.*
- *Click on cell B7.*

Your Functional Arguments window should look like the one pictured. Note that if it is easier for you to type the cell numbers instead of clicking on them, that works just as well. (We find that, with a tablet, it is frequently easier to type than to click.)

- *Click OK.*
- *Copy this formula across to the other two products.*

Values of $5.00 should show up as the sales price for Doodads, $7.00 for Whatchamacallits, and $3.95 for Thingamabobs. If so, then you have just created your first logical test in Excel. Great work!

Let's take just a second to review what we just did. The logical test said that if the revenue without further processing was equal to the net realizable value, then we wanted to show the sales price as the sales price without further processing. Because that was *not* a true statement for Doodads, Excel moved on to the alternative we gave it in the "Value_if_false" instruction and used the sales price after further processing from cell B7. That's all there is to it!

Now, if we had three conditions instead of only two, we could have put another "If" function in that third box. For example, let's say that we wanted to see if reported EPS was good, bad, or okay. Now, this isn't on our spreadsheet anywhere, but if you want to actually try it, type a value into cell I5. You could start with $0.75 and then change it to $1.25 and see how the function changes. We could set up our If function to first check if EPS was negative. If yes, then say "Bad." If not, then look to see if EPS was less than $1. If yes, then say "Okay." If not, then say "Good." The final statement in Excel would look like this: =IF(I5 < 0,"Bad",IF(I5 < 1,"Okay","Good")). This is called a *nested if-then statement*. If we had four conditions, we could have nested yet another If function inside the third box of the second function, etc. Just think of the possibilities!

While you are pondering the vastness of the Excel universe and all of the possibilities that If functions provide, take a look at the calculated sales price of Whatchamacallits and Thingamabobs. Notice that for Thingamabobs, we need to be careful because we are indifferent between selling as-is and processing further. You see, Excel always applies the logic in the If function in the order that it appears. In this case, the first condition was: if revenue without additional processing is equal to the NRV, then use that sales price. Excel calculated that those numbers were equal for Thingamabobs and stopped. It didn't even look at the other part of the argument. So, you would need to be very familiar with your company policy before you set up this kind of a statement. Does management prefer to sell as-is when possible or process further? The argument for whichever choice the company prefers needs to come first. You might want to play with it and see if you can get that formula to work both ways. When you are done, change it back to the original equation so that your numbers in the next steps will match ours as we go on.

After you're familiar with the If function, you can test your handiwork by changing the cost of additional processing on Doodads to $2.00 from $1.25, as we did before. When you do, the shading should shift down from cell B17 to B16 and the sales prices should change from $5.00 to $3.50.

The last step in finishing this table is to calculate gross revenue. Because the costs will also change based on how much processing we do, we'll need to use more If functions to calculate additional cost only when we choose to process further. Let's do it!

- *For the Gross Revenue row, use a basic formula to multiply the sales price on row 20 by the units of production on row 8 for each of the three products.*
- *Calculate a total Gross Revenue using the Sum function in E21. (You should get $415,470.)*
- *In cell B22 start an If function:*
  - The logical test will be to see if the sales price on row 20 equals the sales price on row 7 (B20=B7). We had to use this test instead of the one we used for the sales price because otherwise there would be additional costs under Thingamabobs either way.
  - The Value_if_true will be the cost of additional processing multiplied by the units of production (B6*B8).
  - The Value_if_false will be zero. (Do you know why?)
- *Click OK.*

> **Tip:**
>
> The most common way to add a single underline on top and a double underline on the bottom is to select the cell you want to format, right-click, then click on the drop-down arrow to the right of the Borders tool in the upper pop-up box, and select Top and Double Bottom.

- *Drag that formula across the other two products.*
- *Calculate a total additional processing costs in E22. (You should have $40,625.) Use a simple cell reference to pick up the joint costs from the "Joint Cost Allocation Ratio" row. (For example, in cell B23, put in* +B14 *.)*
- *Calculate the total joint costs in E23 and make sure that it matches the value in B10.*
- *Calculate Gross Margin for each product using a simple formula to subtract both additional costs and joint costs from gross revenue.*
- *Calculate the total Gross Margin in E24.*
- *Format the Gross Margin row so that it is easy for users to see that this is the final value by having one line on top and a double underline on the bottom.*
- *Depending on which version of Excel you are using, you may need to do additional formatting to make sure that the table is easy to read.*

Wrapping Up Our Excel Work

And that wraps up our Excel lesson for this chapter. As you move into the Wedgewood case, think about when and how you could use conditional formatting and the Max, Min, and If functions. Judicious use of these powerful tools can help you quickly get answers when your input data changes. Be sure to keep the other tools you've learned up to now in mind as well. Now, let's move into Wedgewood!

Wedgewood Candle Co.

Determining Joint Versus By-Products

"Come in, Li," Josey called, covering up the mouthpiece on her headset. "I'll be done in just a minute."

Li sat quietly, enjoying the view outside the controller's window while she waited for her boss to finish her conversation. After a few minutes, she heard Josey say good-bye and turned her attention back to the office. "What can I do for you, Josey?" she asked.

Josey smiled. "I have an important assignment for you, Li. One I think you'll enjoy. We have been thinking about starting a special line of candles made from beeswax instead of paraffin. They will be much more expensive candles, because beeswax isn't cheap, but they will be more ecologically sustainable and should appeal to our customers who prefer to buy 'green.'

"We've been in contact with a possible supplier, but our negotiations hit a snag, and that's where you come in."

Li's confusion showed on her face. "Why would you need a staff accountant to smooth out a negotiation snag?" she asked.

"I'm glad you asked," Josey smiled again. "It seems that Mr. Caleb Jefferson, the owner of the apiary, or bee yard, has no idea what he should charge for his beeswax. We've made all sorts of offers, but he's worried that we are trying to cheat him. He says that he wants to see the numbers himself, and that's where you come in."

"You want me to show him the offer numbers?"

Josey smiled. "No, Li. I want you to walk through his numbers with him so that he can actually see his costs and make a decision."

"You are sending me to work for Mr. Jefferson?" Li's voice seemed alarmed. "Am I not doing a good job?"

Josey sighed. "Let me try this again. First, I'm not firing you and I'm not trading you to another company. As a show of good faith in our negotiations, the executive team has offered to help Mr. Jefferson calculate his product costs so that he will feel comfortable with our offer. He's an expert at bees, but very bad with numbers. So, I'm going to have you compute his costs for honey, beeswax, honeycomb, and propolis, and then walk him through your calculations. Does that make more sense?"

Li nodded. "Good," Josey continued, "Do you know anything about beekeeping?" Li shook her head. Josey nodded, "I didn't either, but here is a bit of information I gathered on the different products sold by beekeepers." She handed Li a page of notes. (These are entitled Notes on Apiaries and are included at the end of the chapter after the assignment pages.)

Josey continued, "Here are the production numbers that he provided." She handed Li a set of figures. (This is the first spreadsheet in the workbook entitled **C6 Joint and By-Product Costing**.) "His total production numbers for last year. . . . " She paused while she scanned through her notes. "Ah, here it is. He spent a total of $65,000 on production last year, up to the split-off point. After separating the different products, he continues to process his honey and sells it in jars to local stores and individuals. He really should process the beeswax further as well because he would make more money doing so, but he doesn't have the capital to set up the operations to heat and strain the wax. The honeycomb gives him the same profit whether he sells it in bulk or processes it and jars it for retail sales. He tends to sell it all in bulk though, because he doesn't think that the extra work is worthwhile. Propolis cannot be processed further, so he just sells what he has accumulated at the end of each month. He uses the 100% gross margin method in accounting for his by-products." Josey noted the slightly confused look on Li's face. "That means that he doesn't assign any joint costs to his by-product, just to his main products. Usually the net realizable value method is pretty straightforward when some products are being processed further and others aren't. Perhaps that would be the one to use. Mr. Jefferson will be coming by Thursday morning at 11:00 to go over the numbers with you, so make sure you are ready."

Li nodded. "I will be ready."

"Good. Let me know if you have any questions or problems."

Stop here and answer questions 1 through 4 on assignment pages 6-15 and 6-17 before continuing.

Rapid Review:

Many production processes end up creating more than one product. For example, lumber mills often produce various sizes and grades of building lumber, but also produce the wood chips, sawdust, and scrap wood that can be sold as-is or processed into another product. Another good example is mining. Most mining operations focus on a primary metal (copper or silver, let's say), but in the process of searching for that specific metal, they are find other types of metal that they can sell as well. The principal products are called the ***main products***. For example, a meat processing plant will sell steaks, roasts, ribs, and other cuts of meat as its primary products. The meat processing plant can also produce hamburger, organ meat, meat meal used in dog food, leather, bone meal used as fertilizer, and a variety of other products. Which products are main products and which are ***by-products*** is generally determined by the amount of revenue that product produces. Something considered a by-product may become a main product if the market for it increases substantially.

After determining which products are main and which are by-products, the next question is how to allocate the joint production costs (DM, DL, and MOH) to the different products being produced. Any time you get multiple products from one process, you have to find a way to allocate the joint costs among all of the products created. For example, the cost of going into the forest, cutting down the trees, transporting them to the lumber mill, and replanting the forest are all joint costs for a lumber mill. While we are undertaking all these activities, we don't know if our time is spent on board-feet of lumber or bags of wood chips for garden mulch. Since we need to know our costs to assign a sales price and track our expenditures, we have to figure out how much of those joint costs to allocate to each of the products in the final sales mix. There are several methods that can be used to allocate these costs. The easiest is the units of production method. Another common method, the net realizable value method, is most effective when some of the products are processed further (beyond the joint costs) and some are not. As a final note, remember that the final production cost per unit will include both the allocated joint costs and any costs to process after the joint process ends.

Allocating Joint Costs

"I don't know, Li," Jordan said with a frown. "I don't think he's going to buy it."

"Why not?" Li asked defensively. "I did everything right, and I showed my work very carefully. Even someone who does not understand accounting should be able to follow my process."

Jordan held up his hands. "Hey, don't get me wrong. Your work looks great, but given what Josey told you I don't think this guy is going to buy the first set of numbers you throw at him. I think you're going to have to show him a couple of methods, and then let him choose the one he feels most comfortable with."

Li thought for a moment and then nodded. "You mean that I need to give him the final say in how we make the calculations."

Jordan nodded. "Right. The Net Realizable Value method is very straightforward, but it also *looks* really straightforward. Maybe if you showed him a more complex method.... "

Li jumped. "You make a good point. I'll show him the Constant Gross Margin Method results as well and perhaps he will find that easier to accept."

Jordan shook his hand back and forth. "I don't know that he will prefer that method. I just think that he will prefer being allowed to choose the method that he uses for his business. That would certainly show him that we are acting in good faith."

"Okay. I will do it. Thank you for your suggestion."

Stop here and answer questions 5 through 7 on assignment page 6-19 before continuing.

Rapid Review:

The Constant Gross Margin method is another common way of allocating joint production costs. Under this method, you again start with the total sales revenue you expect each product to bring, less the ***separable*** (or additional processing) costs. You then add up the total revenue from all of the main products and subtract the total separable costs and the total joint costs. This gives you a total gross margin for all of the joint (main) products, and you can convert that to an overall gross margin percentage by dividing that gross margin by the total sales revenue.

To allocate the joint costs to each product, you then multiply the total sales revenue for each product by the overall gross margin percentage. This gives you a target gross margin for each product. If you subtract the gross margin from total sales revenue, you get COGS for each product. Finally, you subtract from that COGS any separable costs for each product. You are now left with the allocated joint costs.

One nice feature of this method is that it has a check figure built in. To check your calculations, calculate the cost/unit for each of the joint (main) products and determine the gross margin by subtracting that total from the sales price. If that gross margin percentage is equal to the total gross margin you calculated at the beginning of the process, then you have done it correctly. All of the products should end up with that same percentage.

Determining Profitability Under Varying Assumptions

"So, you see, Mr. Jefferson, these numbers clearly show that our company's offer is more than fair."

Mr. Jefferson looked up with a frown. "Of course they do. How else would you show them to me?" He paused for a minute. "Of course, looking at the math, I don't really see any problems with your calculations. It does make sense, doesn't it?" Li nodded but kept silent as Mr. Jefferson continued to think. "I'll tell you what, though, I'd like to have you answer a couple more questions, just to be sure."

Li contained a sigh and smiled instead. "Of course. What would you like to see?"

"Well, I'd like to see what happens to your Gross Profit numbers if you increase the sales price of the beeswax by $1. I'd also like to see what happens with the old price if I can double my production. Can you do that?"

"With my spreadsheet, it won't be any problem at all."

Stop here and answer questions 8 and 9 on assignment page 6-21.

Rapid Review:

One challenge with these methods is that they are based on the current condition of the company. If sales price or costs change, or the quantity demanded changes, then not only will profit change, but so will the cost allocation. A wise controller will anticipate these changes and set up his or her worksheets in Excel so that any change can be easily incorporated. In fact, if you have linked everything accurately, then it should take you only a few seconds to revise your allocations when you receive updated information.

This page is
intentionally blank.

Name:

Questions

Note: *For questions and problems that require calculations, attach a copy of your spreadsheet to the related assignment page and hand it in to your instructor.*

Determining Joint Versus By-Products

Q-1. Which are the joint (main) products, and which one is the by-product?

Joint (main) products:______________________________

By-product: ______________________________

Q-2. Using the information provided by Mr. Jefferson, calculate the amount of the joint cost that should be assigned to the joint (main) products using the Net Realizable Value method for allocating joint costs.

Name:

Q-3. Using this method, what will be the total cost per pound for each joint (main) product? (Be sure to include costs to process further, if applicable.)

Tip:

Keep in mind that as a small business owner, Mr. Jefferson might not have the resources to process everything further, even if it makes sense to do so.

Q-4. What is the total gross margin ratio (total gross margin divided by total revenue) for each of the joint (main) products?

Name:

Allocating Joint Costs

Q-5. Using the information provided by Mr. Jefferson, calculate the total cost that should be assigned to the joint (main) products using the Constant Gross Margin method for allocating joint costs.

Q-6. Using this method, what will be the total cost per pound for each joint (main) product?

Q-7. What is the gross margin ratio for each joint (main) product using this method?

Name:

Determining Profitability Under Varying Assumptions

Q-8. Calculate the new cost per pound for each joint (main) product using the Constant Gross Margin method, assuming the sales price of the beeswax increases by $1.

Q-9. Calculate the new cost per pound for each joint (main) product under both allocation methods assuming Mr. Jefferson can double his production of all products and that the price of beeswax remains $3.50/lb.

Name:

Problems

Critical Thinking Issues

Problem #1

"Very interesting," Mr. Jefferson said with a frown. "Very interesting. I guess you guys aren't trying to cheat me after all. I'll have to give the offer from your company a lot more thought. Anyway, thank you for your help."

"It was my pleasure, Mr. Jefferson," Li said with a smile.

"Before I head back to work, I have to ask you one last thing. Which of these methods do you think I should use to run my business and set my prices?"

Which method do you think Li should recommend to Mr. Jefferson? Explain.

Name:

Problem #2

a. Using the total costs you calculated in question 9, and assuming that Mr. Jefferson wants to make a 200% gross profit on each of his products, how much should he charge for each of his joint (main) products using both methods?

b. Based on your answers and the price that Wedgewood is offering ($3.50 per pound), do you think Mr. Jefferson will accept Wedgewood's offer? Explain.

Name:

Ethical Issues

Li frowned as she looked at the numbers in front of her. Something in her calculations of the Constant Gross Margin method didn't look quite right.... She had checked her numbers several times, but she still didn't feel comfortable with the values that she was getting. After several more times checking the links in her spreadsheet, she stood up in frustration. "Perhaps if I take a walk," she thought to herself. She left her office and wandered out of the building and into the well-maintained grounds that surrounded Wedgewood's office building, separating it from the nearby factory.

As she quietly walked around the fountain, she continued to consider the problem she was having. For some reason, the costs assigned to the beeswax seemed low to her. Something had to be wrong with her numbers, but that only left one possibility.

She stopped and looked up at the statue of the company founder in the middle of the grounds. She stared at him for a moment, then nodded. There was only one answer. The price that the company had offered to Mr. Jefferson wasn't right. It couldn't be right. It was the one input in her spreadsheet that didn't come from Mr. Jefferson, and it was in Wedgewood's best interest to lowball their estimate and get the beeswax for below normal market price.

She walked back to her office and spent some time on the Internet looking for the normal price of beeswax. After a few minutes she sat back in her chair with a sigh. She had found what she was looking for. The company's offer was too low; it didn't match the normal market prices for raw beeswax, which was generally at least $5 per pound. Now, what was she going to do about it?

"Why," she thought to herself, "did I take Jordan's suggestion? If I had only calculated the value using the Net Realizable Value method then I would not have found the error. But now that I know, what do I do? Should I hide it from Mr. Jefferson, shifting the values so that he doesn't notice? Do I explain why this Constant Gross Margin method is better, more accurate, and recommend that he take our offer? Do I tell him the truth or let him find the truth for himself? What should I do?"

Name:

Problem #3

a. Figure out the gross margin *per pound* of beeswax for both the Net Realizable Value and the Constant Gross Margin Methods, based on your answers to questions 1 through 7. Figure out the gross margin **ratio** *per pound* as well. What would the gross margin and gross margin ratio per pound of beeswax be if Mr. Jefferson processed his beeswax further? Finally, determine the total profit Mr. Jefferson would recognize from selling the raw wax and the refined wax under both methods.

b. What does this suggest to you? Assume that Li has turned to you for advice as a friend. First, make a list of at least three possible options that Li could consider when she becomes aware that Wedgewood is offering a very low price to Mr. Jefferson. (Be sure to keep this list and turn it in with your assignment.)

1.

2.

3.

Name:

c. Next, choose two options that would be the best for Li and explain the pros and cons of both options.

1. ______________________________

(Pros) ______________________________

____

____

(Cons) ______________________________

____

____

2. ______________________________

(Pros) ______________________________

____

____

(Cons) ______________________________

____

____

d. Finally, make a recommendation for which one of these two options you think she should choose and defend your recommendation.

____

____

____

____

____

____

____

Name:

Problem #4

Assume that Li has decided to take her concerns to Wedgewood's management and ask them to improve the offer to at least the normal market price. What arguments could she use to convince management to accept her suggestion?

Notes on Apiaries

A bee yard or bee farm is called an apiary. Beekeepers create hives that are in square, portable containers. Because farmers and orchard owners need pollination in their fields, and because the population of pollinators (including bees, bats, and birds, among other species) is declining, they will allow the beekeeper to place hives in their fields. Sometimes the beekeeper does this for free and sometimes he or she charges the farmers a fee for the pollination service. In the case of Mr. Jefferson's operation, he has not been collecting revenue for placing hives.

Bees generally don't fly much more than about three miles from the hive. Therefore, if only one crop is planted in an area—orange groves, for instance—the honey can be considered to have come from that crop (e.g., orange blossom honey).

The main assets involved in beekeeping are: movable hives, protective clothing, a smoker (which is used to pacify the bees during collection and inspection), and the queens.

In addition to the revenues from placing hives, beekeepers are able to sell several products produced by their bees. These products include:

- Honey: the main product of the hive,
- Beeswax: a yellow-brown wax secreted by bees that is melted down and purified,
- Honeycomb: a combination of raw honey and beeswax,
- Propolis: resin collected from tree buds used by bees to strengthen the hive, and
- Royal jelly: a bee secretion fed to bee larva, especially those that become queen bees.

Mr. Jefferson hasn't found a market for the pollination services or royal jelly yet. He is investigating these markets at the same time he is looking into selling beeswax to Wedgewood.

ALLOCATING SERVICE DEPARTMENT COSTS

This page is intentionally blank.

CHAPTER 7

Allocating Service Department Costs

Objectives

Excel Skills

- Hiding rows and columns
- Using row height to hide cells
- Formatting cells so they are invisible to users
- Freezing the spreadsheet

Accounting Skills

- Discussing the need to reallocate service costs
- Using the direct allocation method
- Using the sequential allocation method

Mastering Excel

Hiding Rows and Columns

Sometimes we get a little carried away with our spreadsheets. It happens. It's just part of being accountants. We get so excited by rows and rows of data that we end up making our spreadsheets so big that we can't really use them very well. And anyone who isn't an accountant not only can't use them, but actually gets intimidated by them. So, to help overcome this problem, we are going to spend some time learning how to make these mega-spreadsheets easy to read without losing any of our data or any of our carefully created equations. Let's start by hiding rows and columns. Open the workbook called **C7 Excel Practice Sets** from your downloaded files and let's get started.

The accountant for the Stuffed Animal Emporium did a wonderful job creating a spreadsheet that shows the direct and sequential methods for allocating service department costs. Her first table shows the various departments, budgeted office hours, sales visits, and overhead amounts for the company. This is all of the information she needs to allocate the service department costs. Although this is important information,

Tip:

We've copied only the results here for you to look at and format; the formulas are not there. However, you could use this spreadsheet to refresh your memory of these methods by working through the various methods on your own spreadsheet and comparing your answers to those here.

Tip:

Remember, to select a set of rows, you click on the row number at the far left of the spreadsheet and then hold down the left mouse button and drag down to the last row you want to select. Do the same for columns. You can also hide rows by selecting the rows and then using the Format command in the Cells section of the Home tab.

now that the other calculations have been made, she doesn't really need to see it to write a journal entry or to create a report. She's done what she needed to with it, and now she doesn't have to show it anymore. One option would be to delete it, but in most cases the accountant would have linked his or her spreadsheet to these basic numbers. Deleting it would break all of those links and make the rest of the spreadsheet useless. So, instead, let's just hide it.

- *Select rows 2 through 11 by clicking on the row numbers at the far left of the spreadsheet.*
- *Right-click (anywhere in the highlighted section) and then click Hide.*

Those rows should have immediately disappeared, but they aren't gone. If you look at the row numbers, you can see that our list now jumps from 1 right to 12 because rows 2 through 11 are hidden. Since they are only hidden, you can still use the numbers in those hidden rows in formulas and they will still update if they have formulas in them. If you need to bring them back so that you can update information or check details, the process is simple.

- *Highlight rows 1 and 12.*
- *Right-click (anywhere in the highlighted section) and then click Unhide.*

The other way you can do this is to just double-click.

- *Select rows 1 through 12.*
- *Move your cursor over the split between rows 12 and 13.*
- *Double-click.*

All the rows should be back to their normal height again. Go ahead and practice hiding them again (or click the Undo button) so that rows 2 through 11 are hidden as we move forward.

Using Row Height to Hide Cells

From time to time, you may want to hide a row, but you can't use the Hide command. The most common reason for this is when you have used those numbers in a graph. If you hide rows in a graph, Excel removes them from the graph. Let's see how this works. Go to the second spreadsheet in your workbook (called Cost per minute of Machine A). This spreadsheet presents the number of minutes per day for a year that Machine A has been used to stuff animals. In the next column are the related costs to run the machine. There is also a nice graph of the two columns to the right. Finally, the monthly cost totals are presented in column D. While the graph looks pretty good, it's hard to read through all of those figures. So, it might be nice to see the graph, but only read through the last day of each month along with the monthly totals. To do this, it would seem logical to hide the rows you don't need. Let's see what happens when you hide January 1 through January 30. Go ahead and try it.

Did you see that the graph disappeared entirely? Press the Undo button to get the graph back. If you think about it, it makes sense that since we hid the rows where the graph appears, that the graph would disappear along with those rows. So, let's try hiding February 1 through 27 instead. We should be able to do that without losing the graph. Once you've done it, take a look at your graph. You now have a gap where February's data should be. By some strange twist of programming, hidden rows can be used in most functions and formulas, but they don't show up on graphs. Press the Undo button again and we'll show you a sneaky way around this problem.

It's going to be easiest to start somewhere other than January so you can practice this. Let's start with February.

- *Select rows 33 through 59.*
- *Right-click and select Row Height....*
- *Change the row height to* 0.1 *(be sure to put in that decimal).*

Notice that the rows have now become so small that they might as well be hidden. The visible row numbers now jump from row 32 to row 60, but there is a bit of a greyish line or small gap between those rows. That is where your tiny, tiny rows are. If you check the graph, your data are still there. Go ahead and do the remaining months, except January. We'll be right here when you're done.

If you tried to shrink the January rows, you probably noticed that your graph disappeared, shrunk along with the rows. Since that obviously won't work, here are the steps you can use to shrink those rows as well.

- *Click on the upper border of the graph. You need to find the exact spot where your cursor changes to a black plus sign with arrows going all four ways like this ✥.*
- *Drag the graph down so the top is even with row 60 (which should be just below row 32).*
- *Adjust the height of rows 2 through 31.*

We resized our graph so it would show in our screenshot, but here's what it should look like.

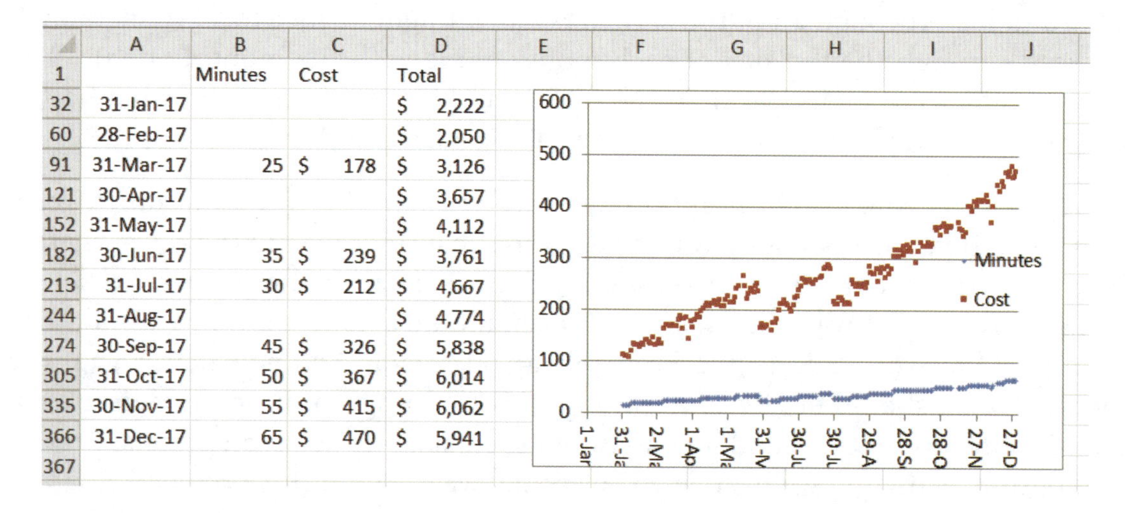

	A	B	C	D
1		Minutes	Cost	Total
32	31-Jan-17			$ 2,222
60	28-Feb-17			$ 2,050
91	31-Mar-17	25	$ 178	$ 3,126
121	30-Apr-17			$ 3,657
152	31-May-17			$ 4,112
182	30-Jun-17	35	$ 239	$ 3,761
213	31-Jul-17	30	$ 212	$ 4,667
244	31-Aug-17			$ 4,774
274	30-Sep-17	45	$ 326	$ 5,838
305	31-Oct-17	50	$ 367	$ 6,014
335	30-Nov-17	55	$ 415	$ 6,062
366	31-Dec-17	65	$ 470	$ 5,941
367				

Notice that it appears you have hidden rows even though they are really only very small. If you wish to display those rows again, you can't just unhide them using the Unhide command. Instead, you'll need to resize the heights of those rows to a normal size (typically around 14.25). The steps are the same as before; just use the new value. Alternatively, you can also expand these rows the same way you expanded hidden rows.

- *Select rows 32 through 60.*
- *Move your cursor over the split between rows 32 and 60.*
- *Right-click, select Row Height, and type in* 15.

Formatting Cells To Be Invisible

The next formatting trick does not remove or shrink rows, but rather allows us to simplify our spreadsheet for those who aren't excited by extensive accounting equations or row after row of data. This time, we're just going to make the information invisible, but we'll leave it there so that we can still get to it when we need to.

To do this, let's go back to the Service Department Allocation spreadsheet. Even after hiding the basic information, there is still a lot of information on the page that may not be helpful for the users. For example, the accountant left herself some notes on what steps to use. Let's hide that information from a casual viewer, but leave it there for the accountant to use.

- *Click on A13.*
- *Right-click.*
- *Click on the drop-down arrow to the right of the Font Color icon (A ▾).*
- *Choose White (the uppermost left color in the color box).*

Those words are no longer visible on the spreadsheet, since white ink on white paper (or the electronic equivalent thereof) makes it look invisible. However, if the accountant needs to remind herself what is in that cell she can easily get to the information by either clicking on the cell and looking at the formula bar (as pictured below) or by highlighting the cell and changing the font to red, black, or blue.

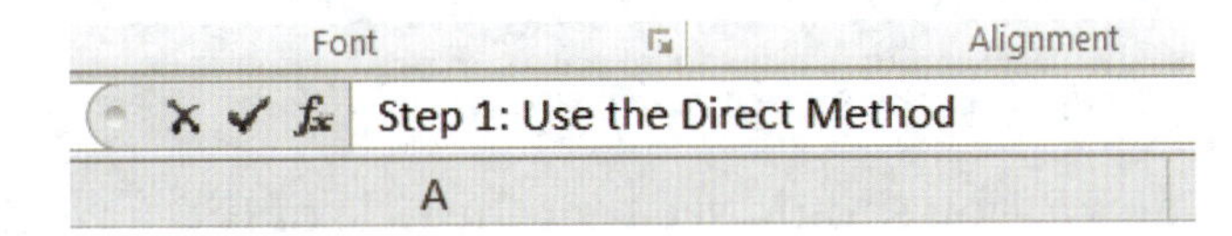

If we want to format all the cells that have a step in it this way, there is yet another shortcut.

- *Click on A13 again (if necessary)*
- *Find the Format Painter icon ( ) in the Clipboard section of the ribbon.*
- *Double-click on that icon.*

This copies the format that is found in the active cell.

- *Click on each cell that contains a step.*

This quick formatting tool paints the format from one cell onto the others we click on. If the Format Painter is active, you will see a plus sign and a paint brush. Just imagine how useful *that* little trick can be when working on a big spreadsheet, especially since Excel defaults to a basic number format. When you are done copying formatting style, press [Esc] or click on the Format Painter icon again.

Freezing the Spreadsheet

Our final trick for making information easier to read in Excel is used when we need to have all of the information accessible and visible. In many cases, we are still tweaking or updating data and equations as we go. In this scenario, we are back to having a very large spreadsheet with lots of data, and it can be very easy to get lost in so much information. The worst part of this scenario is trying to remember what information should be in which column or row, especially as you move further and further from cell A1.

While we can't fix this problem by removing data, we can make it possible to keep track of the row and columns headings so that no matter where you go in your spreadsheet you still know what you are seeing or what information you should be typing. To demonstrate this trick, let's start by freezing the top two rows.

- *Click on cell A13.*
- *Switch to the View tab of the ribbon.*
- *Click on Freeze Panes in the Window group of the ribbon.*
- *Click on the Freeze Panes choice in the drop-down menu.*

As you scroll up and down, you should see that the title of the spreadsheet and the two method titles stay at the top but that the rest of the rows move up and down. If you scroll down to row 49, you can now see the heading and the final totals at the same time, making it much easier to consider the two methods and which might give you the best answers.

What we just showed you is the easiest, and probably most common, way to use the Freeze Panes command. However, there are lots of other options. For example, unfreeze your spreadsheet.

- *Click on Freeze Panes in the Window group of the ribbon.*
- *Click on the Unfreeze Panes choice in the drop-down menu.*

Now, let's set up our spreadsheet so that we can always see the column titles, but so that we can see the row titles as well. To do this:

- *Click on cell B13.*

- *Click on Freeze Panes in the Window group of the ribbon.*
- *Click on the Freeze Panes choice in the drop-down menu.*

Now, if you place your cursor in cell B13 and scroll up and down or scroll off to the right, all of your titles will remain in the same place: the columns and the rows. Isn't that cool?

Once you've made all of these changes, go ahead and resize your columns as we've done in previous chapters. You should now have a spreadsheet that looks similar to this:

	A	B	C	D	E	F	G	H	I	J	K
1	**Stuffed Animal Emporium - Production and Service Department Allocation Worksheet**										
12	***Direct Method***						***Sequential Method***				
46		Horses and	Teddy Bears	Dinosaurs	Zoo Animals			Horses and	Teddy Bears	Dinosaurs	Zoo Animals
47	Support Costs Allocated	$59,030	$335,148	$21,347	$559,974		Support Costs Allocated	$50,759	$314,501	$17,746	$592,494
48	Units Produced	10,000	81,000	2,500	197,000		Units Produced	10,000	81,000	2,500	197,000
49	Support Cost/unit	$5.90	$4.14	$8.54	$2.84		Support Cost/unit	$5.08	$3.88	$7.10	$3.01
50											

Before we wrap up, we just want to give one warning about freezing the spreadsheet. This is a great tool when you are showing your monitor to someone or trying to keep track of a lot of data on your monitor. But it only works on the monitor. If you print your file, it won't just print the portion of the screen you are seeing and it won't move your headers down to the rows you are currently looking at. It is going to print the actual spreadsheet. If you want to change what prints you will need to use the Hide command.

Wrapping Up Our Excel Work

Another Excel lesson has come and gone. We hope that you can put some of these new tools to work as you start on another fun project from Wedgewood Candle Co. Remember to think about how your work looks on screen as well as on paper. Now, as you are working, you can make notes, add extra steps to really carefully walk through your equations, and hide them when you are getting ready to print your work or email it to you instructor. This way, you have all of the information you need, but your work stays neat, clean, and succinct!

Wedgewood Candle Co.

Discussing the Need to Allocate Service Costs

"It's starting to be a problem, Jeremiah. We have to do something about it."

Jeremiah looked across the conference table at his aunt, Jennifer Wedgewood. Jennifer was the chair of Wedgewood's Board of Directors and also the youngest daughter of company founder Pierce Wedgewood. She was the only one of Pierce's children still actively involved in management, and sometimes Jeremiah wished that she would relax a little bit and let his generation take care of things. For now, though, he had no choice but to deal with her. After all, since she was still actively involved with the business, her brothers and sisters just went along with her. There was no way she was going to lose a fight about company policy!

"I see your point, Aunt Jenni, but I really don't see what we are going to do about it."

Jenni sighed. "Fix it, Jerry. I'm tired of listening to the complaints about how the service costs are being allocated to the production departments. The managers don't think it's fair, and after looking at the numbers I have to agree with them. How can you just divide up the total costs by the two product lines and call it fair?"

Peter Wedgewood, the Marketing Director, jumped in. "I don't see the problem either, Aunt Jenni. I mean, my department sells all of our products. Why shouldn't the costs be allocated equally to the two lines?"

Maria, Jeremiah's niece and Wedgewood's COO, jumped in. "I agree with Aunt Jenni. We need to do something about the allocation. I mean, I agree that allocating the service department costs is important to our decision making process, especially since we use full costs to determine bonuses, but there has to be a better way of doing it." She looked at Peter. "I mean, think about your department, Uncle Peter. Isn't your team spending a lot more time pushing the new specialty products than they are the more established pillar candles?"

"Well, yeah, I guess we are," he frowned, and then looked at his brother. "Sorry, Jerry," he said. "I think you're going to have to redo the allocation."

Jeremiah sighed. "How?" he asked. "The accounting staff is already stretched thin trying to keep up with the product costing and the reporting for the new line. Not to mention the monthly reports the bank is requiring because of the rather large line of credit we are using to get the new line up and running. Our department is just not big enough to handle any additional workload."

"Then hire someone, Jerry," Jennifer said. "And get them working on this new project."

"Yes, ma'am. I'll get right on it."

Using the Direct Allocation Method

"This will be your office," Jordan said as he switched on the lights to the small room. "It's not big, but at least there's a door." He turned to smile at Demitri Washington. "Probably a big change from a carrel at the library, isn't it?"

Demitri smiled shyly before answering in his southern drawl. "Everything's different up here, Mr. Leavitt. It's a far cry from Louisiana, but my wife insisted that I find a place outside of the humidity and the bugs, so here I am."

"We're glad to have you, and you can just call me Jordan. We're pretty informal around here. It's one of the nice things about a small company." He gestured towards the desk chair, waited for Demitri to sit down, then sat across from him. "Now, though, you need to get to work. We keep things informal and fun, but we also get a lot done. There are really only three of us—well, four of us now—in the accounting and finance department, and we have a ton to do. Josey, the controller, still takes care of most of the heavy work, but she keeps the rest of us hopping with specific assignments and other basic calculations.

"Normally she would have been here herself, but she's in an all-day budget meeting with the executive team, so she asked me to get you started." Jordan pointed to a stack of papers. "That's the information that we have from our service and production departments about how service costs are being allocated."

Demitri reached out and ruffled through the stacks. After a minute he frowned. "It looks like you assign all of the service costs based on candle inches produced."

Jordan nodded. "We do, but don't judge us too harshly. Remember, there have only been three of us, and we've been stretched pretty thin. Also, we used to only have the one division that made various-sized pillar candles. A while back, we started a second division that produces specialty candles. And we are moving in the direction of adding a third division that makes container candles and a fourth that makes beeswax candles. For now, though, we are just going to worry about allocating service costs between the two existing lines. Now that you're here, we finally have the staffing to do a more accurate job. In fact, that's your first assignment."

Jordan gestured to another sheet of paper (You'll find a copy of the Memo to Demitri about Service Departments located directly after the assignment pages for this chapter). "Josey was able to make that summary for you before her meeting today. I swear that woman never sleeps. Anyway, she put together that information about our two service departments and what she thinks their drivers should be."

Demitri nodded. "Okay, and I'm supposed to allocate the costs?"

"Right. After chatting about it last week with the executive team, she decided that we should probably have two service department pools. We can combine marketing and general office support into one pool and call it "sales support" and then human resources, accounting, and finance into another pool and call it "financial support." She listed what she thinks should be the allocation bases in the memo I gave you. We want you to calculate what the numbers look like using the direct allocation method, and then send your results to Josey."

Stop here and answer questions 1 through 3 on assignment page 7-13 before continuing. You can find a partial template for these questions in the Wedgewood Company files you downloaded.

Rapid Review:

Up to this point, we have focused on production costs, but those are not the only costs that a company incurs in order to deliver a product. In addition to production costs, most companies also have significant ***period costs***. Period costs are all of the selling and administrative costs that allow a company to function. Advertising, marketing, office support, salaries for those not involved in production, research and development, and accounting fees are all examples of period costs. These costs cannot be included in our inventory or in our cost of goods sold. Instead, they are expensed immediately as part of net income. However, from an internal perspective, they should be included in setting sales prices. If you don't set your sales price high enough to cover these costs, then you won't be in business for very long!

The most straightforward method for allocating service costs (also known as *administrative overhead* when it is being allocated) to the units produced is known as the ***direct method***. Using the direct method, the company allocates each administrative cost pool directly to the production lines using cost drivers. In this case, you estimate the total drivers used by each production department, then add them up to get a total cost drivers used by production. You then calculate the percentage of the total cost drivers each production department used and allocate the administrative cost pool to the production lines using that percentage.

Once you have allocated all of the administrative cost pools to your product lines, you can add the production costs to get a total cost for that particular line and then divide by the units produced to get the cost per unit. You can then use that number as part of your decision-making process when setting sales prices.

Tip:

Because managerial accounting isn't regulated, the terminology changes from company to company, textbook to textbook. The sequential allocation method is sometimes called a step-down, stepwise, or step method.

Using the Sequential Allocation Method

Josey frowned as she examined the numbers Demitri had handed her. Demitri tried not to squirm as he watched her, but he worried that her frown must mean that he'd done something wrong. Finally, he couldn't stand it anymore, "Anything wrong, ma'am?" he asked.

Josey shook her head to clear her thoughts as Demitri's question reminded her that he was watching her. She smiled reassuringly as she looked up. "Not with your spreadsheet, Demitri," she said lightly, "but looking at these numbers, I'm starting to think that perhaps the direct method isn't the best way to allocate these costs." She drummed her pencil on the table and her frown returned as she stared down at the printout.

"How about the sequential allocation method?" Demitri asked. "We could try that instead."

Josey beamed at him. "I knew we hired you for a reason. Give that a try and let's see how the numbers look."

"And what's the order for the sequential allocation?" Demitri asked.

"Hmmm. I'm not sure. Why don't you do it both ways and see what you think? Sales and general administration provide about 1,000 hours of support to the financial group, so that will be the driver when you allocate that cost first. As for allocating the financial support costs first...." Josey looked at her computer. "Let's see, we are using payroll costs as the driver, I think." She tapped a few more keys and then looked up at Demitri. "The payroll for sales and general admission support was $300,000 that period, so you'll need to use that value for your calculations. Do you need anything else or have any questions before you go?"

Demitri shook his head, already deep in thought. "No, I don't think so. I'll let you know if I get stuck."

Stop here and answer questions 4 through 7 on assignment page 7-15 before continuing.

Rapid Review:

The sequential method is the other common method for allocating service costs to the production lines. This method recognizes that the administrative departments support not only production, but each other as well. For example, the accounting department not only helps track production costs but also tracks the costs of the human resources (HR) department and the marketing department. By allocating the costs of accounting directly to the production departments, we lose information. We miss the fact that accounting is spending a ton of time helping HR track the costs of new employees and that the new employees have all been hired for the new line. If you think about it, that means that accounting is really spending more time and money on the new line than on the old ones, and more of its cost should be allocated to that new line.

(continued on the following page)

Rapid Review *(continued)*:

The sequential method allows us to take that kind of support into account. When allocating the service department costs, we start out by deciding which administrative department most supports the other administrative departments. In our example, we would have to decide if accounting helps HR the most or if HR helps accounting more. If we decide that accounting helps HR the most, then we would start the allocation process by allocating the accounting costs to HR and marketing *and* the production departments. After we've made that allocation, we look at HR and marketing. Since marketing probably doesn't help HR at all, we allocate the new HR costs (including the portion of accounting already allocated) to marketing *and* the production departments. We keep doing this, sequentially allocating each administrative department's costs to all of the other departments until we have allocated everything to the production departments.

Name:

Questions

Note: *For questions and problems that require calculations, attach a copy of your spreadsheet to the related assignment page and hand it in to your instructor.*

Using the Direct Allocation Method

Q-1. What is the total amount of administrative overhead (support costs) that needs to be allocated between the two lines?

Q-2. If the direct method of allocating support costs is used, how much of the sales support costs should be allocated to financial support?

Tip:
Practice all the formatting techniques you've learned so far to make this spreadsheet easy to read and printable.

Q-3. If the direct method of allocating support costs is used, how much of the cost is allocated to the standard line? To the specialty line?

Standard line:

Specialty line:

Name:

Using the Sequential Allocation Method

Q-4. If Sales support is allocated first, and the sequential method is used, how much of the sales support costs should be allocated to financial support?

____

____

Q-5. Assuming that sales support is allocated first, how much of the total service department costs should be allocated to the standard line? To the specialty line?

Standard line: ______________________________

____

Specialty line: ______________________________

____

Q-6. If financial support is allocated first, and the sequential method is used, how much of the financial support costs should be allocated to sales support?

____

____

Q-7. Assuming financial support is allocated first, how much of the total service department costs should be allocated to the standard line? To the specialty line?

Standard line: ______________________________

____

Specialty line: ______________________________

____

Name:

Problems

Critical Thinking Issues

Demitri knocked on Jordan's door. "Demitri," Jordan said with a smile. "Come on in. How go the calculations?" he asked as his new colleague settled into a chair.

"Just fine," Demitri answered, "but I have a question."

Jordan leaned back and crossed his hands behind his head. "I might have an answer. Try me!"

"Well, I have the costs that Josey wants, but what should I do with them?"

Jordan frowned. "What do you mean?"

"Well, these numbers don't really give us much information, do they? So, what should I do with them?"

Jordan nodded. "Ah, now I see." Jordan leaned over and tapped a few keys on Demitri's computer and then pointed to a few numbers. "Well, here are the total production numbers for each of the departments from last quarter. Why don't you come up with a full cost per candle?"

"Why would I do that?" Demitri asked.

"Because that's the whole point, my friend, "Jordan answered with a laugh. "Why allocate costs if we can't determine the total spent to really produce an item?"

Name:

Problem #1

Assume that Wedgewood produced 7,500,000 candle inches of the standard candles with total production costs of $7,553,681. What is the full cost of a four-inch candle under the direct allocation method? What about using the step method and allocating sales support first? The step method and allocating financial support first? Which method do you think provides the most accurate allocation of service costs? Write a short memo to Josey defending your choice. Use the space below to create an outline of your memo before you create it in Word. When you have completed the memo, attach a copy of it to this sheet and hand it in to your instructor.

Name:

Problem #2

Would your answer to Assignment #1 change if Wedgewood produced 2,500,000 candle inches at a total production cost of $2,657,894? Why or why not? Amend your memo, if necessary, explaining how volume affects your answer. When you have completed the memo, attach a copy of it to this sheet and hand it in to your instructor.

Name:

Ethical Issues

Demitri looked over his numbers again and nodded. He had done a good job, with the allocation and the calculation of the full product prices. Now he could call it a night. He turned off his computer and gathered his things to leave.

It was late, well past the normal closing time, so the building was quiet as he walked to his car. However, by the door he met a well-dressed man, probably in his late 30s, looking out towards the parking lot. He was standing right in the doorway, so Demitri politely said, "Excuse me," as he tried to get past.

The man looked at him, smiling. "Ah," he said. "You must be Demitri."

"Yes, sir," replied the new employee, his southern manners helping him mask his annoyance. After a long day at the office, he really just wanted to leave. He held out his hand. "And you are?" he asked.

The man shook his warmly. "I'm Stephen Pontz, manager of the pillar candle line."

"It's a pleasure to meet you, sir," Demitri said with feeling. "I'm sorry to bug you, but would you mind if I slipped by? It's late, and my wife is probably worried about me staying away so long on my first day."

"Of course, of course. We definitely need to get you to your wife. But I have a quick question for you. Have you finished running the numbers for the service allocation?"

"Well, yes sir, but how did you.... "

Stephen laughed. "This is small company, my friend. Word travels fast, especially with something as important as this. Tell me," he said, suddenly serious again. "Did you transfer a lot of the service costs out of my division?"

"Some, sir, but because your division is so much larger than the others, you still ended up with a large share."

Stephen frowned. "Hmmm. Is there.... " he paused, looking out the door for another minute. "Is there anything I can do to help make that change?"

"What do you mean?"

"Well, my division has been struggling to make its numbers recently, and I think a lot of it has to do with the service allocation. My line has been around the longest, so I'm expected to be efficient and run a high margin—keep a high margin, actually. No one expects," he said softly, "the new lines to be successful yet. I think they could handle a bit more of the service costs. After all, we are all spending a lot of time helping them get up and running.... " He looked meaningfully at Demitri.

Name:

"Are you asking me to shift some of your costs to the other divisions?" Demitri asked, surprised.

"Asking? That's probably too strong a word." Stephen said as he opened the door and started to walk out. Demitri followed. He stopped at the edge of the parking lot. "But," he said with meaning. "Do keep in mind, my friend, that my father-in-law is the CEO and Jenni Wedgewood, the Chairman of our Board of Directors, is my wife's godmother. I have a lot of pull around here, and I'd love to see a young man like you be successful." With that he nodded and walked quickly to his car, leaving Demitri standing on the curb.

Problem #3

What options does Demitri have in dealing with Stephen's request? Who will be affected by his decision? Think outside the box as you answer these questions and make your lists as extensive as possible.

Name:

Problem #4

What do you think is the best way for Demitri to handle this situation? Explain why your chosen solution is better than the other options available to him.

Wedgewood
Candle Co.

To: Demitri Washington

From: Josey Wedgewood

CC: Jordan Leavitt

Date: October 15, 2016

Re: Thoughts on Service Department Allocations

I think that we can lump all of the general administrative support and sales and marketing overhead into one service department pool and call that "sales support." We can combine the accounting, human resources, and finance departments and call that "financial support." Last year, the sales support pool totaled about $400,000 and the financial support expenses were about $375,000.

We could allocate the sales support based on staff hours. For the production divisions, the basis for the sales support group would be:

Standard Line - 6,000 hrs
Specialty Line - 9,000 hrs

The financial support group's costs should be allocated based on payroll expenses, since the main internal support is for payroll issues. The driver values are:

Standard Line - $401,250
Specialty Line - $214,500

It would be very helpful if a spreadsheet could be designed that would allow us to input our figures each period and get the allocation amount automatically.

DETERMINING TRANSFER PRICING

This page is intentionally blank.

CHAPTER 8

Determining Transfer Pricing

Objectives

Excel Skills

- Naming cells
- Using the rounding functions
- Using absolute cell references

Accounting Skills

- Gathering the data for a transfer pricing decision
- Calculating transfer prices

Mastering Excel

Naming Cells

As our Excel workbooks become larger, including more and more individual spreadsheets, it can become difficult to find key pieces of information. While we can use the formatting tools to highlight this information on each spreadsheet, colors and fonts don't make it any easier to reference those numbers in other spreadsheets. Say, for example, that we want to reference net income as part of a financial analysis. Since net income is such a key number, we will need to access that information often on each of our spreadsheets. As we learned in Chapter 3, the steps needed to pull information from one spreadsheet to another in a workbook are simple, but that doesn't mean that they don't become time consuming. So, if we plan to use a number often, we can name the cell where that number appears for the first time. Then, in later spreadsheets and equations, we can use the name as a reference. If we were to name the cell in the Income Statement that show net income as "NI" we wouldn't have to keep going back to our Income Statement spreadsheet each time we need to refer to that number.

Open up the workbook called **C8 Excel Practice Sets** from your downloaded files, and we'll show you how to use this shortcut. The first spreadsheet in our workbook shows

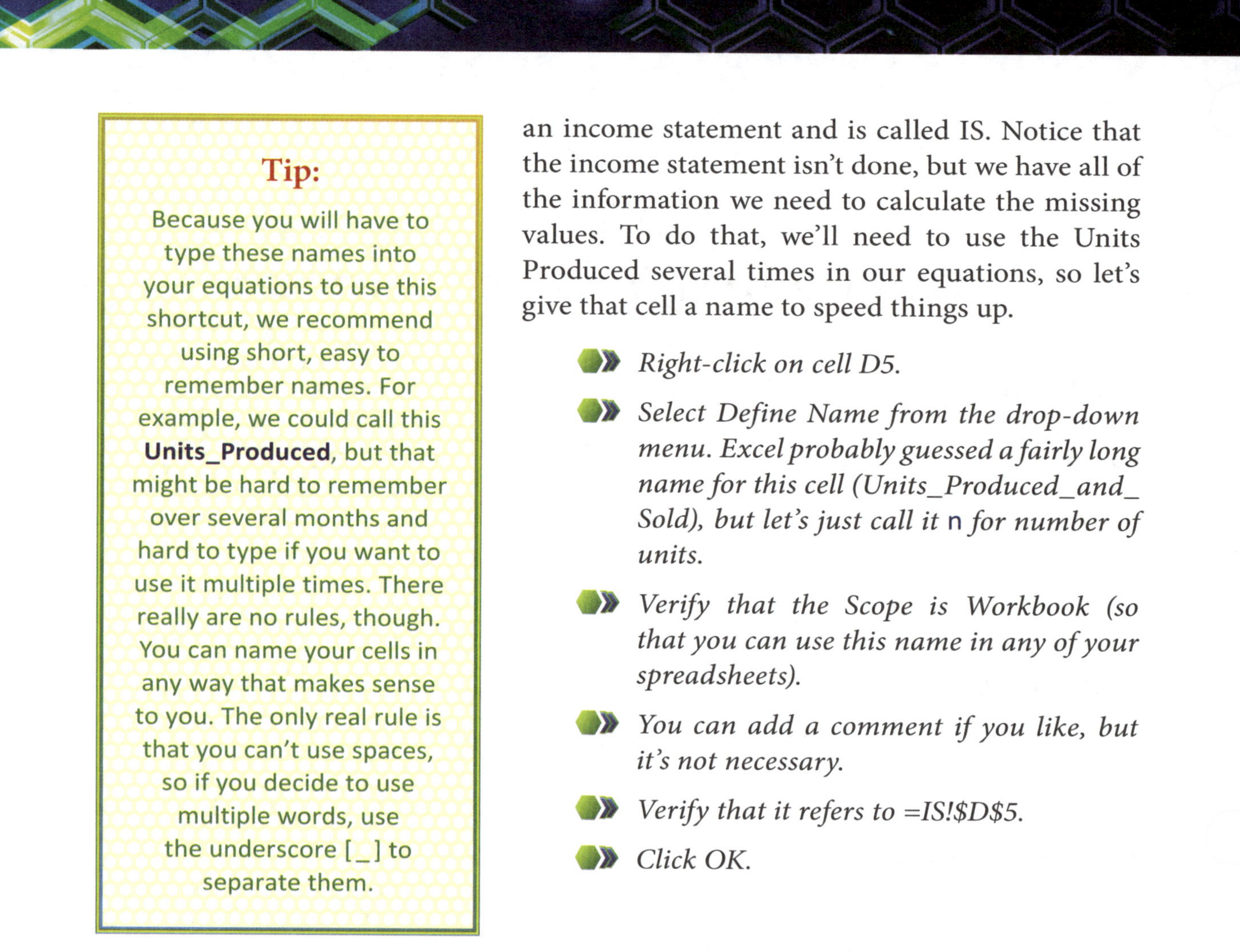

Tip:

Because you will have to type these names into your equations to use this shortcut, we recommend using short, easy to remember names. For example, we could call this **Units_Produced**, but that might be hard to remember over several months and hard to type if you want to use it multiple times. There really are no rules, though. You can name your cells in any way that makes sense to you. The only real rule is that you can't use spaces, so if you decide to use multiple words, use the underscore [_] to separate them.

an income statement and is called IS. Notice that the income statement isn't done, but we have all of the information we need to calculate the missing values. To do that, we'll need to use the Units Produced several times in our equations, so let's give that cell a name to speed things up.

- *Right-click on cell D5.*
- *Select Define Name from the drop-down menu. Excel probably guessed a fairly long name for this cell (Units_Produced_and_Sold), but let's just call it* n *for number of units.*
- *Verify that the Scope is Workbook (so that you can use this name in any of your spreadsheets).*
- *You can add a comment if you like, but it's not necessary.*
- *Verify that it refers to =IS!$D$5.*
- *Click OK.*

Now when you look at the top-left part of your screen, to the left of the dialogue box you'll see the name of this cell (n). It should look like the picture shown here.

n	*fx* 500000
	A	B
1	Some Company	
2	Pro Forma Statement of Operating Income	

Go ahead and name the cell next to it. Use the name Price for this one. Now let's use those names.

- *Click on Cell B5. Type the following formula:* =n*price *and then press [Enter].*

You should have noticed that autocomplete kicked in and tried to guess which named cell or function you wanted to use. When that pops up, make sure the correct one is highlighted then press [Tab] and Excel will autocomplete the name for you. Because of this help, you can use longer names if you need them.

While this process is probably more effort than it is worth when you are working on only one spreadsheet, it becomes a very useful shortcut when you are working on another spreadsheet or tab. Instead of going back to the IS tab for the number of units produced, you can just type in n on any spreadsheet in the workbook. We'll demonstrate how well that works in just a minute. For now, name cell E7 Unit_COGS and then name cell E9 Unit_VSA. Of course, these are the names that make sense to us. You are welcome to select names you will remember for these cells.

Now use the names to calculate the total cost of goods sold and total selling and variable selling and administrative costs in the income statement. Your formulas should look like the ones pictured here when you are done.

	B
5	=n*Price
6	
7	=n*Unit_COGS
8	**=+B5-B7**
9	=n*Unit_VSA
10	264000
11	**=+B8-B9-B10**

To view your formulas, you can press [Ctrl] [~] (hold the [Ctrl] key down while pressing the tilde [~], which is above the [Tab] key).

A final note about named cells: Excel provides several options to help you use these shortcuts. In the Formulas tab of the Excel ribbon, you'll find a Defined Names area with several tools. In addition to the Define Name command that we have already discussed, you'll also see a Use in Formula command, which will give you a list of all of the names in your workbook for easy use when creating formulas and a Name Manager, which allows you to edit names (a very useful option if you cannot remember the original name or if you accidentally chose the wrong cell reference for the name) or delete names (which can be handy if you have too many named cells).

Using the Rounding Functions

Naming cells can make it much easier to find key pieces of information in our spreadsheets, but it doesn't fix problems with that information. One of the biggest issues we have in accounting is rounding numbers, typically to the nearest penny. For example, let's say that we have calculated a unit price of $1.75342. It's great, theoretically, to have such an accurate estimate, but it can cause some problems. First, it's hard to read. Most people in business tend to think of values in terms of dollars or, at most, pennies. We don't want to think about anything further than that, especially

Tip:

You can also visually round numbers when formatting your cells. One of the options Excel provides is the number of decimals to display. The default for the Financial and Accounting formats is 2 decimal places, but you can easily change to however many you prefer.

if we need to do any calculations with that number. Second, there are often tax or GAAP rules that require numbers to be rounded to the nearest dollar or penny. That doesn't affect calculations as much in cost accounting, but it's often nice to follow the same convention.

When working in Excel, there are two ways to round numbers. The first is to just visually round the values. Using the Increase Decimal and Decrease Decimal commands ( ) in the Number group of the Home tab on the Excel ribbon, we can force Excel to show exactly the values we want: dollars or pennies. However, that doesn't actually change the value in Excel. It only changes what we see.

Visual rounding has the benefit of leaving all of that key data in place for use later, making future calculations and estimates more accurate. However, it can also lead to problems. If you add up enough small values (like $0.10) you will eventually get to a total above $0.50, which rounds up instead of down. This can throw off a balance sheet or trial balance by $1, and you won't see why because of the visual rounding. Another example can be easily seen from our unit price of $1.75342. Let's say that we round that value in Excel to $1.75 and use that sales price for our customer. In Excel, when we sell one million units, we will show total revenues of $1,753,420, but in reality we'll only get $1,750,000. While that difference ($3,420) seems immaterial, it can throw off your calculations and your pro forma balance sheet very quickly.

Tip:

Before starting the next example, you might want to format the cells in the Target Price spreadsheet and change the column widths to make everything easy to read.

To avoid this problem, we can force Excel to actually round our values using one of the round functions: Round, Roundup, or Rounddown. Each of these functions works in about the same way, so which function you use will depend on the questions you are asking and how the final number will affect your business. For example, if you are setting a price or calculating a breakeven point, you will probably want to round up. If you are estimating a safety margin or calculating a CM/unit, you will probably want to round down. If you are following GAAP in creating a set of financial statements, then you will probably want to use the generic round function. Let's try these different options in calculating a target price for our practice company. Go to the Target Price tab in your workbook. You'll see a generic setup for calculating the target price.

- *In B2, type* =Unit_COGS *and press [Enter]. (Remember to use the autocomplete function.)*
- *In B3, add a formula that multiplies cell B2 by 72%. Using the Increase Decimal command, format this cell to see at least four decimals.*

Now we want to add these two values together, but to the nearest penny. Let's use the roundup function, since that's the most useful option in setting a price. As we go, keep in mind that the same basic steps are used for the Rounddown and Round functions as well.

- *Click in cell B4.*
- *Click the drop-down arrow to the right of the AutoSum in the Editing group of the Home ribbon.*
- *Click on More Functions.*
- *Search for or scroll down and find Roundup (in the Math & Trig category).*
- *In the Number dialogue box type* sum(B2:B3).
- *In the Num_digits dialogue box type* 2.

> **Tip:**
>
> Instead of typing B2:B3 when doing your formula within a function, you can use the mouse to select the cells just like you do with a regular formula.

Here's what it should look like when you are done.

	A	B
1	Target Price Calculations	
2	COGS	$ 3.16
3	Markup	2.2752
4	New Price	$ 5.44

The 2 in the Num-digits dialogue box tells Excel that you wanted to round the result to two digits to the right of the decimal. You can enter any positive number up to 14. You can also use negative numbers to round to the left of the decimal, showing the nearest $100 or $1,000 dollars. Let's take a quick look at how that works.

- *Somewhere on your spreadsheet, add a header called* Units.
- *Under that, enter* 1,375.

- *Next to the first header, add a header called* Price.
- *Under that, enter* $19.25.
- *Next to that header, add a third header called* Monthly Total.

Under that, use the Rounddown function to multiply the units by the price and type -3 *in the Num_Digits dialogue box.*

We weren't as specific that time, but hopefully you were able to figure it out without any problems. Here's what our solution looks like after a little formatting. (Now that you are comfortable with many of the formatting skills in Excel, hopefully you are no longer content with just raw numbers on a white page.)

Units	Price	Monthly Total
1,375	$ 19.25	$ 26,000

Absolute Cell References

Having difficulty finding information or dealing with unrounded numbers are not the only problems we can have with large spreadsheets. It can also be difficult to manage your equations, especially when you are trying to refer to a key piece of information like net income. When we copy equations in Excel, it helpfully moves the cell references too, moving down or to the right as you copy your work. That's because Excel thinks of references a little differently than we do. For example, take a look at the Monthly Total that we just calculated. What we see is +F2*G2. (Your cell references may be different, depending on where you input this information.) What Excel reads is "two cells to the left * the cell immediately to the left." So, if you were to copy that equation to the adjacent cell to the right, you would now have $500,000, which is $19.25*$26,000 (rounded down, since Excel copied the entire formula).

In many cases, that's what we want Excel to see as we are copying and pasting our work, but sometimes this is a problem. Say, for example, that your price is set for the whole year and you won't be changing it. If you want to estimate total revenue for each month, you would have to copy that same price for each month in order for the equations to work correctly. But there's a better way that also allows you to copy equations from worksheet to worksheet or throughout a worksheet and still calculate your total price or net income. How? By using absolute cell references!

Absolute references change what Excel reads. Instead of seeing "two cells to the left * the cell immediately to the left," a permanent reference Excel reads as "two cells to the left * $F$1." No matter how you copy and paste that equation, it will always multiply two cells to the left of the cell the equation is in to the value in F1. The dollar signs tell Excel that you don't just mean the cell to the left; you mean the specific value in a specific cell. Here's how to use it.

To the left of your Units column, add a column called Month.

- *Under that, enter* January.
- *Mouse over the lower right corner of the cell containing January until you find the black box and your cursor turns into a plus sign, then click and drag down another 11 rows. This should fill in the months through December (another fun Excel shortcut).*
- *Add units for each month, starting with February, as follows:* 1427, 1832, 1716, 1963, 1393, 1281, 1583, 1872, 1626, 1500, 1225.
- *Sum these months. Your check figure is 18,793.*
- *Click on your original calculation for January's monthly total and press the [F2] key.*
- *Move your cursor to the cell reference in the formula that points to the price (G2 in the formula bar in our example).*
- *Press the [F4] key and then [Enter].*

Our formula is pictured here. The $ that signals absolute cell references should now appear in the reference to the price.

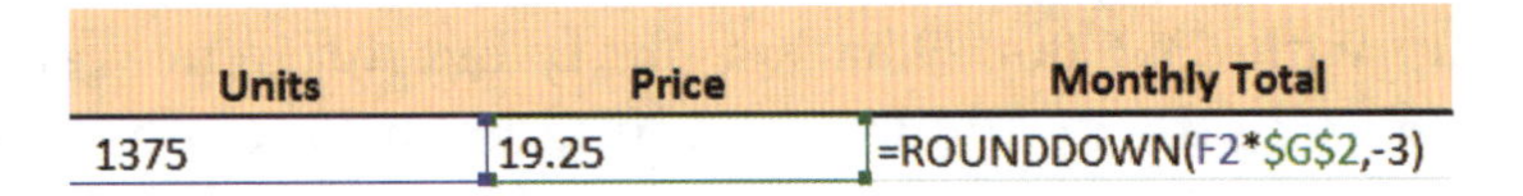

Units	Price	Monthly Total
1375	19.25	=ROUNDDOWN(F2*$G$2,-3)

- *Now drag your Monthly Total down to fill out the table, just like you did with the months.*

Pretty cool, isn't it? If you were to try that without the permanent reference, you would end up with a bunch of 0's. Think of how useful this would be when doing a ratio analysis. You could link once to net income or current assets, and then copy that cell into every ratio that uses that key number. And you don't have to keep jumping back and forth from spreadsheet to spreadsheet.

Before we wrap up, there is one more thing you should know about permanent references. The way we have used them here will keep the reference to cell G2 no matter where we copy the formula. However, you can also lock just the column or just the row. If you click on January's equation again and move your cursor to the price element (now $G$2) and press the [F4] key again it would show G$2. This means that, if you copy the cell, the new references will always refer back to row 2, but can move from column to column. So, if you copied the equation into cell H8, you would now reference H2. You will have that same link in every cell in column H as you copy your equation. This can be a very handy trick when you are looking at cross-sectional data (such as quarter to quarter).

If you press the [F4] key a third time while on the price element, you would see $G2. Now the column is locked, but the row can change. So if you copied the equation into H8, you would now reference G8. No matter where you copy the equation across row 8, it would always refer back to column G.

You may want to take a few minutes and play with this feature right now. Make sure you are comfortable with all of the different versions. Other than the Excel basics, these are probably the single most time saving features you will ever use in Excel.

Wrapping Up Our Excel Work

As we wrap up our discussion of Excel, we want to take just a moment to give you a final warning about the rounding functions. These are great tools, but they can also cause problems in your spreadsheets if you aren't careful. Let us show you what we mean.

If you copy your equation for the Monthly Total all the way through the total row, you end up with $361,000. That is because Excel took the total annual sales of 18,793 units, multiplied it by the price, then rounded it down to the nearest $1,000 (just as we told it to). If, on the other hand, you use the Sum function to sum the monthly values, you end up with $356,000. That's a pretty big difference, and something to keep in mind when using the Roundup and Rounddown functions. Keep in mind too that because we rounded down, every monthly total was lower than the actual total, so using the Sum function makes it significantly lower. Here's a comparison of the different methods.

Months	Units	Price	Monthly Total	Monthly Total	Monthly Total
January	1,375	$ 19.25	$ 26,000	$ 26,000	$ 26,469
February	1,427		$ 27,000	$ 27,000	$ 27,470
March	1,832		$ 35,000	$ 35,000	$ 35,266
April	1,716		$ 33,000	$ 33,000	$ 33,033
May	1,963		$ 37,000	$ 37,000	$ 37,788
June	1,393		$ 26,000	$ 26,000	$ 26,815
July	1,281		$ 24,000	$ 24,000	$ 24,659
August	1,583		$ 30,000	$ 30,000	$ 30,473
September	1,872		$ 36,000	$ 36,000	$ 36,036
October	1,626		$ 31,000	$ 31,000	$ 31,301
November	1,500		$ 28,000	$ 28,000	$ 28,875
December	1,225		$ 23,000	$ 23,000	$ 23,581
Year to Date	18,793		$361,000	$356,000	$ 361,765
			copied	summed	no rounding

Here's a comparison of the different methods. The first monthly total column in our picture is the equation we were using copied all the way through the total row, so the final number is the year-to-date units multiplied by the price. The second monthly total column uses the formula through December then sums the rows. In the final monthly total column, there is no rounding at all. Notice that the first method yields an answer that is relatively close to the correct answer. When using rounding, this is the best way to go. But anytime you use rounding, you are giving up accuracy for easy to read numbers. With that food for thought, you are ready to head back to Wedgewood and help Josey with some transfer pricing problems.

Wedgewood Candle Co.

Gathering the Data For a Transfer Pricing Decision

"Josey, can I talk to you for a minute?"

Josey turned to see Maria Wedgewood, her slightly built, red-haired cousin coming down the hall. Maria was the current COO of Wedgewood and, despite her small size, she carried a lot of weight around the company. "Sure, Maria, what can I do for you?"

"Walk with me for a minute, if you don't mind," Maria said as she continued on down the hall, leaving Josey to catch up. When she did, a moment later, Maria continued. "We need to talk about what we're doing with SWC, Inc." She stopped suddenly at an office, poked her head in, and said, "James, I'm going to need that report by the end of the business day tomorrow." With that, she was off again, and Josey found herself hurrying to catch up.

"What about SWC?" Josey asked, a little out of breath as she tried to keep up with her cousin's quick pace. "The company is doing well."

"Yes. Yes. I know," Maria said curtly, quickly signing something that a secretary held up for her as they neared the corporate offices. "Buying into the soy wax production business was a great decision. However, now we need to use their product."

"But I thought we decided not to do that. The wax is too soft to make our normal candles, and we didn't want to lose their eco-friendly image by adding normal paraffin wax to make them stand up."

Maria nodded. "Correct, but now we have a new line of specialty candles, so we don't have to stick with our original brand image. We think we can easily create a container candle with pure soy wax. We can advertise it as 'Made in America with eco-friendly, renewable resources.' In other words, it's a *green* candle. We even thought about putting it in green recycled cardboard packaging. That should really help us make headway in certain markets."

Josey nodded. "That makes sense. How can I help?"

Maria smiled. "I'm so glad that you put it that way. The advertising and production groups are already thinking about things from their end, but we need to make sure that the accounting numbers work out as well. Since SWC is our subsidiary, we need to think about how we are going to price the wax that we get from them."

"Can't we just use the normal sales price?" Josey asked.

Maria stopped as they got to the door to the executive conference room. "That's the one hang-up with this decision. The soy wax is very expensive relative to our normal paraffin, so our line supervisors and division manager are pushing back. They don't want to take responsibility for such an expensive product. On the flip side, the managers at SWC don't want to sell us anything for less than their normal price. I need you to work out a logical number that both sides will be happy with."

Josey frowned. "I believe there are some tools that I can try. I'll have to do a little research to refresh my memory, but it shouldn't be a problem. By the way, how much wax are we talking about here?"

"Here is a copy of a memo from SWC." She handed Josey a piece of paper. "I have already forwarded you an email with their income statement. (The memo is included at the end of the chapter, after the assignment pages; the spreadsheet is in the files you downloaded for this chapter.) I think that for the first year, we are talking about purchasing 500,000 pounds of wax. That may go up in subsequent years, provided we can come to some sort of agreement with SWC. I know you'll do your usual excellent work on this." She looked at her watch. "I've got to get into this meeting before I miss any more. You'll let me know when you have some answers? Good," she said without waiting for an answer and slipped through the door.

Josey stared after her cousin for a minute, then shook her head and chuckled softly. That was Maria all right. She headed back towards her office to begin making some preliminary calculations.

Stop here and answer questions 1 and 2 on assignment page 8-13 before continuing.

Rapid Review:

Transfer pricing sets prices for the units sold within the company instead of outside the company. When we set a normal sales price, we try to cover all of the costs allocated to that product. When we set a transfer price, we try to strike a compromise between covering the costs of the producing division and assigning costs to the receiving division. Since the units aren't really being sold and the company's overall revenues don't change, there are no rules for setting these prices; however the process can cause political tension between the managers of the selling and purchasing divisions.

The first step in setting a transfer price is to determine the relevant cost per unit of the units actually being transferred as a reference point for the negotiations between managers. Although the relevant costs are typically the variable costs, there can be differences. For example, if a commission (which is a variable cost) is not paid on transferred units, then it is not relevant. However, if a fixed cost will be incurred or can be avoided on the transfer, then that cost becomes relevant. For example, if *selling* to an internal division allows us to avoid hiring a new member of the sales team, then that cost is relevant.

Calculating Transfer Prices

"Fong," Josey said as she stepped into the young woman's office. "I have a job for you."

"Yes, Ms. Wedgewood?" Fong asked as she stood up to greet her boss.

"It's still just *Josey*, Fong. But let's not worry about that. I have a set of numbers here from Maria. She needs some transfer prices calculated for using some of the soy wax from SWC. I started the process, but I need to move on to some other projects. Can you finish up for me?"

Fong smiled. "I would be happy to help," she said.

"Excellent. Calculate the transfer price using both the variable-cost and full-cost methods. Also, determine what the logical range would be for a negotiated transfer price—I'm thinking it might make sense to just let the two managers hammer it out themselves."

"That should not be a problem," Fong said. "I will get these done for you as quickly as I can."

Stop here and answer questions 3 through 7 on assignment pages 8-15 and 8-17 before continuing.

Rapid Review:

While there are no rules for assigning a transfer price, there are some commonly used methods for helping to set these prices. To use the ***Variable Costing*** method, we add a target markup to the relevant variable costs incurred in producing the product. The markup used depends on the company and its policies. One option is to use the standard markup percentage. Another method is to add in the standard markup per unit as a dollar amount.

Remember that all of these numbers are just parts of a negotiation process. None of them are required or more valid than the others, so both departments involved will have to focus on their negotiating skills rather than on the numbers themselves.

Name:

Questions

Note: *For questions and problems that require calculations, attach a copy of your spreadsheet to the related assignment page and hand it in to your instructor.*

Gathering the Data For a Transfer Pricing Decision

Q-1. Using the information provided, what is the total variable cost per pound of the soy wax? Are all of these costs relevant to the transfer pricing decision? Why or why not?

Q-2. Using the information provided, what are the total fixed costs for SWC per year? Are all these costs relevant to the transfer pricing decision? Why or why not?

Name:

Calculating Transfer Prices

Q-3. What is the operating profit per pound (operating income divided by pounds of wax sold) of the wax currently? Round your answer to the nearest penny.

____

Q-4. Using the information provided by Maria, what should the transfer price be using the variable-cost method, assuming a 25% markup? What would the transfer price be if Wedgewood wants to give SWC the same operating income per pound they currently have? Round the *markup* up to the nearest penny in both calculations. How does this compare to SWC's current selling price?

____

____

____

____

____

____

____

Q-5. Assume no selling and administrative variable costs are going to be paid on the inter-company transfer, how does this change your answers to Q-4? Again, round the *markup* up to the nearest penny in both cases.

____

____

____

____

____

____

____

Name:

Q-6. What would be the logical range for a negotiated transfer price (still assuming no variable selling and administrative costs)?

Q-7. What would be the relevant cost per pound to SWC if Wedgewood wanted to purchase 1,000,000 pounds per year?

Name:

Problems

Critical Thinking Issues

Problem #1

Maria, the COO, would like to mandate the price, but Josey feels that it would be better to let the managers work out the details themselves. She has asked you to consider the prices using the variable cost and full cost method as well as the logical range for a negotiated transfer price and make a formal recommendation regarding the method the team should choose for setting the transfer price. The two companies have determined that there will be no variable selling or administrative costs. Also assume that the amount transferred will be between 500,000 and 750,000 pounds per year.

Write a memo that outlines your recommendation. Keep in mind that you will need to be persuasive, since you have one important manager on each side of the debate. Use the space below to create an outline of your memo before you create it in Word. When you have completed the memo, attach a copy of it to this sheet and hand it in to your instructor.

Name:

Problem #2

Examine the **Critical Thinking** spreadsheet in your workbook. In the first four columns is a table for calculating the company's overall profit on the transferred units. Notice that the first row, Transfer Revenue, is not applicable (NA) to Wedgewood because Wedgewood will not have transfer revenue for these units. Instead, it will show the transfer cost for the units it purchases. For SWC, on the other hand, the formula will multiply the number of units transferred times the transfer price after you input those values over in Column G. For transfer cost the setup is reversed; Wedgewood will have a cost while SWC will not. Finally, only SWC will have a manufacturing cost, since it is the division producing these units.

The final column in this table shows the totals for the entire company. Since SWC is owned by Wedgewood, the final total (the value in the bottom-right-hand corner of this spreadsheet) shows how the final combined financial statements of these two companies will be affected by the transfer.

You know what the manufacturing cost per pound is from Q-5 and you used that amount again to solve Q-6. Go ahead and enter that value into cell G2 now. Enter 500,000 in the amount to be transferred. You should show a cost of $290,000 now. Input the transfer price you calculated in the first part of Q-4. What is the benefit or cost to Wedgewood? To SWC? To the companies combined?

Benefit/Cost to Wedgewood: ______________________

____

____

Benefit/Cost to SWC: ______________________

____

____

Benefit/Cost to combined companies: ______________________

____

____

____

Change that answer to the transfer price you calculated in the second part of Q-4 and answer these questions again.

Next use the transfer prices you calculated in Q-5. What if the transfer price were zero? Or $1,000 per pound? Does this change your answer to Problem #1? Write a short paragraph explaining why or why not.

Name:

Ethical Issues

Pierce Wedgewood stopped by Josey's office as she was just getting settled after lunch. "Josey," he asked. "Do you have a minute?"

Josey smiled and invited Pierce in, but inwardly she was sighing. Pierce was the grandson of her uncle Jeremiah, the company CFO. He had recently graduated from college and was working on his MBA, which often gave him an "I know best" attitude that grated on everyone around him. However, he was good with people and a decent manager. He had recently been named as the manager of the new specialty candle line, and he was always monkeying with processes and procedures to match whatever they were teaching him in his MBA classes. It got very annoying, especially for someone with both a CPA license and a Master's of Accountancy degree like Josey. She really just wanted to put him in his place, but that wouldn't be very good politics. You can't really get away with telling off the grandson of your boss without a very good reason. But maybe today he would finally give her that reason....

"...so, I was wondering if you would help me get ready for this negotiation."

Josey felt embarrassed that she hadn't been listening, but she had no idea what he was talking about. "I'm so sorry, Pierce," she said sheepishly. "I was still gathering my thoughts, so I missed a lot of what you just said. Could you ask your question again?"

"Sure. I was saying that I've never actively negotiated before, and I was wondering if you could help me out before the meeting this afternoon."

"Well, I don't negotiate that much either," Josey said. "Your grandfather would actually be a better choice if you want advice. He negotiates all the time."

"Oh, I know. I've already gotten some advice from him. What I need now are the numbers."

"I gave you the numbers," Josey said, confused. "I sent them to both you and the manager of SWC."

"I don't want those summary numbers," Pierce said, shaking his head. "I want the more detailed numbers for the calculations your team ran." He slipped into his know-it-all tone, "I know all about the variable-cost and full-cost methods, and I know you must have run those numbers. And I want them."

Josey frowned, both at his tone and his question. "Well, I guess I could send those out...."

"No, no, no," Pierce said. "I don't want you to *send them out*; I want you to just give them to *me*. Come on, Josey, these guys are nice and all, but they aren't family like we

Name:

are. Besides, they are experienced negotiators. I just want something that will even the playing field for our negotiations."

Problem #3

Is there an ethical issue in this scenario? Defend your answer.

Name:

Problem #4

What do you think Josey should say to Pierce? Assume that she feels it would be unfair for her to provide these numbers to only one of the participants in the negotiations. What could she say to him to convince him that she is right?

INTERCOMPANY MEMORANDUM

TO:	MARIA WEDGEWOOD, COO OF WEDGEWOOD CANDLE COMPANY
FROM:	EMILIO RUSSO, CONTROLLER OF SWC, INC.
SUBJECT:	OPERATING RESULTS
DATE:	DECEMBER 5, 2016

Maria,

It was nice chatting with you on the phone last week. We are very excited about the possibility of Wedgewood adding a new container line of candles using our soy wax. As you can see, though, from the numbers below, we have very little negotiating room on the transfer price. Our normal wholesale price of $1.35 per pound is really as low as we can comfortably go and still have any chance of a reasonable operating income, especially since this is our only product.

Here are the figures for last quarter. You should know that we sold 800,000 pounds of soy wax that quarter. We started the period with 150,000 pounds in beginning inventory and finished the quarter with 250,000 pounds in inventory. Our applied MOH of $0.15 per pound covers our fixed manufacturing costs for the budgeted production of 3,000,000 pounds this year. We have the capacity to produce 4,000,000 pounds a year, but we normally only sell about 3,200,000 pounds per year. Our sales staff is paid a 20% commission and our other selling and administrative costs are fixed. Please let me know if you need any more information.

Emilio

PERFORMING CVP ANALYSIS

This page is intentionally blank.

CHAPTER 9

Performing CVP Analysis

Objectives

Excel Skills

- Creating and using line graphs
- Using other types of graphs
- Performing What-If Analysis

Accounting Skills

- Performing basic cost-volume-profit (CVP) analysis
- Using CVP calculations to make business decisions

Mastering Excel

Creating and Using Line Graphs

Up to this point, we have focused our discussion of Excel on calculations and formulas, and while those are useful tools, they aren't always the most effective at helping with our most important job: providing information for management. As accountants, especially managerial accountants, we should be focused on providing useful information in a way that the managers we work with can quickly incorporate it into key business decisions. More often than not, that can be done more effectively with pictures than with tables. And that's what we're going to discuss in this chapter.

CVP analysis naturally lends itself to pictures. What could be easier to explain, to any manager, than a CVP graph? Not much, especially if it is done correctly. So, how exactly do we create a graph in Excel? Start with some basic data. Open your **C9 Excel Practice Set** workbook and go to the Line Graphs spreadsheet. You'll notice that there isn't much information there at this point. In fact, all we've given you is fixed costs, unit variable cost (VC/Unit), and unit sales price (Sales Price/Unit). Luckily, that's all we need. The first step is to create a table. Let's get started.

» *Starting in A5, create four (4) column headers:* Units Produced, Fixed Cost, Total Cost, *and* Total Revenue.

- *Type 0 in the first cell of our new table (A6).*
- *Link cell B6 to the Fixed Costs given (C1) and make it an absolute reference by pressing F4 before pressing [Enter].* (You should end up with =$C$1.)
- *In cell C6, multiply the units produced by the VC/Unit, then add the Fixed Costs. Again, use an absolute reference for the VC/Unit so that we can copy our equation through our table.* Your equation should look like this: =(A6*$C$2)+B6.
- *In cell D6, multiply the units produced by the Sales Price/Unit. Again be sure to use an absolute cell reference when picking up the sales price.* Your equation should look like this: =A6*$C$3.

At this point, your table should look like the one pictured here.

	A	B	C	D
1	Fixed Costs		$800,000	
2	VC/Unit		$10	
3	Sales Price/Unit		$30	
4				
5	Units Produced	Fixed Cost	Total Cost	Total Revenue
6	0	$ 800,000	$ 800,000	$ -

Once you feel comfortable with these first steps, we can move on to the other three rows we'll need to make our graph.

- *In cell A7, add 25,000 units to the zero in cell A6. That is, enter this equation in cell A7:* +A6+25000.
- *Highlight cells B6 through D6 and copy them to cells B7 through D7.*
- *Copy A7 through D7 down two more times.*

Hopefully, you should now have a table that looks like ours.

	A	B	C	D
1	Fixed Costs		$800,000	
2	VC/Unit		$10	
3	Sales Price/Unit		$30	
4				
5	Units Produced	Fixed Cost	Total Cost	Total Revenue
6	0	$ 800,000	$ 800,000	$ -
7	25,000	$ 800,000	$ 1,050,000	$ 750,000
8	50,000	$ 800,000	$ 1,300,000	$ 1,500,000
9	75,000	$ 800,000	$ 1,550,000	$ 2,250,000

You'll notice that we did a little bit of formatting to make our table easy to read. It is so much easier to read a table with good formatting. Our data set is pretty simple, but it is more than enough for us to practice making graphs. You can follow the same procedures we're about to use to create a line graph for any reasonable amount of data. So, let's get started.

- *Highlight the last three columns of your table, including the headers. Don't highlight the Units Produced; we'll use those in a minute.*
- *Under the Insert tab of the Excel ribbon, under the Charts area, click on the Insert Line Chart icon.* Both Excel 2010 and Excel 2013 presentations are shown here.

Excel 2010

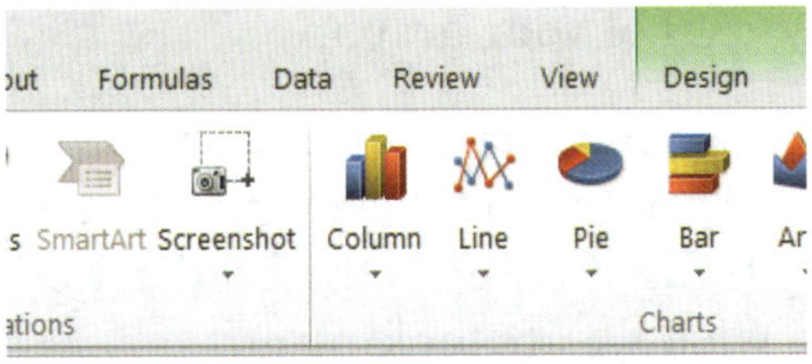

Excel 2013

- *Choose any of the graph options that appear, although the first one is usually the best choice for now, since you'll want to make changes to the formatting later.*
- *Right-click on the values along the x-axis (they should appear as 1, 2, 3, 4) and choose the Select Data option from the menu that appears.* The following window appears.

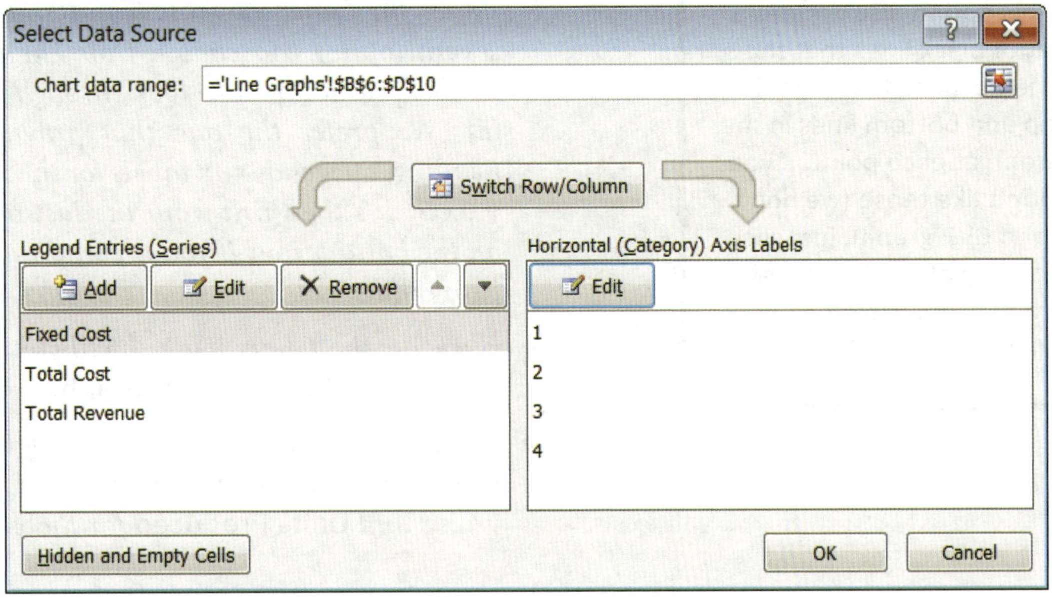

The left portion of the window [titled Legend Entries (Series)] displays the costs and revenues that we want to show in our CVP graph. The right portion of the window [titled Horizontal (Category) Axis Labels] contains Excel's guess about what the number along the bottom should be. But in this case, we don't want to use Excel's guess. Instead, we want the graph to show the company's levels of production. Here's how to replace Excel's numbers with the ones you want.

- *Click on the Edit option directly under the Horizontal (Category) Axis Label title.*
- *Highlight cells A7 through A10.*
- *Click OK or press [Enter] on your keyboard.*
- *Click OK again on the Select Data Source box.* You should now see our actual production estimates along the x-axis of your graph.

You now have a basic CVP graph. You can see the total cost line, the fixed cost line, and the total revenue line. In addition, you have the breakeven point where the total cost and total revenue lines cross. The only thing missing is the header. Let's go ahead and add a header so that we can easily see what we are looking at.

- *Click anywhere in the graph. A set of Chart Tools should appear at the end of the normal ribbon tabs at the top of your screen.*
- *Click on the Design tab.*
- *In the Chart Layouts area, select the chart format that seems the best fit. (In Excel 2013, these layouts appear as options under the Quick Layouts icon.) You have several options to choose from, and can scroll up and down to look through them all. We prefer the one that provides a heading, a legend, and labels for the x and y axes. It's the third from the last option on the bottom row, if you are interested in using that one.*
- *Click on the Chart Title, highlight those two words, then type* CVP Graph.
- *Click on the two Axis Titles, highlight the words, then type in* Dollar Values *for the y-axis and* Units Produced *for the x-axis.*

Tip:

This option also creates a set of black lines that show the distance between the top and bottom lines in the graph at each point. If you don't like those (we don't for a CVP graph), just click on any of the black lines and press [Delete]. The lines should disappear.

You should now have a CVP graph that looks similar to the one here.

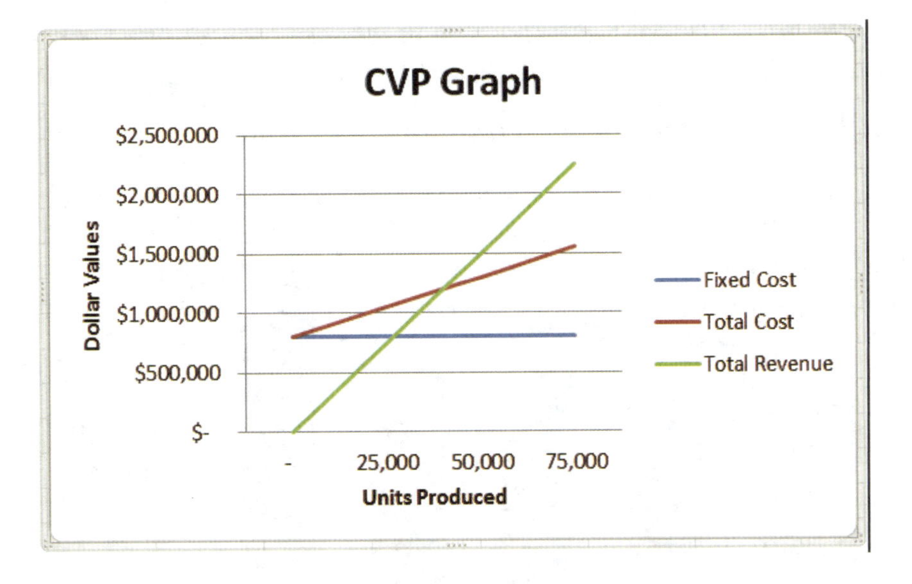

If you need to, you can use the options in the Insert tab of the Excel ribbon to add arrows (use the shapes option in the Illustrations area) and labels (use the Text Box option in the Text area) to mark the breakeven point and the profit and loss areas.

You also have many options to adjust formatting, text styles, and layout that can make your charts more interesting and easier to read. While we encourage you to play around with these options and see what they can do, we also want to warn you to be careful with these kinds of formatting tools. It is easy to get so caught up in choosing options that you spend too much time creating one graph!

Using Other Types of Graphs

In addition to line graphs, Excel offers several other types of graphs. We want to mention two others: bar graphs and pie charts. The type of graph you choose will depend on the type of information you want to convey and on the interest of your audience. Line graphs, like the one we just made, are best for showing progress over time or as quantity increases. Bar graphs are typically best for showing relative value (company sales vs. competitors' sales) and pie charts work well for demonstrating allocations (how much revenue comes from each product). Let's look at these two fundamental graphs.

In Excel, switch from the Line Graphs spreadsheet to the Data spreadsheet. The first table (in green) shows the revenues and expenses of one department of an example company for the four quarters of last year. Let's put the data into a bar graph so that we can more easily see the relationship between revenues and expenses.

- *Highlight the table.*
- *On the Insert tab of the Excel ribbon, choose the Column icon in the Charts area. In Excel 2013, select the Insert Column Chart icon.*
- *Click on the first option for a traditional bar chart.*

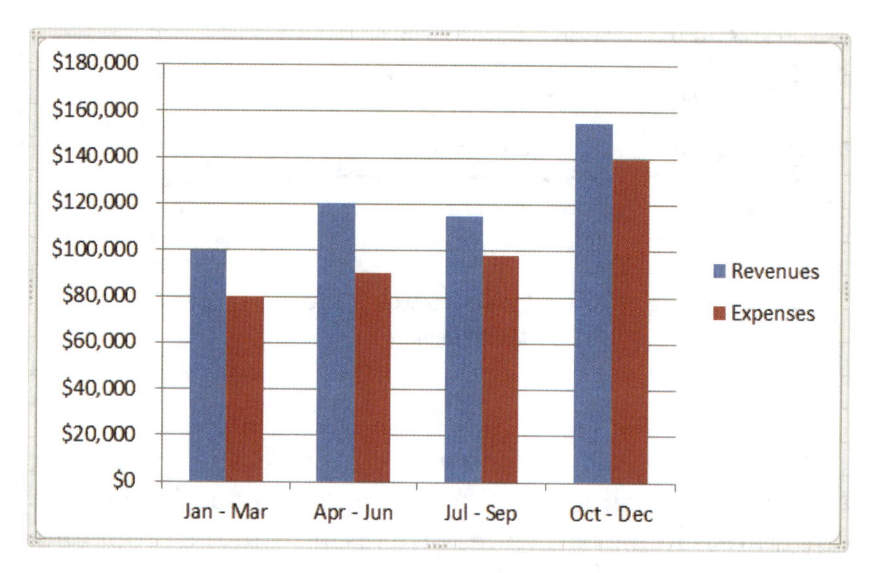

That's all there is to it! You now have a simple bar chart that quickly shows that revenues are increasing, but so are costs. This company needs to get to work to improve the spread between revenues and costs. If you'd like, you can add a title to the chart, you can click on it and move it around, and you can even make it 3D if that is easier for users to visualize.

Tip:

Excel actually provides two styles of bar charts. What we typically think of as a bar chart (with vertical bars) is called a *column chart* in Excel. If you prefer horizontal bars, use the *bar chart* option. The formatting choices are similar, so you can use these same steps to make both types of bar charts.

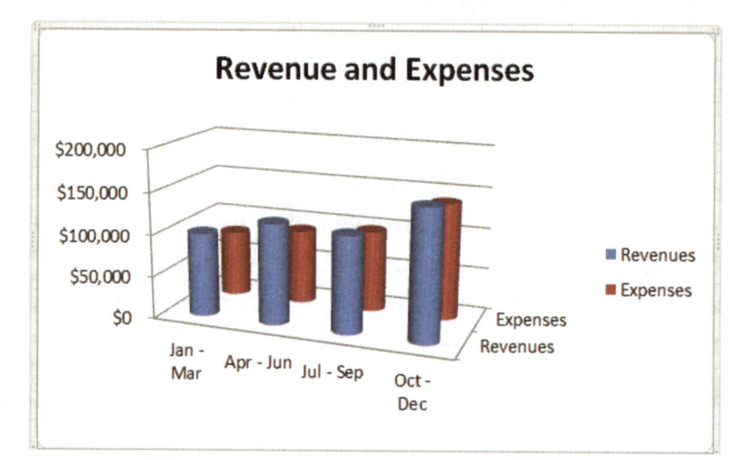

Since we are going to be making another chart in just a minute, let's move this graph into a separate spreadsheet. That should make it easier to see the data and get it out of the way of other charts we might want to make.

- *Right-click in the white space at the bottom or right of the bar graph.*
- *Click Move Chart.*
- *Select the New sheet option and type in a label like* Rev. vs. Exp. Chart.
- *Click OK.*

Your chart will now appear in a new spreadsheet that Excel has placed immediately in front of the Data spreadsheet. Any time you move a chart or graph to a new spreadsheet, Excel will place it right in front of the spreadsheet with your information. If you don't like it there, you can easily move the spreadsheets around.

- *Click and hold on the Data spreadsheet tab at the bottom of your Excel workbook.*
- *Slide the spreadsheet to the left until you see a black arrow appear between the Line Graphs and Rev. vs. Exp. Chart tabs.*
- *Release the mouse.*

Now that we have space in our spreadsheet again, let's go ahead and create a pie chart using the overhead cost data in the purple table.

- *Highlight the purple table.*
- *On the Insert tab of the Excel ribbon, choose Pie in the Charts area. In Excel 2013, select the Insert Pie or Donut Chart icon.*
- *Click on the first option for a traditional pie chart.*

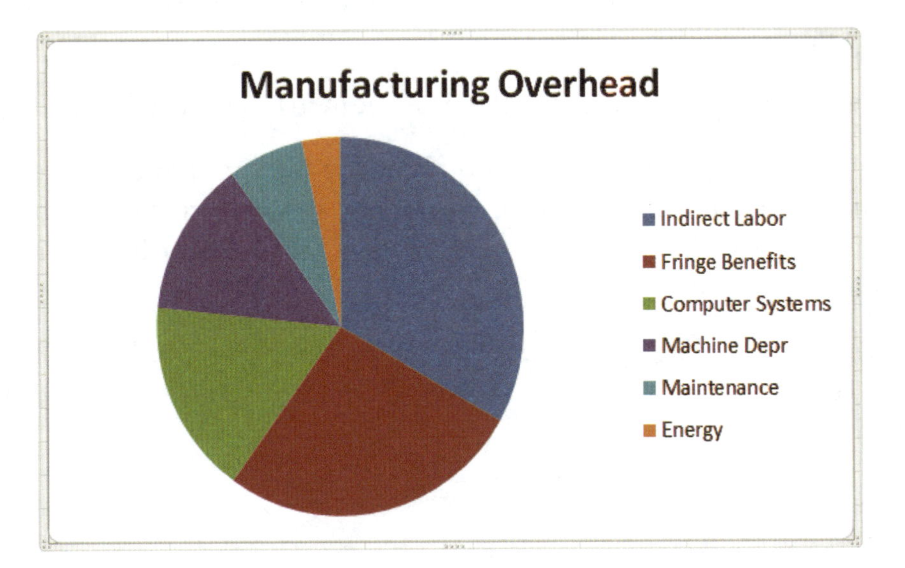

Again, that's all there is to it! You now have a pie chart of the company's cost structure, easily demonstrating which cost pool has the greatest impact on the company's overhead. You also have lots of different options for sprucing up this chart or highlighting key information. You should take some time to become familiar with the other options, now that you know the basics, but not so much that you forget to work on the other parts of your assignment (in school or at work).

Creating a CVP Table Using What-If Analysis

Now that we've walked through the process of making graphs, let's turn our attention back to tables for a few minutes. Up to this point, we've focused on creating tables using or calculating data that we provide, then formatting it step-by-step as needed. But Excel provides us with another tool, a What-If Analysis, which can automate the formatting and calculations for some kinds of analyses. Again, CVP provides us with an excellent example for this tool, so we can continue our discussion using this same method.

The first step in using the What-If Analysis tool in Excel is to write down, in detail, the most flexible version of the equation that you want to use to relate two different values. In CVP analysis, for example, we can use the following equation to relate contribution margin to operating income:

$$\text{Operating Income} = (\text{Quantity} \times \text{Contribution Margin}) - \text{Fixed Costs}$$

But that's not the most flexible way to write out our equation. Why? Because contribution margin is the result of subtracting variable costs from the sales price:

$$\text{Contribution Margin} = \text{Sales Price} - \text{Variable Costs}$$

Because of this, the best, most flexible way we can write out the equation for operating income is:

$$\text{Operating Income} = \text{Quantity} \times [\text{Sales Price} - \text{Variable Costs}] - \text{Fixed Costs}$$

With this equation we can dig down into all of the factors that will affect operating income: quantity of units sold, sales price chosen, variable costs per unit, and fixed costs for the company. That is the flexibility that we want to have for our what-if analysis to be really effective.

» *Switch to the CVP spreadsheet of our practice workbook.* You'll notice that we've given you a set of data and basic equations necessary for performing a CVP analysis.

These simple equations (CM and operating income) are enough to show you the basic effects of changes in any of the values. For example, what happens if variable costs go up by $1 per unit? Go ahead and try it. You should now have a contribution margin of $77 and operating income of $170. Once you get those figures, go ahead and change your variable costs back to $22.

While those simple equations are nice, there is so much more that we can do. To start, let's set up a table that will answer most CVP questions in more detail than you have probably seen before (courtesy of Excel's What-If Analysis).

- *In cell C6, type the header* Sales Price.
- *Select cells C6 through K6.*
- *Merge and center these cells, then format them as a header.*
- *In cell A8, type the header* Quantity Sold.
- *Select cells A8 through A18.*
- *Merge and center these cells, then format them as a header.*
- *In cell C7, type in* 80.
- *In cells D7 through K7, type in a formula that adds five dollars to the number to the left (i.e., in cell D7 the formula is* =C7+5*). You should end up with values ranging from 80 in cell C7 to 120 in cell K7.*
- *Format cells C7 through K7 as currency with no decimals.*
- *In cell B8, enter* 5.
- *In cells B9 through B18, type in a formula that adds one unit to the value above it (i.e., in cell B9 the formula is* =B8+1*). You should end up with values ranging from 5 in cell B8 to 15 in cell B18.*

Tip:

Sometimes it can be useful to adjust the orientation of a heading, especially when you are trying to cover several wide cells (such as cells A8 through A18 in our example). To change the orientation, right-click on the cells and click on the Format Cells option. Now, click on the Alignment tab of the Format Cells box that appears. At the far right, you will see an orientation box. Just click on the red diamond and drag it to the angle that you want your text to have.

Here's what our table looks like after completing these basic steps. (See top of the following page.)

	A	B	C	D	E	F	G	H	I	J	K
1	Quantity Sold	$ 10									
2	Selling Price	$ 100									
3	Variable Costs	$ 22									
4	Contribution Margin	$ 78									
5	Fixed Costs	$ 600									
6			Selling Price								
7	Operating Income:	$ 180	$80	$85	$90	$95	$100	$105	$110	$115	$120
8	Quantity sold	5									
9		6									
10		7									
11		8									
12		9									
13		10									
14		11									
15		12									
16		13									
17		14									
18		15									
19											

Now comes the fun part.

- *Select all of the cells from B7 through K18.*
- *Go to the Data tab of the Excel ribbon.*
- *Click on What-If Analysis in the Data tools group.*
- *Select Data Table.*

Before we do the next couple of steps, we want to explain what we are doing. In the first cell of the table, B7, we have our equation for Operating Income. Along the top row (C7 through K7), we have the sales prices that the company is considering. Down the columns (B8 through B18), we have the quantities that the company might be able to sell. After selecting the Data Table command, we need to tell Excel which parts of the equation in B7 we want it to test as What-If's. Excel will then use each of the combinations from the row and column to recalculate the equation in B7. For the variables we don't tell Excel to change (like Variable and Fixed Costs in our example), Excel will automatically use the same values every time, linking automatically to B3 and B5. Isn't that awesome? Okay, back to the process.

- *For row input cell, select cell B2. This is the variable from the equation in B7 that we want Excel to replace with the values in the top row of the table (C7 through K7). So, Excel will substitute our alternative selling prices into the equation, replacing the one in cell B2.*

- *For column input cell, select cell B1. Again, this is the variable from the equation in B7 that we want Excel to replace with the values in the far left column of the table (B8 through B18). So, Excel will substitute our alternative sales quantities into the equation, replacing the one in cell B1.*
- *Click OK.*
- *Format the table so that the calculated values (C8 through K18) are shown as dollar amounts and negative values are in parentheses and red.*

	A	B	C	D	E	F	G	H	I	J	K
1	Quantity Sold	$ 10									
2	Selling Price	$ 100									
3	Variable Costs	$ 22									
4	Contribution Margin	$ 78									
5	Fixed Costs	$ 600									
6			Selling Price								
7	Operating Income:	$ 180	$ 80	$ 85	$ 90	$ 95	$ 100	$ 105	$ 110	$ 115	$ 120
8	Quantity sold	5	($310)	($285)	($260)	($235)	($210)	($185)	($160)	($135)	($110)
9		6	($252)	($222)	($192)	($162)	($132)	($102)	($72)	($42)	($12)
10		7	($194)	($159)	($124)	($89)	($54)	($19)	$16	$51	$86
11		8	($136)	($96)	($56)	($16)	$24	$64	$104	$144	$184
12		9	($78)	($33)	$12	$57	$102	$147	$192	$237	$282
13		10	($20)	$30	$80	$130	$180	$230	$280	$330	$380
14		11	$38	$93	$148	$203	$258	$313	$368	$423	$478
15		12	$96	$156	$216	$276	$336	$396	$456	$516	$576
16		13	$154	$219	$284	$349	$414	$479	$544	$609	$674
17		14	$212	$282	$352	$422	$492	$562	$632	$702	$772
18		15	$270	$345	$420	$495	$570	$645	$720	$795	$870

You should have something that looks like the one pictured above. Wasn't that fast and easy?

Okay, you might be wondering why we are so excited about this process. Well, there are a couple of reasons. First, did you see how quickly Excel created all of those equations and values for us? While we might be fast, none of us can make that many equations, properly linked, so quickly. Second, we now have a wide range of sales prices and quantities that aren't linked to our basic information but instead to the table, which means that we can change our best guess at quantity and sales price without affecting our table. Although most of the time we want our equations to automatically update as we input new numbers, sometimes we don't want that to happen. In this case, the company can easily estimate what its variable and fixed costs will be. They have the contracts and the information from past years to make very good guesses, but the amount they can actually sell depends on too many factors to easily make a good prediction (competition, market strength, economic growth, etc.).

And they are probably trying to find the best sales price in order to maximize their profits, so they don't want to be linked into just one option quite yet. That's where this kind of table becomes so useful.

In addition, the table makes it really easy for us to see what the company should *not* do. For example, there is no way for the company to make a profit selling only five or six units in this range of possible prices, and it would be very difficult to make any money selling only seven units in this price range.

The table also makes it easy to find the company's breakeven points at each sales price. Can you see them? For example, if the company sells eight units for $100 each, the company's operating income will be $24. Because they can't sell seven units at $100 and breakeven, eight units at $100 each is the company's breakeven point. Other breakeven points are seven units at $110 each and nine units at $90 each. When we look for CVP in a textbook problem, sales price and quantity are held constant, but in the real world there is usually some range of sales price and quantity that allow us to breakeven or make a target profit.

The final benefit of these What-If tables is the ease with which we can adjust them. For example, perhaps $80 is an unrealistically low selling price. We believe the minimum selling price is $90 and want to check values above that. Change the amount in cell C7 to $90. Now your selling prices should range from $90 to $130, and your whole table changed automatically to show the effects of this change.

The analysis also lets us examine the effects of other common CVP questions. What happens if the company's variable costs increase by $3? Change the variable costs in cell B3 to $25 and find out. Again, everything updated automatically, and because of the red and black formatting, it is easy for us to see where all of the new breakeven points are. Go ahead and play around with it a little bit, then change the variable costs back to $22. You can also change the fixed costs from $600 to $700 or $550. Again, the table will update automatically.

As a final change, try changing the sales price in cell B2 to $120. This time, nothing happens. Why not? Because the table is using the selling prices from cells C7 to K7 and not our best guess or last year's value from cell B2. Nothing happens if you change the quantity sold in cell B1 either. Again, the table is not using the value in B1, it is using the values in B8 through B18. You can, of course, link your equations within the range of possibilities to the best guesses. For example, instead of starting with $80 in C7, you could start by linking G7 to the company's best guess in B2. You could then subtract $5 as you move to the left and add $5 as you move to the right in the Sales Price values. Then, as the company changes its best guess, you would still get a range of prices around that best guess.

Like most of the Excel tools we've discussed, all we have time for are the basics. You can create, combine, and play with different options and possibilities to get the very most from your spreadsheets.

Wrapping Up Our Excel Work

With that, it's time to move on from practicing Excel to practicing managerial accounting with the Wedgewood Candle Co. As you work out Wedgewood's CVP questions, keep in mind the tools and tricks that we've discussed. They will make the process much easier for you to do, and much easier for everyone else to understand.

Wedgewood Candle Co.

Performing Basic CVP Analysis

"Demitri," Josey called after the young man as he walked past her office.

"Yes, ma'am," Demitri said in a slow southern drawl as he came back to her office door. "What can I do for you?"

Josey shook her head. "For one thing, you can stop calling me 'ma'am,' as we've discussed before."

Now Demitri shook his head. "Sorry, Ms. Wedgewood," he said. "My mama worked hard to instill respect into her kids," grinning he added, "and she's scarier than you are, ma'am."

Josey started to laugh. "Demitri," she said after a minute, "you're a treasure. Just do the best you can. I actually didn't stop you to talk about your language."

"Really? Well, that's something anyway. What can I do for you, *ma'am*?" Demitri emphasized the last word and grinned impishly.

"You can do a basic CVP analysis on the new line of soy candles. I have to present to the Board tomorrow about how the line is doing. I could go through budgets and our most recent Income Statement, but I'm sure they'll be much happier with the visual effect of a CVP analysis."

Demitri nodded. "That makes sense to me. It's always easier to see something drawn out than to just look at a bunch of numbers, especially for non-accountants."

"Exactly. I had planned to do it myself today, but I have to get this report finalized for the bank, and I'm the only one who can do that. I'll email you the information I gathered, and you should be able to do the analysis without any trouble." (A copy of the email from Josey is included at the end of the chapter, after the assignment pages. Operating results for last quarter are on the second tab of the student workbook for this chapter.)

"Thanks, ma'am...I mean, *Ms. Wedgewood*. I'll get right on it."

Stop here and answer questions 1 through 6 on assignment page 9-17 before continuing.

Rapid Review:

Cost-Volume-Profit (CVP) analysis is one of the most commonly used methods for assessing business performance. A full CVP analysis is comprised of several pieces, each of which is dependent on first breaking down the fixed and variable costs of the division, product, or business. A fundamental concept in CVP is the ***contribution margin (CM)***. The CM is derived by subtracting all of the variable costs from the sales price and it represents the amount each unit contributes towards covering fixed costs or providing net profits for the period. For example, let's say that a company sells snow cones during the summer at a local ballpark. Each snow cone sells for $1.50, with $0.40 of variable costs (ice, cup, flavoring, and a few seconds of employee time). That means that each snow cone sold contributes $1.10 ($1.50 revenue less $0.40 variable cost) to the company's bottom line. We first use that $1.10 to pay off our fixed costs (rent on the snow cone machine, electricity, the manager's salary, etc.). After we have met all of those costs, then each snow cone sold provides $1.10 in profit.

This simple example is the basis of CVP analysis. Once you have determined the fixed and variable costs, you can calculate the ***breakeven point*** (how much you have to sell to cover the fixed costs) by dividing the fixed costs by the CM/unit. You can also calculate the ***safety margin***, which is the amount sales can drop before you start losing money, by subtracting the breakeven point from current sales. Suppose the snow cone stand has fixed costs each month of $5,500 and typically sells 6,000 snow cones. With a contribution margin of $1.10, the company has a breakeven point of 5,000 snow cones ($5,500/$1.10) and a safety margin of 1,000 snow cones (6,000 - 5,000). Simple, right?

Using CVP Calculations to Make Business Decisions

Josey put down her laser pointer and motioned for Jordan to turn the lights back up, then she turned to the Board. "As you can see, the line appears to be doing well, making a solid profit and easily covering both its own costs and some of our general overhead. That's the end of my formal presentation. Does anyone have any questions?"

Jenni Wedgewood, the Chairman of Wedgewood's Board, turned to her older siblings. "Any of you still awake enough to ask questions?" she quipped.

George shook his head. "Jenni, do you always have to treat us like we've all got one foot in the grave? I mean, you aren't really that much younger than we are."

"Humbug, George. I'm almost ten years younger than you are. That keeps me down in the double digits, and that's a lot."

George frowned. "Double digits, huh? I'll have you know that I'm nowhere near 100, thank you, and I'm still sharp enough to help make decisions around here." He looked around the room. "I think the paint is still just fine, so let's stop arguing about it and get out of here."

Jenni just stared at him for a moment. "Paint?" she asked incredulously. George glanced at Josey and winked.

"Well, don't you think the paint is still fine?" he asked, turning back to Jenni. "I'm not sure why you insisted we decide about something like paint, but I think we can just leave it for now." Jenni continued to stare at him in shock, her mouth open. George finally started to laugh, as did the other four siblings that made up Wedgewood's Board.

"He got you that time, Jenni," Priscilla Mullen, Pierce Wedgewood's third child said with a chuckle. Priscilla had white hair that stuck out at odd angles. She looked to Josey like a grandmother right out of a storybook rather than a Board member of a large private corporation. Josey nodded to herself as her great-aunts and great-uncles bantered with each other. This was a very good sign. If they had been worried about the new line, there wouldn't have been any joking.

After a few minutes, Peter Wedgewood, Josey's dad and the Marketing Director jumped in, stopping the playful argument. "Now that everyone has a good idea about how the new line is going, I'd like to ask a couple of questions." The room grew quiet and Jenni motioned for Peter to continue. "Josey, can you tell us what the effect would be if we were to make some changes to our sales plan?"

"I can try, Dad. What would you like to know?"

"Well, I'd like to encourage our sales force to push them a little bit. If we increased the sales commissions on these candles by 20%, I think we could increase sales by 5%. Alternatively, we could spend an additional $150,000 in fixed advertising, which would raise our sales by about 4%. Would either of those increases in cost be worthwhile? Which would be better for us?"

"Give me a minute, and I'll run the numbers right now." Josey turned to her laptop while the Board discussed some other ideas.

Stop here and answer questions 7 through 9 on assignment page 9-19 before continuing.

Rapid Review:

CVP analysis is probably best used to see how changes in prices, costs, or volume will affect profit. Although this can be done with simple formulas, it's easier to visualize what is happening with a CM Income Statement that shows the per-unit prices and costs in one column and total revenue and costs in another. Because you set this up in CM format by separating variable and fixed expenses, you can quickly calculate the changes and see the effects of any changes or new estimates. If you use formulas in Excel for all of your calculations, then when you want to make a change you just type in the new information and all the amounts will update automatically. We recommend that you create a separate CM Income Statement for each scenario and label them carefully!

You can also do some of these calculations using a ratio called the ***degree of operating leverage***, which is calculated by dividing the total contribution margin on all units sold by the total operating income. This ratio can be used to quickly assess the impact of changes on company profits by taking the percentage change in sales multiplied by the degree of operating leverage. The result will be the percentage change to net income. To determine the projected operating income, just multiply this percentage by the original operating income.

CVP is frequently used in business for two reasons. First, the calculations are simple to perform. Second, the results are intuitive and can be easily explained. This makes it a powerful tool worth learning and remembering.

Name:

Questions

Note: ***For questions and problems that require calculations, attach a copy of your spreadsheet to the related assignment page and hand it in to your instructor.***

Performing Basic CVP Analysis

Q-1. What is the contribution margin ratio for the new line of container candles?

___

___

Q-2. What is the breakeven amount for the container candle line in dollars and units? (Make sure you round up your answers to the nearest unit.)

___

Q-3. What is the safety margin for the container candle line in both dollars and as a percentage?

___

Q-4. What is the degree of operating leverage for the container candle line?

___

Q-5. How much would operating income increase if sales increased 15%?

___

___

Q-6. Create a clearly labeled CVP graph for the new line, including each of the following:

a. Fixed costs

b. Total costs

c. Total revenue

d. Breakeven point

e. Loss and gain areas

Name:

Using CVP Calculations to Make Business Decisions

Q-7. What would be the effect on the container line's net income if the company increased sales commissions by 20% and sales by 5%? (Be sure to state your answer in terms of how much the net income *changes*.)

Q-8. What would be the effect on the container line's net income if the company increased their advertising expense (a fixed cost) by $150,000 and raised sales by 4%?

Q-9. Which option, increasing sales commissions or advertising expense, would you recommend Wedgewood's management choose?

Name:

Problems

Critical Thinking Issues

One of the greatest benefits of a CVP analysis is that you can perform it with minimal information. For example, the second spreadsheet in the Excel workbook for this chapter contains the Operating Results from the Container Candle Division for Quarter 2 of the following year. Other than the new numbers, the only difference is that the department has not provided you with the number of units sold or any other per-unit information.

Problem #1

Assuming that the breakdown of fixed versus variable costs has not changed over the year, perform the following analyses:

a. Calculate the division's new breakeven point (in sales dollars only).

b. Calculate the division's margin of safety percentage.

c. Calculate the division's operating leverage and determine the dollar effect of a 15% increase in sales on operating income.

Name:

Problem #2

Knowing how to perform a CVP analysis without per-unit data can be useful to both internal and external stakeholders. In a short memo to Demitri, explain what circumstances might arise that would require you to do CVP without knowing the number of units sold or unit prices. Use the space provided below to draft an outline of the memo, then print the final memo to hand in to your instructor.

Name:

Ethical Issues

Demitri looked at the numbers, frowning. He couldn't quite put his finger on it, but something in his CVP analysis didn't feel quite right.

After looking at it for almost an hour, he found it. He had accidentally transposed one number. Instead of showing the MOH cost/unit as $0.53, he had typed them in as $0.35, increasing the CM/candle by $0.18. He picked up the phone to call Josey, then stopped as he noticed the clock. She wouldn't be in her office. She would be in the boardroom, right now, showing the Board his incorrect numbers.

What was he going to do? He couldn't interrupt a Board meeting, could he? A new employee walking into an important meeting to tell everyone that he had made a dumb mistake like this. It would be career suicide! He looked at the numbers again. It wasn't really that big of a mistake, was it? It was only about $0.18 per unit, and it only changed the breakeven point by less than 9,000 units. From what he remembered from his audit class, that was not even material. Perhaps it would be better to just let it go. Chances are no one would notice, and he could always fix it next quarter.

Problem #3

Who will be affected by Demitri's decision? In answering this question, think outside of the box and consider individuals outside of the department and even Wedgewood. Would your answers be different if he'd used $0.75 instead of the $0.35? Why or why not?

Name:

Problem #4

Assume that Demitri sent you an email asking for advice on how to deal with this dilemma. Write an email back to Demitri suggesting two possible options. Discuss both the options and the consequences of each of your two suggestions. Which of the two options do you recommend he choose and why? Would your answers be different if he'd put in $0.75 instead? Why or why not? Use the space provided below to draft an outline of the email, then print the final email to hand in to your instructor.

Wedgewood
Candle Co.

MEMO

To: demitri@wedgewoodcandles.com

From: josey@wedgewoodcandles.com

Subject: CVP analysis on the container line of candles

Demitri,

Attached is a breakdown of the container candles we sold and the operating results from last quarter (available in the Excel workbook for this chapter). See what you can do with a CVP graph, but please do the basic CVP equations as well: breakeven, margin of safety, and degree of operating leverage. Thanks! The Manufacturing Overhead is 40% variable, the Selling and Administrative costs are 90% fixed, and the rest are commissions. I think that will give you everything you need. Just keep in mind that this division has been making product to order, so there is no beginning or ending inventory.

Josey

CHAPTER 10

PERFORMING VARIANCE ANALYSIS

This page is intentionally blank.

CHAPTER 10

Performing Variance Analysis

Objectives

Excel Skills

- Selecting non-contiguous cells
- Using the Clear command
- Creating hyperlinks

Accounting Skills

- Calculating sales variances
- Calculating the overall cost variances
- Calculating the rate and efficiency variances

Mastering Excel

Selecting Non-Contiguous Cells

One of the reasons nonaccountants have difficulty understanding Excel spreadsheets is the formatting (or lack of it). It is so easy to lose information within the large tables of data that accountants so often give to nonaccounting managers. When you create a full master budget, payroll spreadsheet, or a set of historical data for analysis, you often have hundreds of lines and dozens of columns of information. And somewhere in all of that is the information that your team or your supervisor needs to make an important decision or conduct a more detailed analysis. Because this is such an important issue, we are going to discuss it one more time with a new set of tools.

In the past, we've talked quite a bit about general formatting that will help to highlight or set apart key data, but in this chapter we discuss advanced tools that you can use to highlight data for other users or to make it easy for you to highlight key figures while you are working. Let's get started.

Go ahead and open up the workbook called **C10 Excel Practice Sets** from your downloaded files. Can you see what we are doing? Since we made this spreadsheet, it actually makes sense to us, and if you were to take a little time to check our equations and read through the assignment in column M, you probably would be able to make sense of everything as well. But do you really want to take that kind of time? Probably not. You, like most managers, are probably thinking that it would be a waste of your time to dig through our spreadsheet to see what we are doing and why, which is exactly our point with this chapter. What can you do, beyond using colors and number formatting, to really make your data easy to find and use?

Let's start formatting this spreadsheet by making it easy to see where the answers to the questions are. Any time a manager (or a professor) asks you for specific information, you want to make sure that they can easily find it. Now, you can click on each cell one by one, finding the answers to each question and making them stand out. But you can also do it all at once, which is less time-consuming.

Like most programs, you can select multiple items at one time by using the [Ctrl] key and then clicking on the cells you want to examine.

- *Click on cell E13 and then,*
- *While holding down [Ctrl]*
- *Select the following cells: G14, G16, C19, C22, E24, E25, H30, and H34.*

These cells answer each of the questions that are asked in the assignment (in column M). You'll notice that, just as with a set of contiguous or touching cells, Excel provides you with an average of the cell values, a count of the highlighted cells that contain information, and the sum of the cell values in the lower-right corner of the spreadsheet. You can also right-click on any one of these cells, select Format Cells, and format them in any way you wish. You'll need to be careful what you choose for this example, though, because some of the values are negative numbers, some are percentages, and some are dollar amounts. To be safe, you'll probably just want to change the color and put a box around them. We decided to do the following:

- Bold
- Bright green fill color

You can see our results in the picture on the following page, but you should choose whatever formatting makes the most sense to you.

	A	B	C	D	E	F	G	H
1								
2			Actual		Flex -Constant Mix		Static Bud	
3	Sales - A - Q	1,250		1,406		1,500		
4	Sales - A - $	$12	$15,000			$10	$15,000	
5	Sales B - Q	625		469		500		
6	Sales B - $	$48	$30,000			$50	$25,000	
7	Variable - A	$6	($7,500)			$6	($9,000)	
8	Variable - B	$35	($21,875)			$35	($17,500)	
9	CM - A	$6	$7,500		$9,492	$4	$6,000	
10	CM - B	$13	$8,125		$3,164	$15	$7,500	
11	Total CM		$15,625		$12,656		$13,500	
12								
13	CM Variance				$2,125			
14	Budget Avg CM						$ 6.75	=
15								
16	CM Vol Var.						(844)	overall whi
17				Sum of	$ 2,125			sold:
18				two separate variances				planned:
19	Flex Budget Variance		$2,969					difference
20				formulas for this is below				times wtd
21	Market Size		50,000				20,000	budgeted
22			3.75%	actual share			10.00%	
23								
24	Market Share Variance				($21,094)			
25	Market Size Variance				$20,250			
26					($844)	This is the CM Vol Var split into two p		
27				sales mix variance:	Actual Units	Budgeted Units	Budgeted CM	SMV
28				Product A	1,250	1,406	$4	($625)
29				Product B	625	469	$15	$2,344
30								$1,719
31				sales price variance:	Actual CM	Budget CM	Actual Units	SPV
32				Product A	6	4	$1,250	$2,500
33				Product B	13	15	$625	($1,250)
34								$1,250

When you select several cells at once, even though they are not contiguous, you can format them all exactly the same. Pretty cool, right?

Using the Clear Command

Unfortunately, though, Excel is not very forgiving when it comes to selecting non-contiguous cells. If you click on an incorrect cell, Excel won't let you unselect that cell. That means that you either have start selecting cells again (first clicking on any cell without holding the [Ctrl] key to release those cells you had already selected) or go ahead and format all of the cells (including the incorrect one) and then use the Clear command to make sure that the incorrect cell doesn't match the ones you are trying to emphasize.

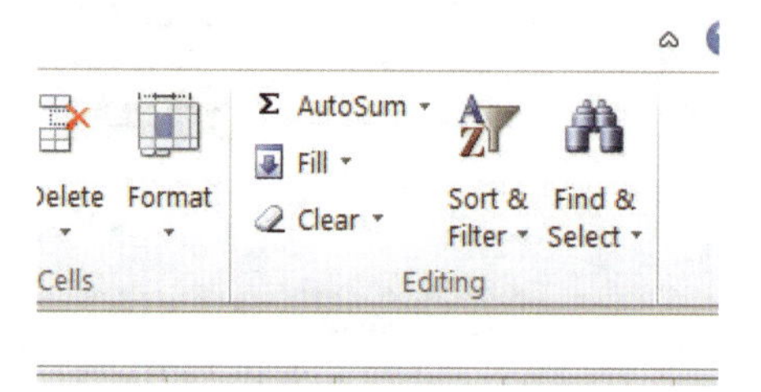

Let's say, for example, that you wanted to format cells C11, E11, and G11 with a double underline. Go ahead and select those cells using the [Ctrl] key, then also select cell G10 as if you had mistakenly clicked on that cell when trying to click on G11.

Unfortunately, you can't unselect cell G10 by just clicking on it again like you can in most Internet drop-down menus. Now, in this case with only three cells, starting over is not a big deal; but, if you had selected 20 different cells and then discovered you had mistakenly selected a wrong cell, you probably would like an option other than starting over. Here it is.

- *Format all four of these cells with a double underline.*

Now all of the cells look like the final cell in a calculation, even G10, which isn't a total.

- *Select G10.*
- *Click on the Clear command in the Editing area of the Home tab of the Excel ribbon.*
- *Choose the Clear Formats option.*

That's it. It's a very simple command, but a very useful one. You'll notice, though, that this command not only clears the lines but all other formatting (number style, rounding of decimals, colors, etc.). While that might be stripping more than you want, it can be very useful when you decide to start formatting from scratch.

Even more useful is the Clear All option, since that removes everything in the cells you have selected. We have often used that command when we don't just want to change formatting or don't just want to change information, but want to start from scratch without having to open a new window or spreadsheet.

Using Hyperlinks

Reformatting the cells that contain key information is a great way to make that information easier to find, but that isn't always enough for those who aren't comfortable with Excel (or for those very complicated spreadsheets that only you understand!). In these situations, you may have to go even one step further to help users find the information they need. That sounds surprising when you end up with a spreadsheet like ours with totals that are double-underlined and highlighted in green. Luckily, there is one more tool we can use in Excel to make information easy to find. In fact, we're going to make it almost impossible to miss. Take a look in column M to see what we were asked to find in our spreadsheet. The numbers that we asked you to highlight are the answers to these questions. But which answer goes with which question?

The best way to answer this last question, and to make our information super easy to find, is to add hyperlinks. Let's do that with these questions. We'll start by giving labels to each question, then use those labels to easily identify each answer, adding a quick link in Excel so that one click will take us right to each answer. Let's get started.

- *Right-click on cell M2.*
- *Select Hyperlink from the pop-up menu.*
- *Under Link to: on the top-left side of the Insert Hyperlink dialog box, select Place in This Document.*
- *Under Type the cell reference: type in* D13.

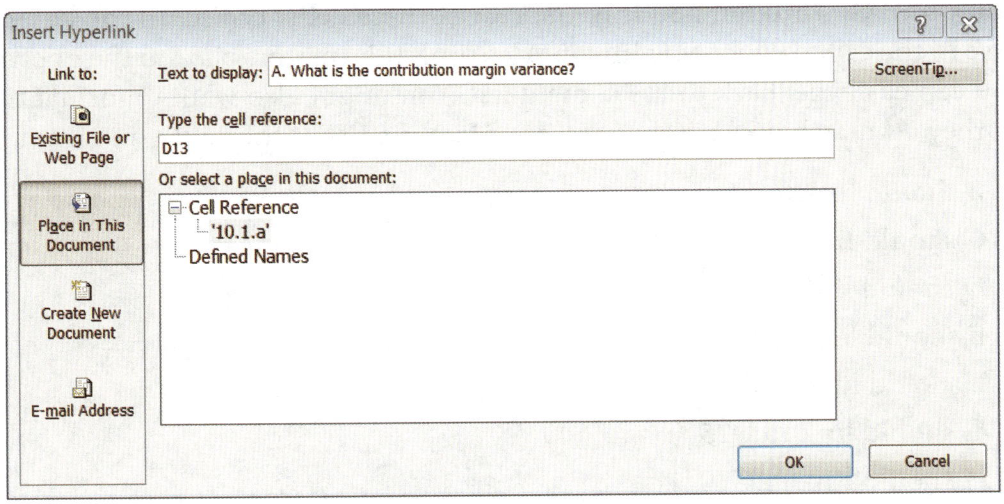

Insert Hyperlink
Link to:
Text to display: A. What is the contribution margin variance?
ScreenTip...
Existing File or Web Page
Type the cell reference:
D13
Place in This Document
Or select a place in this document:
Cell Reference
'10.1.a'
Defined Names
Create New Document
E-mail Address
OK
Cancel

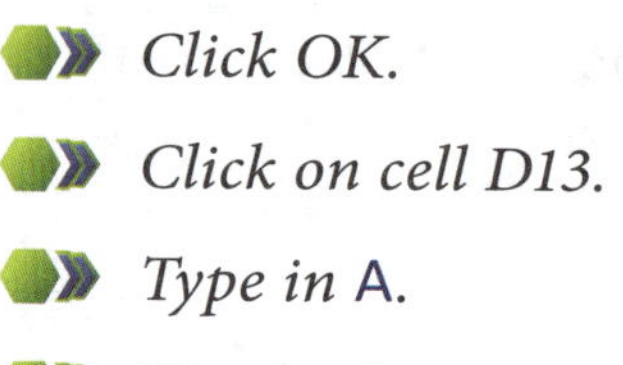

- *Click OK.*
- *Click on cell D13.*
- *Type in* A.
- *Use the format painter to make it match cell E13.*

We chose the cell to the left of the actual answer (D13) instead of the cell with the actual answer (E13) because of the effect of hyperlinking on a cell. Once you hyperlink a cell, clicking on that cell will immediately move you to the new location. That makes it very difficult to change the contents of the cell. In this case, we're going to link this cell back to the list of questions so that we can quickly travel back and forth between our questions and the answers to those questions. Because we want to have a return link, we don't want to link directly to our work. If we did, then the hyperlink would make it difficult to change the formatting or the formulas in the answer. Of course, if you aren't going to add a hyperlink back to your question or table of contents, then you can hyperlink directly to your answer.

Let's go ahead and add the hyperlink back to the question.

- *Right-click on cell D13.*
- *Select Hyperlink from the pop-up menu.*
- *Under Link to: on the top-left side of the Insert Hyperlink dialog box, select Place in This Document.*
- *Under Type the cell reference: type in* M2 *(for some reason, Excel won't just let us just click on the cell; you have to type the reference instead).*

Now you have a hyperlink to the answer and another link from the answer back to the question itself. Go through and link the rest of these cells, typing in the letter of the response in the cell to which you link it. Also, link the answers back to the questions so that you can easily get back to the content list. You might also want to format the cells so that they all match up with the answers. Here is a list of the cells you want to link:

- B should link to F14
- C should link to F16
- D should link to B19
- E should link to B22
- F should link to D24
- G should link to D25
- H should link to G30
- I should link to G34

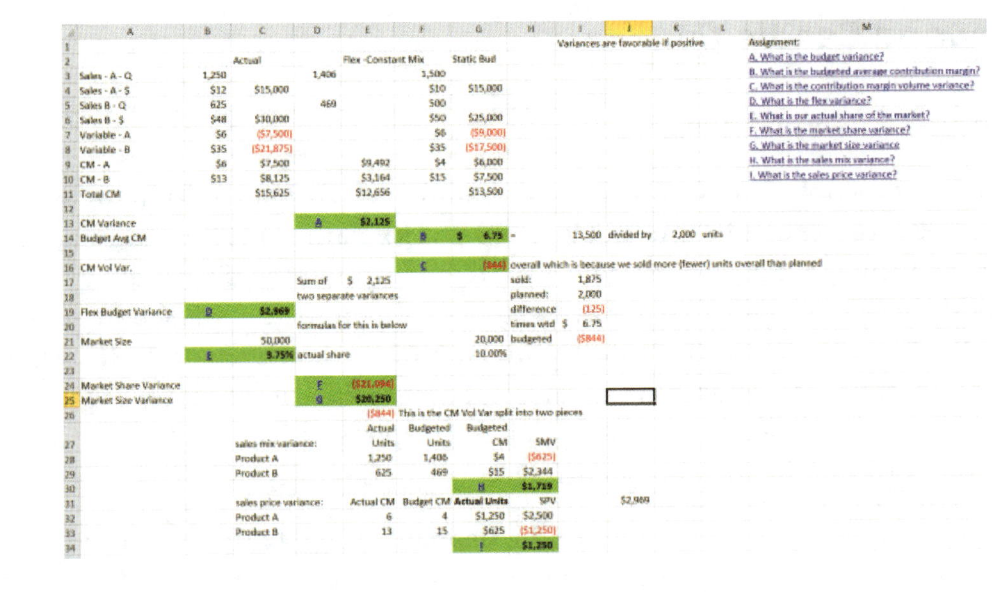

	A	B	C	D	E	F	G	H	I	J	K	L	M
1									Variances are favorable if positive				Assignment:
2			Actual		Flex -Constant Mix		Static Bud						A. What is the budget variance?
3	Sales - A - Q	1,250		1,406		1,500							B. What is the budgeted average contribution margin?
4	Sales - A - $	$12	$15,000			$10	$15,000						C. What is the contribution margin volume variance?
5	Sales B - Q	625		469		500							D. What is the flex variance?
6	Sales B - $	$48	$30,000			$50	$25,000						E. What is our actual share of the market?
7	Variable - A	$6	($7,500)			$6	($9,000)						F. What is the market share variance?
8	Variable - B	$35	($21,875)			$35	($17,500)						G. What is the market size variance
9	CM - A	$6	$7,500		$9,492	$4	$6,000						H. What is the sales mix variance?
10	CM - B	$13	$8,125		$3,164	$15	$7,500						I. What is the sales price variance?
11	Total CM		$15,625		$12,656		$13,500						
12													
13	CM Variance			A	$2,125								
14	Budget Avg CM					B	$ 6.75	=	13,500	divided by	2,000	units	
15													
16	CM Vol Var.					C	($844)	overall which is because we sold more (fewer) units overall than planned					
17				Sum of	$ 2,125			sold:	1,875				
18				two separate variances				planned:	2,000				
19	Flex Budget Variance	D	$2,969					difference	(125)				
20				formulas for this is below				times wtd $	6.75				
21	Market Size		50,000				20,000	budgeted	($844)				
22		E	3.75%	actual share			10.00%						
23													
24	Market Share Variance			F	($21,094)								
25	Market Size Variance			G	$20,250								
26					($844)	This is the CM Vol Var split into two pieces							
27			sales mix variance:		Actual Units	Budgeted Units	Budgeted CM	SMV					
28			Product A		1,250	1,406	$4	($625)					
29			Product B		625	469	$15	$2,344					
30							H	$1,719					
31			sales price variance:		Actual CM	Budget CM	Actual Units	SPV		$2,969			
32			Product A		6	4	$1,250	$2,500					
33			Product B		13	15	$625	($1,250)					
34							I	$1,250					

Now when users want to see, for example, what the sales mix variance is, they can click on "H" in the Assignment column of the workbook and it will take them right to the answer on the workbook. And once they are done with that information, they can click on the link to come right back to the content list! Pretty nifty, right? As a final note, you can easily combine this technique with the other formatting concepts you have already learned. For example, you could name the cells you want to link to and have the hyperlink take you directly to the cell that was named.

> **Tip:**
>
> Using named cells is the only effective way to hyperlink between spreadsheets. You can try to type in the name of the new spreadsheet along with the cell reference, but it is very easy to make a mistake. If you name the cell, however, then you can find that name in the Defined Names list in the large white box in the Insert Hyperlink dialog box. Just click on the appropriate name and you are all set.

Wrapping Up Our Excel Work

Now that you have learned a bit about how to make your answers easy to find within a large complicated spreadsheet, it's time to return to Wedgewood and help Josey out again. Remember to make your spreadsheets as user-friendly as possible. The more time you save upper management, the faster you'll become part of upper management!

Wedgewood Candle Co.

Calculating Sales Variances

"I want answers, people. We were supposed to make nearly $400,000 in gross margin from the new container candle line, not lose money! Explain to me how this happened!" Sherman Wedgewood thundered. The Board had appointed Sherman as CEO of Wedgewood three years ago after Jennifer stepped down to serve as Chairman of the Board for health reasons. As the oldest grandson of the company founder, Sherman had been the natural choice within the family, but he had a fierce temper when things went wrong. Understandable, probably, given the responsibility he felt for maintaining the livelihood of so many members of the Wedgewood family.

"We're still not sure," Josey answered in a reasonable tone, trying to calm her uncle down. "We just barely finished calculating the numbers this morning. We haven't had time to analyze them yet."

Sherman's face was starting to turn purple. "Numbers this bad should have been a priority!" he thundered. "Do I have to...?"

"Sherman, that's enough," Jennifer's quiet voice stopped the CEO cold. "You know as well as I do that Josey is good at her job. She'll get the analysis done and back to us as soon as she can, but we have to give her time. Perhaps if you had let her do her work instead of calling her into this emergency meeting, we would have the numbers that we need."

"Yes, Aunt Jenni," Sherman said immediately, although he almost choked on the words. The others in the room hid smiles. No one argued with Aunt Jenni, the Chairman of Wedgewood's Board of Directors and the youngest of company founder Pierce Wedgewood's children.

Sherman took a couple of deep breaths to calm down, and then turned back to the group. "Does anyone have any specific suggestions or ideas that might help Josey's search for the problem?"

The room went quiet. "Well," Josey finally said, "Let me give you some good news. I had a few minutes to at least start my search, and it doesn't look like the problem is with our sales. Take a look at these sales and gross margin numbers, and then we can discuss it." The summary Josey distributed is included at the end of the chapter, directly after the assignment pages.

Stop here and answer questions 1 through 5 on assignment pages 10-13 and 10-15 before continuing.

Rapid Review:

Variance Analysis is one of the most powerful tools available for determining how to improve operations in a company. The foundation for this analysis includes three versions of the CM income statement. The first, commonly known as the ***Static Budget***, is based on the annual budget and includes estimates for units sold, sales prices, and fixed and variable costs. The second, commonly known as the ***Flexible Budget***, is based on actual units sold, but uses the budgeted amounts for sales prices and fixed and variable costs. The third doesn't actually have a name, but consists of the actual results of the period in a CM Income Statement format. Variance analysis is performed by comparing the results of these three income statements.

The only difference between the Static and Flexible budget are the units sold, therefore all differences between these two budgets are due to shifts in sales volume (known as ***Volume Variances***). The differences between the Flexible budget and the actual results are everything *except* volume. Therefore, the differences between the Flexible budget and the actual results can pinpoint changes between planned and actual prices, costs, and quantities (Flexible Budget Variances). The overall difference between the budgeted profit from the Static Budget and the actual profits is the sum of these two types of variances (known as ***Budget Variances***).

As a final comment, remember that every variance you calculate is going to be either favorable or unfavorable. A ***Favorable Variance*** improves our profit, leaving it higher than we thought it would be. We signal this type of variance by making it positive and putting an "F" after the value. An ***Unfavorable Variance*** reduces our profit, leaving it lower than we thought it would be. We signal this type of variance by making it negative and putting a "U" after the value. Make sure you use these signals for all of the variances you calculate. After finding the variances, companies focus on improving the favorable variances and reducing or eliminating the unfavorable variances. But be careful. Improving profits for the wrong reasons, like by purchasing substandard parts, is not a good decision, even though it may result in a favorable variance next period. Likewise, decreasing profits for the right reasons, for example implementing a new maintenance schedule that will reduce downtime in the long run, may be a good decision even though it results in an unfavorable variance.

Calculating the Overall Cost Variances

"You're right, Josey," Sherman said, his voice much calmer after hearing the good news about sales. "I reviewed the numbers you showed us. The flexible budget sales results are higher than the static budget results, which means we sold more candles than we planned to, right?" As Josey nodded, he continued. "And actual sales results are higher than the flexible budget, which means our selling price was higher than we planned, right?" Again, he waited for Josey's nod before he continued. But this time his face started to turn red. "So exactly what," he continued visibly trying to control his frustration and anger, "happened to expenses?!"

Josey shrugged her shoulders. "I don't know yet. I need to dig into the numbers much more before I'll know. If the Board doesn't have any other questions or suggestions, then perhaps you wouldn't mind letting me get back to my calculations."

Sherman looked around the room. "Any additional questions or comments before we excuse Josey and move on to other business?"

A young man, sitting nervously in the back, tentatively raised his hand. "Yes, Percy?" Sherman asked. "I was hoping to hear from you."

"Well," Percy began. "I don't have any specific ideas, but I do know that I've had quite a few discussions with purchasing about the costs of the glass containers and fancy lids that go into this line of candles and a couple of discussions with HR about the new hires that are being assigned to my division." Percy Wedgewood, the first of the fifth generation to become a manager at Wedgewood, had only recently graduated with a degree in management and was still working on his MBA. Because of his energy and enthusiasm, not to mention his training, he had recently been assigned as the manager of the container candles division.

Sam Rindlesbacher, the HR Director, jumped in. "I've heard your complaints, Percy, and I really don't think that we've given you any apprentice candlemakers that are worse than those going to other divisions."

Percy shook his head. "I disagree. We are having a terrible time with them, and I'm sure that is driving up costs."

"No. I know that you are getting the same number of new recruits as everyone else.... " Now Sam's face was the one turning purple.

"Enough." As before, Aunt Jenni's calm voice cut through the debate before it could turn into an argument. "This isn't helping. Before we can start finding solutions or assigning responsibility, we need to know what happened." She turned to Josey, who was still standing by the white board where she had jotted down her calculations for the sales variances. "Do you have what you need, dear?" she asked her grand-niece.

"Yes, ma'am," Josey replied with a nod. "I'll get you some basic numbers on direct materials and the apprentice wages right away, then I'll move on to more detailed analysis."

"Good. And if you need anything else, please let us know." Sherman jumped back in, finally picking up his responsibility as CEO.

Josey nodded to him and the other members of the leadership team and quietly left the room. Back in her office, she added more information to the original report. (You can find this information on a spreadsheet entitled C10 Variance Analysis). Then she sat down to start crunching the numbers that the Board needed.

Stop here and answer questions 6 through 9 on assignment pages 10-15 through 10-19 before continuing.

Rapid Review:

After calculating the overall budget variances, it is useful to dig into the details. The first step in this more detailed analysis is calculating the total cost variances. We start by calculating the budget variances for DM and DL, subtracting the budgeted amount to be paid for these items in the Static Budget from the actual amount paid. We then start to break down the overall variances to determine what caused the changes: the amount we sold or the amount we paid. The changes in the amount we sold cause ***Volume Variances*** and can be calculated as the difference between the Static and the Flexible budget amounts. The changes in the amount we paid are called ***Flexible Budget Variances*** and can be calculated as the difference between the Flexible Budget and CM Income Statement amounts. Note that we don't really try to investigate the MOH variances at this point. The differences in MOH are often caused by our allocation method rather than real changes, making it much harder to determine if anything has really changed or if we just need to improve our allocation method.

Calculating Rate and Efficiency Variances

"Aunt Josey?" Percy asked tentatively from her doorway.

"Ah, Percy," she said briskly to her nephew, motioning him in. "Come in and sit down. Do you have the numbers I asked for?" she asked.

Percy handed her a sheet of numbers. "I only brought the actual numbers. I assume you have the budgeted numbers, since you created the budget for me."

Josey frowned. "Well, I can look them up, I guess, but it would have been nice to have them here. It would have saved me a step, especially with the Board and the Executive Team so excited to get the final analysis."

Percy frowned. "I guess I didn't think about that."

Josey smiled. "Don't worry about it, Percy, but do keep in mind that the more you can do to make life easier for upper management, the faster you will become part of upper management." She turned her attention back to the list of numbers. "Now," she said. "I'd better get to work. Anything in particular you want to point out to me?"

"Well, I'm glad that you are looking into the DM costs, Aunt Josey, but I still think you're going to find more answers in the DL."

"Maybe, but that's not what my quick analysis showed. I'll get back to you with what I find."

Josey set to work with the numbers Percy had brought her and those she already had from her budget (once she found them). She created a spreadsheet that compared the static budget to the actual results and then she inserted a flexible budget in the middle of the two. (You can find this on the Budgets tab of your workbook for this chapter.)

Stop here and answer questions 10 and 11 on assignment page 10-21.

Rapid Review:

After calculating the overall cost variances, it is time to start drilling down into the differences between the Flexible Budget and the actual results. Remember that the difference between the Static and Flexible budgets is always due to changes in volume. If we sell a different quantity than planned, then we know that the DM, DL, and MOH costs are going to be different. They have to be, because as variables costs, they automatically change when we change the number of units sold. So, what we really want to know is how they changed from what we thought they should be for the real number of sales to what we actually paid.

As we mentioned earlier, variances in the MOH are frequently caused by an allocation problem. However, at this point we can really start to examine the DM and DL variances in detail. Some of the differences will be caused by the prices and wage rates we paid (price and rate variances, respectively). We calculate these variances by subtracting the actual amount paid (found in the actual results) from the actual inputs multiplied by the standard amount paid. Because the amount used is held constant, we can see how changes in costs affected our profit. We then calculate the differences caused by the quantity of raw materials or labor hours we used (quantity and efficiency variances, respectively). We calculate these variances as the budgeted cost (found in the Flexible budget) from the actual inputs multiplied by the standard amount paid. Because the price per unit is held constant, we can see how changes in usage affected our profit.

Name:

Questions

Note: *For questions and problems that require calculations, attach a copy of your spreadsheet to the related assignment page and hand it in to your instructor.*

Calculating Sales Variances

Q-1. What is the overall budget variance for container candles?

Q-2. What was the container candle division's sales volume variance?

Q-3. What was the container candle division's flexible budget variance?

Q-4. Using only the revenue figures provided, determine if the sales volume was higher or lower than budgeted? How do you know?

Name:

Q-5. Using only the revenue figures provided, determine if the sales price was higher or lower than budgeted? How do you know?

Calculating the Overall Cost Variances

Q-6. The budgeted amount of fixed MOH was $200,000; the actual amount shown is $300,000. What, if anything, does this tell us about the actual amount of manufacturing overhead incurred?

Name:

Q-7. a. What are the budget, volume, and flexible budget variances for direct materials?

budget variances ______________________________

____

volume variances ______________________________

____

flexible budget variances ______________________________

____

b. Which of these variances will be the most informative and why?

____

____

____

____

____

____

____

____

____

____

____

____

____

____

Name:

Q-8. What are the budget, volume, and flexible budget variances for direct labor?

budget variances ______________________________

____

volume variances ______________________________

____

flexible budget variances ______________________________

____

Q-9. Does the problem appear to be in materials or labor? Why?

____

____

____

____

____

____

____

____

____

____

____

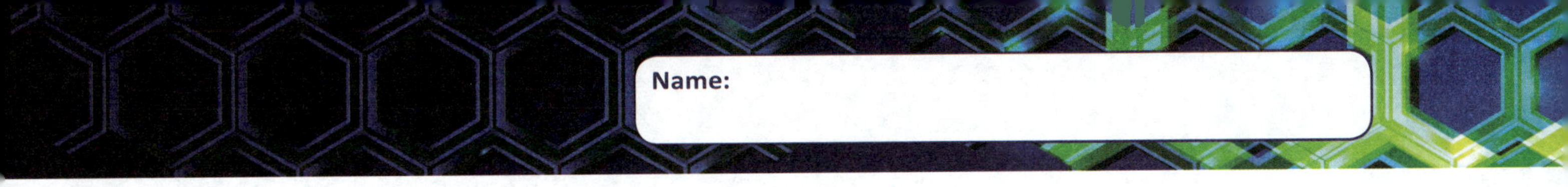

Calculating Rate and Efficiency Variances

Q-10. Create a table in Excel showing the breakdown by item of each raw material's price and quantity variances.

Q-11. Create a table in Excel showing the breakdown of the Apprentice Labor rate and efficiency variances.

Name:

Problems

Critical Thinking Issues

"I'm telling you, Aunt Josey, you are still looking in the wrong spot." Percy seemed adamant about his opinion.

"The numbers don't agree with you, Percy. I've looked at the numbers and the raw materials variance seems to be the biggest problem."

"But they don't account for everything. I still think that we are missing something obvious. What about the candlemaker and Candle Master labor? Did you look at those variances?"

"Not really. You didn't mention them as a possible problem and they have more experience, so I moved on. Do you think they might be an issue?"

"Well, I just have a gut feeling that what we are looking for is in the labor variance, despite what Sam says. Can you at least look?"

"Sure. The other numbers are all done, and I've got some time. I'll look into it."

Problem #1

After looking at all of the variances, what do you believe to be the root cause of the problems Wedgewood is having with their new line? Defend your answer.

Name:

Problem #2

Based on your assessment of the variances, write a memo to Sherman explaining why the line is struggling and what could be done to address the issues. Make sure that you keep your audience in mind (an irate CEO) as you write your answer and keep your memo succinct and helpful. Use the space below to draft an outline of your memo before you prepare the final version to hand in to your instructor.

Name:

Ethical Issues

"I knew I was right! Just look at those numbers. The problem is really with the staff." Percy was positively glowing with enthusiasm about his line. "When's the next meeting of the executive team? I want to show Sherman that I was right."

"Let me get this straight," Josey said with a slight smile on her face. "You want to go into the meeting and tell Uncle Sherman he was wrong, that the line is doing just fine, right to his face? Even with these numbers?"

Percy noticed her smile and frowned. "Well, yeah. Don't you think I should? This is actually a labor issue. These young employees don't really know what they are doing, and that's what is causing the waste. Once they are fully trained, most of the issues we're having with materials will go away."

Josey shook her head and laughed. "Are you kidding? Nobody talks to a CEO like that, not even one that's their uncle."

"But, Josey, I don't have time for tact here. They are talking about closing my line, shutting it down. I'd be back as an assistant in the executive office or even working as a supervisor in someone else's line. I can't do that, not when I know that I'm doing a good job. We can't let them close the line!" Josey grabbed him by the shoulder and pulled him around to look at her. "Percy, what are you saying exactly? Where is your focus? Are you worried about the line being closed and the company losing money or about losing your job and your status? Where are you loyalties?"

"Um, well..." Josey's question had him stumped for a minute before he caught himself. "With the company, of course," he said just a little too quickly. "I mean, after all, we have a duty to our shareholders...."

Josey held up a hand. "Percy, the executive team and the Board *are* the shareholders, and so are we. This is a family business, not a company in the Fortune 500. More importantly, we're a *small* family business, which means that we're all more hands on, and much more involved in the company, than the shareholders of the companies that you studied in college."

"Well, if it is a family business, then I should be even more free to express my opinions...."

Josey was shaking her head again and Percy stopped talking. "Fine, Josey, what do you think I should do?"

Name:

Problem #3

What incentives does Percy have to fight to keep the line open?

What incentives does he have to allow the executive team to close the line?

Which incentives do you feel are more important to Percy?

Do you agree with his focus? Why or why not?

Name:

Problem #4

How do you think that Percy should appropriately handle his belief that he is managing his line well, regardless of what the variance analysis shows?

Report for Board of Directors Meeting

Prepared by Josey Wedgewood

The following report shows the static budget, flexible budget, and actual results for the container candles for the quarter just ended.

	Static Budget	*Flexible Budget*	*Actual results*
Revenues	$2,199,000	$3,298,500	$3,307,500
Manufacturing Costs	$1,808,000	$2,612,000	$3,314,175
Contribution Margin	$391,000	$686,500	($6,675)

Wedgewood
Candle Co.

Actual Direct Materials and Labor Costs

Container Candle Line

	Quantity Used	*Total Cost*
Direct Materials		
Container and Lid	187,500	$1,713,750
Wax	1,200,000	$960,000
Wick	177,000	$35,400
Coloring and Scent	1,350,000	$135,000
Clip (1 per candle)	270,000	$2,700
Packing Material	300,000	$42,000
Direct Labor		
Apprentice	10,456	$53,325
Candlemaker	4,500	$45,000
Candle Master	1,500	$27,000

Budgeted Direct Materials and Labor Costs

Container Candle Line

	Est. Quantity/ Candle	*Cost/ Unit*
Direct Materials		
Container and Lid	1.00	$9.00
Wax	5.00	$1.00
Wick	1.00	$0.20
Coloring and Scent	8.00	$0.10
Clip (1 per candle)	1.00	$0.01
Packing Material	1.00	$0.27
Direct Labor		
Apprentice	0.05	$7.50
Candlemaker	0.02	$12.25
Candle Master	0.01	$18.00

CHAPTER 11

MAKING TACTICAL DECISIONS

This page is
intentionally blank.

CHAPTER 11

Making Tactical Decisions

Objectives

Excel Skills

- Using the function keys
- Using keyboard shortcuts
- Final notes

Accounting Skills

- Discussing the difficulties in pricing special orders
- Calculating projected revenues for special orders

Mastering Excel

Using the Function Keys

In previous chapters we have covered all of the basic tools you need to feel comfortable in Excel. We haven't covered everything; that would require a much longer book and much more time and effort. In fact most of us, even those who feel we have "mastered" Excel, are still learning new skills and techniques all of the time. In addition, Microsoft® is constantly updating their software, providing more tools and techniques (and removing some former tools and techniques), requiring us to keep updating and advancing our skills. Keeping up with Microsoft Office Excel is a constant process, but you should now have all of the tools you need to use the basic operations and to learn new tricks and techniques as you need them.

In this final chapter, we introduce some of the keyboard shortcuts and function keys that can greatly speed up your work in Excel. While most people are more comfortable using the mouse, you can move much faster if you know some of these shortcuts. So, this chapter is for those of you who like keyboard shortcuts, and also for the rest of us who are willing to learn some of them so that we don't have to point and click at the same things time after time.

Open up the workbook called **C11 Excel Practice Sets** from your downloaded files, and we'll get started with the function keys. You may remember that we discussed one of these keys, [F4], back in Chapter 8 when we discussed using absolute cell references, but so far we haven't talked about any of the other function keys. The good news is that most of the function keys in Excel perform the same basic functions as they do in other Microsoft Office products (such as Word and PowerPoint). For example, [F1] brings up help in all of the Microsoft Office programs we have used, including Excel. However, in addition to those basic functions, there are tools unique to Excel. Tapping [Alt] [Shift] [F1] will insert a new spreadsheet into your workbook. That doesn't happen in Microsoft Office Word.

Tip:

You'll probably notice that some of the combinations have been left blank. Because of space issues, we have only mentioned those function keys that are the most commonly used or that we believe will be the most helpful. If you want a more detailed discussion of all of the function keys, you can find them online or in a more comprehensive book about Microsoft Office Excel.

If you look at the list we set up in the Functions spreadsheet in Excel, you can see that across the top (in row 2) we have created column headers of "Alone," "CTRL+," etc. These are the combinations of keys you can press with the function keys to perform different tasks. Let's go through each of them so that you can get a feel for how they work. You'll notice that we marked some of the cells in blue. These are the functions that we have found the most useful, so you might want to memorize them.

Tip:

Hiding the ribbon can be a great trick when you are working on a small screen. Once you hide the ribbon, you can bring it back temporarily by clicking on any of the tabs. This will bring up the ribbon long enough for you to choose a command, then the ribbon will disappear. This process can save a great deal of space, but it can also become annoying if you are trying to do a lot of formatting or use several different tools.

Using the [F1] Key to View Menus and Ribbons, or Make a Quick Bar Chart

Pressing [F1] alone brings up Excel's help menu, while pressing the [Ctrl] key along with [F1] will hide the ribbon, and doing it again will bring the ribbon back. Go ahead and try it! Pressing [Alt] and [F1] can be a very quick way to insert a bar chart. You can try this function using the data in the Bar Chart Data spreadsheet. Just click on any of the cells with data and press [Alt] and [F1]. It's just a basic graph, but using the tools we discussed in Chapter 9 you could easily adapt it to what you really want to see. Let's take a look at what the other keys will do.

Using the [F2] Key to Edit Cells

[F2] is probably the most useful keyboard shortcut in Excel. If you have a cell selected, pressing [F2] will bring it up for editing so that you can make corrections without having to redo the cell or without having to double-click. [Ctrl] [F2] will bring up the print dialog. [Shift] [F2] will add a comment box to the selected cell, a very useful tool when you want to make notes for future reference or to send a question or highlight something for another individual. After you press [Shift] [F2], just type in your comment, and then click anywhere else in your document. Since you can also add a comment by right-clicking on the cell, we don't use the [Shift] [F2] function key too often, but the shortcuts for editing and printing are useful ones to memorize.

> **Tip:**
>
> Comment boxes normally appear as a little red triangle in the upper-right box of a cell. If you hover your mouse over that cell, the comment box will appear, and then disappear when you move your mouse again. This makes it very easy to make and use notes without hiding the rest of the spreadsheet. If you want to see all of the notes (to make sure you aren't missing anything), go to the Review tab of the Excel ribbon and click on the Show All Comments command in the Comments group. You can hide them all again with the same command when you are done.

Using the [F3] Key with Named Cells

We do not use the [F3] tool very often, but it can be useful if you use cell names. Pressing [F3] will bring up a list of all of the named cells in your workbook (all of your spreadsheets in this file). You can then select any of them, press OK, and Excel will insert into the cell "=Name", replacing "Name" with whatever name you chose. Let's try it. The third spreadsheet in this file (Income Statement) contains a divisional income statement for Wedgewood. Instead of going to that spreadsheet to find the net income for the division:

- *Choose a blank cell in the Functions spreadsheet.*
- *Press [F3].*
- *Select NI.*
- *Click OK.*

You probably noticed several other named cells in the spreadsheet. You can use any of these for additional practice if you'd like.

[Shift] [F3] will bring up the Insert Function dialog box. If you prefer keyboard shortcuts rather than using your mouse, this is a handy one to memorize.

> **Tip:**
> You can use multiple function keys to really speed things up. One of our favorite combinations is to use [F2] to edit an equation, then [F4] to change a cell reference to a permanent reference.

Using the [F4] Key for Absolute References

[F4] is the key we use to make absolute references. Since we discussed how to use this tool in more in detail in Chapter 8 (see pages 8-7 through 8-8) we won't go through it again here. [Ctrl] [F4] closes the current workbook window, and [Alt] [F4] closes Excel. Note that these options will also bring up the Save dialog box if you haven't recently saved your workbook.

> **Tip:**
> Although it can be a pain to use the Go To command the first time, Excel will remember the places you have gone in the past. Excel will remember where you jumped in each session (from opening to closing the program). So if you know you are going to be referencing one or two cells many times while you work, this tool can really speed things up.

Using the [F5] Key to Go To a Cell, or Find and Replace

[F5] will bring up a Go To dialog box. It will work all the time; you just type in the cell reference that you want to use, but it's most useful when you have named cells, as it also lists the names. (It's also usually too inconvenient to type in the name of another spreadsheet, but you don't have to worry about that if you have named cells.) Go ahead a try it with one of the named cells we have provided. [Ctrl] [F5] restores the windows. This means that the current Excel file will not be maximized in your window anymore, allowing you to resize it and click on other Excel files currently open. Perhaps not the most useful function, but it can be nice to use when you need to copy information from one file to another. [Shift] [F5], on the other hand, opens up the Find and Replace dialog box, which can be very helpful if you need to find key information and haven't marked it very well.

Using the [F6] Key to Switch Between Open Excel Workbooks

Although [F6] is supposed to shift between various places in the Excel window, we haven't found it to be very helpful. The functionality it provides is very limited and there are better ways to do just about everything programmed into this key. The one exception is [Ctrl] [F6], which will switch back and forth between open Excel files.

Using the [F7] Key to Check Spelling in a Worksheet

[F7] brings up spell check. Yes, you can (and should!) spell check your Excel documents. Although [F7] does a few other things (such as opening the thesaurus when you press [Shift] [F7]), they aren't very practical. Of course, if you ever want to know more about this (and the other keys that we are only briefly mentioning), you can do a search online or you can always press [F1]!

Using the [F8] Key to Highlight Cells

[F8] is designed to help you highlight cells without using your mouse. Pressing [F8] at the beginning of a table (say in cell A1) then at the end of the table (say G14) can be a fast way to highlight lots of data without having to click and drag, but it isn't much of a time saver. Pressing [Shift] [F8] can be more useful, since it allows you to select noncontiguous cells without holding down the [Ctrl] key. When you are done highlighting cells, you can right-click on any highlighted cell to pull up the formatting menu or you can press [Esc] so that Excel stops highlighting but still keeps your chosen set of cells highlighted until you press [Esc] again or click on a new cell.

Using the [F9] Key to Perform Calculations and Recheck Formulas

[F9] has Excel perform the calculations in your spreadsheets, updating numbers and values as necessary. Pressing [F9] alone calculates the equations in all cells in all of the spreadsheets in all of your open workbooks. [Shift] [F9] only calculates the equations in the active spreadsheet; [Ctrl] [Alt] [F9] is the same as just [F9] alone, except it forces calculations even if nothing has changed. [Ctrl] [Alt] [Shift] [F9] rechecks your formulas and then forces all calculations again (we didn't put this one in the Functions spreadsheet, since this combination of keys isn't used for other function keys). Typically with today's computing power, you don't need to manually calculate the equations in Excel. Instead, you just let Excel update your equations every time you change a value or other link. But with older computers or with massive spreadsheets that have thousands of calculations, allowing Excel to automatically update your equations with every change can really slow you down. In these situations, it is best to turn off automatic updating and use the [F9] key instead.

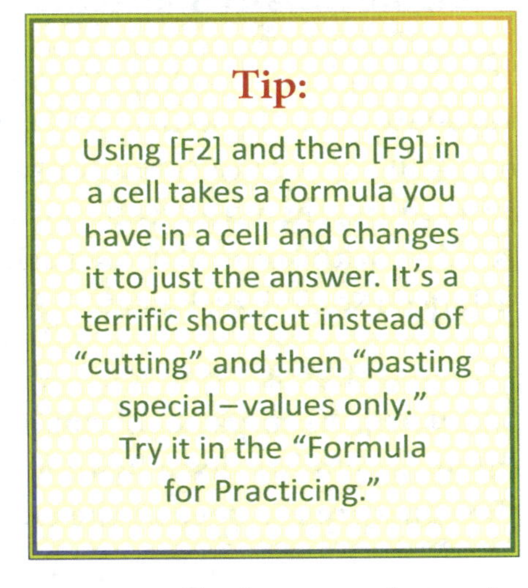
Tip:
Using [F2] and then [F9] in a cell takes a formula you have in a cell and changes it to just the answer. It's a terrific shortcut instead of "cutting" and then "pasting special–values only." Try it in the "Formula for Practicing."

As a final note about this key, [Ctrl] [F9] minimizes your workbook.

Using the [F10] Key for Key Tips and More

Pressing [F10] turns the Key Tips on and off (we'll talk more about these options in the next section). [Shift] [F10] will bring up shortcut menus and dialog boxes that are relevant to the active cell. Finally, [Ctrl] [F10] maximizes your workbook.

Using the [F11] Key to Make a Chart, or Create a New Spreadsheet

Pressing [F11] creates a chart out of your current data, similar to the [Alt] [F1] command. The difference is that [F11] creates the bar chart in a new spreadsheet, rather than as an insert in the current spreadsheet.

[Shift] [F11] creates a new spreadsheet in your workbook just as [Alt] [Shift] [F1] does, while [Alt] [F11] brings up Visual Basic. Visual Basic is a powerful tool, but it is far beyond the scope of this book. With Visual Basic you can code and program within Excel and other Microsoft Office programs, but that is a specialty. In most cases, you can perform what is necessary using the preprogrammed functions in Excel.

Using the [F12] Key to Save, Open, or Print a File

Pressing [F12] brings up the Save As dialog box and [Ctrl] [F12] brings up the Open File dialog box. Pressing [Shift] [F12] will save your file, and [Ctrl] [Alt] [F12] will open the Print dialog box, just like [Ctrl] [F2].

Using Keyboard Shortcuts

Some people like using the mouse for everything, while others prefer using the keyboard. For those that prefer the keyboard, there are several keyboard shortcuts that you can use to speed up your work in Excel. If you prefer to use the mouse for everything, then this section isn't going to help you much, but you might want to be familiar with some of these basic tools just in case you lose or break your mouse and still need some Excel data.

Perhaps the most common keyboard shortcuts are [Ctrl] [C] to copy, [Ctrl] [X] to cut, and [Ctrl] [V] to paste. If you use these tools with [F8], then you can actually move things around in Excel without using your mouse at all. Other common keyboard shortcuts are included in the table on the following page.

Keyboard Shortcut	Result
[Ctrl] [P]	prints the current spreadsheet
[Ctrl] [B]	bolds the text in a cell
[Ctrl] [I].	makes the text italic
[Ctrl] [U]	underlines the text
[Ctrl] [S]	saves a file
[Ctrl] [O]	opens a file
[Ctrl] [L] or [Ctrl] [T]. . . .	creates a table
[Ctrl] [N]	opens a new file
[Ctrl] [H] or [Ctrl] [F] . . .	opens the Find and Replace dialog box
[Ctrl] [Y]	closes the current file
[Ctrl] [A]	highlights all of the concurrent cells
[Ctrl] [Z]	undo
[Ctrl] [Home]	moves to cell A1
[Ctrl] [End].	moves to the last active cell in your spreadsheet
[Ctrl] [~]	shows the formulas in your spreadsheet (the [~] is called a tilde and is usually below the [Esc] key).

We left one formula in the Functions spreadsheet labeled "Leave this formula alone!" so that you can see how the [Ctrl] [~] keyboard shortcut works. It is a great way to quickly look over your work and find mistakes or links to other files.

Practice using the [Ctrl] [~] shortcut. When you are done experimenting with it, press [Ctrl] [~] again to go back to the normal view.

Once you get the hang of these tools, you'll use them so quickly that you won't even think about it.

In addition to these quick commands, Excel has also built in a set of keyboard commands for those who cannot (for whatever reason) use a mouse. If you press [F10] or [Alt], you will see letters pop up along the ribbon in Excel. These are "Key Tips," essentially a keyboard version of the Excel ribbon. You can then press any of the letters you see to move deeper into the ribbon. Let's try an example:

- *Press [Alt] or [F10] to open Key Tips.*
- *Press [P] to move to the Page Layout tab of the Excel ribbon.*
- *Press [O] to open the Orientation drop-down box.*
- *Press the down arrow to change the orientation to Landscape.*
- *Press [Enter] to finalize your change and exit Key Tips.*

Using the Key Tips menu, you can go anywhere on the Excel ribbon using only your keyboard! This can be very handy if you, like us, occasionally run out of battery power on your wireless remote and don't have time to change it or don't have a replacement available.

Final Notes on Excel

There is so much to learn in Excel that people have written thousand-page manuals on it. It's a powerful tool and one that employers expect their new accountants to be able to use effectively and efficiently. Despite all of our work throughout this book, we have only just scratched the surface. One of our goals was to increase your chances of landing a good job because you know both accounting and Excel, and have had a chance to practice both. Now let's get back to Josey and the Wedgewood Candle Company. They need your help one more time.

Wedgewood Candle Co.

Discussing the Difficulties in Pricing Special Orders

"Josey," Peter Wedgewood called as his daughter walked into the restaurant. "Over here."

"Hi, Dad," Josey said as she joined Peter at his table. She gave him a quick kiss on the cheek before sitting down next to him. "How are you?"

"Just fine, just fine. And how's my little girl doing?"

Josey smiled and shook her head. If she lived to be 100 years old, she'd still be a little girl to her dad. "I'm doing fine, too. Work is good; really busy, but I can't complain. I have a good staff now to help with a lot of the work."

"That's great, dear." Peter signaled to a waiter who hurried over to take their order.

Once the waiter left, Josey looked over at her dad. He was getting older and a little heavier, but he still had very playful eyes. "Dad, why are we here?" she asked after studying him for a minute.

"Do we need a reason?" Peter asked, surprised.

"No, but you always have one, and usually one I'm not going to like very much." Josey leaned back and crossed her arms. "Now, tell me what's up."

Peter chuckled. "I never could put one over on you, not even when you really were my little girl. Well, here goes then. I've been contacted by Pierre's Boutique. It's a very large chain in the South, and they would very much like to stock our new line of imprinted candles in their stores. We're talking high-end customers; a great opportunity to not only make some money but also to get our product in front of a nice clientele."

"Sounds great, so what's the catch?" Josey started drumming her fingers on the table. Any time her dad made her wait this long it was not good news.

"Well, they want to make a large order, the first of many, remember, and they would like a special discount."

Josey shrugged. "You offer discounts all the time, Dad. That's your job as Wedgewood's Director of Marketing. Why do you need to talk with me about it?"

"Because of their offer." Peter placed an email on the table. "I presented them with our normal prices and the discount I was willing to offer, and they countered with this."

Josey picked up the email, but had to wait to read it until their food was served. When she did her eyes opened in surprise. "Dad, this is not just a normal discount. They're asking for a huge discount."

"I know. That's why I brought you in on the decision. You know that I'm no good with numbers, never have been. So I thought you could help me make the decision. Just remember, they are offering to buy quite a few candles in exchange for that special price."

"I don't know, Dad. I'm not sure I even need to run the numbers. This is a very low offer. I don't think we would make any profit at all, and I doubt we could raise the price on them later. You might be committing us to a long-term relationship with no profit at all!"

"But think of the marketing campaign it would be! We could sell the imprinted candles in the boutiques as a hook, and then get those wealthy people to buy our normal candles at the normal price."

Josey frowned. "Why would they do that? Wouldn't they just pick up a new batch every time they go into the boutique?"

Peter waived his hand dismissively. "Of course not. These people aren't cost conscious with anything under $100. They won't care. We'll market directly to them and make a bundle on selling them large packages for their large homes. I think it's worth it."

Josey shook her head. There was very little reasoning with her dad once he got an idea like this stuck in his head. At least, not without numbers to back her up. "I'll tell you what, Dad. Let's enjoy lunch, then I'll take these back to the office and run some calculations and scenarios. I'll get you my answers as soon as I can."

"Thanks, Josey," Peter said as he patted her hand. "I knew I could count on you."

Calculating Projected Revenues for Special Orders

"Jordan," Josey called as she hurried up to her senior staff accountant in the hall of the Wedgewood offices. "I need you to run some numbers for me."

"Okay, Josey, what do you need?" Jordan asked.

"Well, we've been offered a special order contract and we need to decide if we should accept the offer or not. Here's their offer and some of our production numbers." She handed him the email she had received from her dad at lunch an hour earlier and the Contribution Margin Income Statement for the imprinted candle line for the last quarter (a copy of the email is included at the end of the chapter, directly after the assignment pages and the income statement is in the workbook you downloaded for this chapter). "One more thing. We sell everything we produce; there is no beginning or ending inventory. Run the numbers, and then let me know what you recommend we do."

Jordan nodded. "No problem, boss. Just one question."

Josey nodded. "Go ahead."

"Well, I haven't talked with anyone in production for a while. Are we at capacity already on the new line or not?"

Josey pursed her lips. "You know, I'm not sure. Why don't you run the numbers both ways, then we'll be ready for whatever questions the executive team asks. Oh, and before I forget, the variable S&A is a 10% commission, so when the sales price drops, so will the variable S&A."

"Makes sense. I'll get these back to you as soon as I can." Josey watched Jordan walk down the hall. She hoped the numbers came out badly. It would be so much easier to convince her dad not to accept this kind of long-term arrangement if the numbers were not in his favor.

Stop here and answer questions 1 through 5 on assignment pages 11-13 through 11-15 before continuing.

Rapid Review:

Tactical decisions can be made regarding many aspects of a business or business process. The methods discussed in your managerial or cost accounting textbook involve several different aspects or versions of these decisions and how to address them. While each method is slightly different from the others, each method comes down to a basic question: is the contribution margin of the proposal positive? If it is, then the company should take advantage of the proposal unless it lacks sufficient capacity to do so. Why? Because the proposal is contributing to the success of the business by at least covering some of the fixed costs and perhaps providing a profit in addition.

In this case, Wedgewood is considering whether or not to accept a special order. If the company has excess capacity, then there are machines and possibly people standing around not doing anything. If the price of the special order will allow the company to put these resources to work and cover all of the variable costs and directly-related fixed costs of the order, then we should take the order (at least from an accounting perspective). The other fixed costs are already being covered by other project or orders, so we don't need to allocate any of them to the special order.

If the company does not have excess capacity, then we would have to bump another job off the line. In this case, the revenue from the special order would need to cover the variable and directly-related fixed costs of the special order as well as the fixed costs allocated to the order being bumped. If not, then we should reject the order (at least from an accounting perspective).

In any case, the accounting perspective is not the last word. Once we decide if the numbers make sense (or don't), we should consider all the stakeholders. How will this affect our employees? Do they want the extra hours? How about our existing customers? Will this special order affect them in anyway? What about the community? The shareholders? Management? Although you can't quantify these considerations, they are nonetheless very important!

This page is

intentionally blank.

Name:

Questions

Note: *For questions and problems that require calculations, attach a copy of your spreadsheet to the related assignment page and hand it in to your instructor.*

Calculating Projected Revenues for Special Orders

Q-1. What are the typical variable costs/unit for each 12-inch imprinted candle?

Q-2. What are the average fixed costs/candle for each 12-inch imprinted candle line?

Name:

Q-3. If the line has excess capacity, what would be the profit (loss) on the special order? What if no sales commissions were paid on the order?

Q-4. If the line is operating at full capacity, what would be the profit (loss) on the special order? What if no sales commissions were paid on the order?

Q-5. Based on your analysis, do you think Wedgewood should accept the special order? Explain your answer.

Name:

Problems

Critical Thinking Issues

Problem #1

Write a memo to Josey's father, Peter Wedgewood, discussing the pros and cons of his suggestion. Your memo should include both quantitative and qualitative characteristics. In writing your memo, assume that the plant has sufficient excess capacity to handle the entire order from Pierre's Boutique. Use the space below to create an outline of your memo before you create it in Word. When you have completed the memo, attach a copy of it to this sheet and hand it in to your instructor.

Name:

Problem #2

After talking with Percy, the manager of the new line, Josey estimates that the imprinted candle line can produce a maximum of 2,200,000 candle inches each year, but is only producing about 2,000,000 candle inches currently. The special order from Pierre's Boutique is for 25,000 12-inch candles. Using these capacity numbers, figure out the profit (loss) on the special order.

Based on this calculation, what do you think the company should do? How much would Wedgewood have to charge Pierre's Boutique to break even in this situation? Explain your answer.

Problem #3

For purposes of this conversation, assume that Wedgewood does not have excess capacity.

"Josey, I know that you don't like this offer from Pierre's Boutique," Peter Wedgewood said as they sat at another restaurant. "But don't you think you've been a little unrealistic? I mean I know a little bit about accounting.... Not much," he conceded as he noticed her rolling her eyes, "but a little. For example, I know that our fixed costs are not going to change if we accept this order. So, even if we are already operating at capacity, I don't think that you should be applying these costs to a new order." He paused as the waiter placed their food on the table. "I honestly think that you are purposefully trying to sabotage a great deal, and I don't understand why."

How should Josey answer her father? Make sure that your answer includes an explanation of the difference between excess capacity and working at full capacity and how that affects the allocation of fixed costs to special order decisions.

Name:

Ethical Issues

"Josey, allow me to introduce Ms. Renee Unité, the Purchasing Director of Pierre's Boutique," Peter Wedgewood said as they approached the table. Josey studied the woman as they shook hands. She was tall, with long brown hair and a nice smile. She was obviously very skilled at making people like her and putting them at ease.

"I am grateful that you could join me for lunch today," Ms. Unité said as they sat back down. The restaurant was one of Josey's favorites, although she usually only came when her dad was paying. It was just a little too pricey for her. Someday she hoped to be able to come here on her own, but for now she just enjoyed going when someone else was taking care of the bill.

The meal was delicious, as always, and the conversation was light and comfortable. At the end of the meal, Josey was surprised when Ms. Unité paid the bill. She had been under the impression that her dad had set up this meeting and would host the meal as part of dining a prospective client. As they left the restaurant, Ms. Unité insisted on driving them back to their hotel, and they settled into her limousine instead of taking a taxi.

Just as the car pulled up to Wedgewood headquarters, Ms. Unité finally spoke about business. "Ms. Wedgewood, I know that you are not, shall we say, thrilled with our offer, but I'm sure we can come to an agreement. I'm planning on taking a small group of business associates with me on a trip to Miami next weekend. We'll enjoy the sights and the food, and talk a little bit about business, of course. I'd love for you and your father to join us. It should be easy for us to figure out a good contract in that environment, don't you think?"

Josey opened her mouth to refuse, but Peter spoke more quickly. "That's a great idea," Peter Wedgewood said, leaving his daughter speechless.

Name:

Problem #4

Review the four principles and four standards of the IMA's Statement of Ethical Professional Practice. (There is likely a copy in your Managerial Accounting or Cost Accounting textbook. However, you can also find this online by Googling "IMA Code of Ethics.") Explain which, if any, of the principles and/or standards Ms. Unité's suggestion might violate. Does it matter that this is a family-owned company instead of one with outside investors?

Name:

Problem #5

Assuming that Josey feels uncomfortable with the idea of this trip, what could she say to convince her dad, who sees nothing wrong with the idea, that neither of them should go and that they should probably reconsider any potential relationship with Pierre's Boutique?

From: Renee Unité
To: Peter Wedgewood
Cc:
Subject: Placing Order

Sent: Mon 1/19/2017 8:20 AM

My Dear Mr. Wedgewood,

I very much enjoyed your presentation to our committee last week. While we do not typically carry candles in our establishments, we believe that your imprinted candle line is of a high enough quality that our customers might be interested in them. With that in mind, we would like to place an order for 25,000 12-inch candles in a variety of colors.

Because of the size of our order, we hope that you would be willing to consider a discount rate of $10.00 per candle. In addition, we would be willing to pay actual shipping charges for overnight delivery once production is done. We want to start stocking these candles in the next 30 days, however, and thus expect the first 2,500 candles from the order by that time with the remaining ones to follow within three months. While I realize this is a sizable discount on your normal prices, I'm sure that you are aware of the types of clients we entertain—and the potential for significant profits if you can interest those clients in making direct purchases.

I look forward to working with you on this and future orders. I'm sure this will be the beginning of a wonderful relationship between our two companies.

Yours truly,
Renee Unité
Purchasing Director
Pierre's Boutique
FINE ACCESSORIES FOR THE HOME

Index of Excel Functions and Commands

Notes

Use this page to accumulate important notes.

Notes

Use this page to accumulate important notes.